Delphi Component Design

Delphi Component Design

Danny Thorpe

ADDISON-WESLEY DEVELOPERS PRESS

An imprint of Addison Wesley Longman, Inc.

Reading, Massachusetts · Harlow, England · Menlo Park, California
Berkley, California · Don Mills, Ontario · Sydney
Bonn · Amsterdam · Tokyo · Mexico City

Many of the designations used by manufacturers and sellers to distinguish their products are claimed as trademarks. Where those designations appear in this book, and Addison-Wesley was aware of a trademark claim, the designations have been printed in initial capital letters or all capital letters.

Fractal Imager copyright (C) Iterated Systems, Inc., 1995—1996. All rights reserved. Fractal Imager, Fractal Viewer, the fern logo, and all other Iterated Systems product names and logos are trademarks of Iterated Systems, Inc., in the United States and other countries. Other trademarks are properties of their respective owners.

The author and publisher have taken care in preparation of this book, but make no expressed or implied warranty of any kind and assume no responsibility for errors or omissions. No liability is assumed for incidental or consequential damages in connection with or arising out of the use of the information or programs contained herein.

Library of Congress Cataloging-in-Publication Data

Thorpe, Danny.
    Delphi component design / Danny Thorpe.
       p. cm.
    Includes index.
    ISBN 0-201-46136-6
     1. Computer software—Development. 2. Delphi (Computer file)
I. Title.
QA76.76.D47T49 1997
005.265—dc20   96-42198
                                                                                                          CIP

Copyright © 1997 by Danny Thorpe
A-W Developers Press is a division of Addison Wesley Longman, Inc.

All rights reserved. No part of this publication may be reproduced, stored in a retrieval system, or transmitted, in any form or by any means, electronic, mechanical, photocopying, recording, or otherwise, without the prior written permission of the publisher. Printed in the United States of America. Published simultaneously in Canada.

Sponsoring Editor: Mary Treseler
Project Manager: John Fuller
Production Assistant: Melissa Lima
Cover design: Ann Gallager
Text design: Kenneth J. Wilson
Set in 10-point Palatino by Vicki L. Hochstedler

1 2 3 4 5 6 7 8 9 -MA- 0099989796
First printing, November 1996

Addison-Wesley books are available for bulk purchases by corporations, institutions, and other organizations. For more information please contact the Corporate, Government, and Special Sales Department at (800) 238-9682.

Find A-W Developers Press on the World-Wide Web at:
http://www.aw.com/devpress/

To
my grandparents,

Adolf Oliver Goldsmith and *Josephine Bristol Goldsmith,*

who teach by example
that with patience, persistence, and a little bit of faith,
you can achieve anything you set your mind to.

To
Lynn, the hostess with the mostest

To
Daev, master of the remote

To
Jan, in emerald green
(and her little dog, too)

who have shown remarkable patience, persistence, and faith
in their efforts to teach me
the intrinsic value of distraction.

Fortunately for this book,
they have not yet entirely succeeded.

Contents

Acknowledgments xi
Foreword xiii
Introduction xv

PART I   Analysis and Design

Chapter 1   The Delphi Programming Model   3

Delphi—10 Years in the Making   4
Lessons Learned   7
Delphi Solutions   12
The Delphi Application Writer—Component Consumer   21
The Delphi Component Writer—Component Provider   28
Summary   33

Chapter 2   Designing Components   35

Balancing Design Priorities   35
Reading a Class Declaration   38
Identifying Tasks and Parts   47
Operating Within the Implementation Bubble   62
Setting the Degree of Extensibility   64
Providing Design-Time Support   67
Summary   68

PART II   Implementation Details

Chapter 3   Virtual Methods and Polymorphism   73

Syntax Review   74
Polymorphism in Action   75
The Virtual Method Table   81
The Dynamic Method Table   83
Redeclaring Virtual Methods   86

Abstract Interfaces 88
Virtuals Defeat Smart Linking 91
Virtuals Enhance Smart Linking 92
Class Reference Types 98
Summary 101

Chapter 4 **Exceptions** **105**

An Exceptional Communication System 105
Exception Syntax 108
Exceptions Change Your Assumptions 114
Rules of Thumb for Implementing Exception Handlers 117
Rules of Thumb for Raising Exceptions 120
Summary 123

Chapter 5 **Run-Time Type Information** **125**

The TypInfo Unit 125
The RTTI Fountainhead 126
RTTI supported types 130
Non-RTTI Types 130
RTTI Data Structures and Pseudostructures 131
RTTI Routines 140
RTTI Example Project: Persistent User Data 143
Summary 151

Chapter 6 **Streaming** **153**

Property-Based Streaming 153
Writing to the Stream with TWriter 158
Reading from the Stream with TReader 168
Converting Between Binary and Text 172
Streaming Opportunities for Component Writers 173
Summary 175

Chapter 7 **Messaging** **177**

Win32 Messaging 177
The Message Loop 179
Receiving Messages 188
Sending Messages 195
Miscellanea 200
Summary 201

Chapter 8 **More VCL Subsystems** 203

FreeNotification   203
Assign and AssignTo   205
Clipboard Support   210
GetPalette and PaletteChanged   211
Graphics   213
Summary   224

Chapter 9 **OLE and COM Interfaces** 225

OLE—Interprocess Communication   225
COM = Abstract Interfaces   226
Delphi OLE Automation Server: Design Strategy   228
Building a Factory   239
Registering the Factory   241
Automating the Application   243
Registering the Application   244
Testing the Automation Server   245
Summary   246

Chapter 10 **Optimization Techniques** 249

Levels of Optimization   249
The Fine Art of Procrastination   252
Memory Allocation Strategies   256
Costs of Value Semantics—Managing Strings and Variants   263
Plain Old Dirty Tricks   270
Summary   271

PART III Design-Time Support Tools

Chapter 11 **Delphi's Open Tools Architecture** 275

The Big Picture   275
Lines of Communication—Interfaces   279
General Design-Time Issues   281
Summary   283

Chapter 12 **Property Editors** 285

TPropertyEditor   285

Standard Property Editors 289
Registering Property Editors 294
Implementing Property Editors 297
Property Editor Rules of the Road 301
Summary 302

Chapter 13 **Component Editors** **303**

TComponentEditor 304
Modifying the Component 306
Registering Component Editors 307
TDefaultEditor 308
Implementing Component Editors 310
Summary 311

Chapter 14 **Experts and Add-in Tools** **313**

Explanation of Terms 313
TIToolServices—Gateway to the IDE 315
Implementing TIExpert 326
Installing and Initializing an Expert 329
Summary 335

Appendix **Win32 Review** **337**

Address Spaces 337
Preemptive Multitasking 338
Long Strings 338
32-Bit Integers 339

Index 341

Acknowledgments

Obviously, this book would not have been possible without a blockbuster Delphi product. Delphi, in turn, owes a lot of its success to the preceding eight generations of Borland Pascal compiler technology and market experience. For all these, we owe thanks to Anders Hejlsberg and Chuck Jazdzewski for continually pushing the envelope and to Gary Whizin and Zack Urlocker for continually pushing Anders and Chuck. Though more than half of Borland has a hand in building some piece of the Delphi product, these four keep the vision coherent, consistent, and competitive.

My debt to the Delphi team runs much deeper than just having a cool product to write about. The Delphi development team and work environment have proven to be a far richer soup of technology and creativity than this student of software could have ever hoped for. This is an environment that values finding and understanding the important questions as highly as finding the right answers. In the words of Professor Chuck, "I don't mind being interrupted to discuss a hard programming question—hard questions show you've done your homework. Easy questions, I mind." I wish to thank the many people at Borland who have provided me with answers over the years and, more importantly, explanations of the lines of reasoning that led up to those sometimes wild and radical solutions. I owe equal thanks to the many more people who have provided me with interesting questions, an endless source of excuses to embark upon yet another quest for enlightenment. Since the quest often imparts more insight into a problem than its solution, I have a large group of customers, beta testers, and Borlanders to thank for unwittingly directing my continuing education.

Thanks to Addison-Wesley's Claire Horne for calling my bluff and seducing me into this new torture machine (book writing), to Mary Treseler for executing the plan with seemingly endless patience, and to John Fuller and the rest of the A-W production staff for their great work in putting this book together. Thanks to Chuck Jazdzewski for taking time out to review and critique the manuscript and to Steve Treffethen for the many hours spent checking technical details in the text and source code examples. Thanks to Ken Henderson and Luk Vermeulen for their detailed reviews of the manuscript and to Richard Haven and Roy Nelson for their comments on the text.

ACKNOWLEDGMENTS

A special thanks to my boss, Gary Whizin, for not throttling me when I first informed him of this after-hours book project (it's hard to define "after-hours" when you're on salary) right in the middle of the Delphi 2.0 schedule crunch. Thanks to my former boss, Delphi QA manager Ramin Halviatti, for having faith in the Delphi QA team to build radical test automation tools to make the highest-quality development tools on perpetually impossible schedules. (I never met a Zombie I didn't like.) Thanks to Eberhard Waiblinger for hauling a math major with a lot more energy than QA experience halfway across the continent to this odd place called Santa Cruz. Thanks to Jim Land for "letting" the student workers do real work, and thanks to the late Dr. Betty Jane Fairchild, whose generosity kicked my career up a notch before I even knew where the notches were.

It's all about opportunity—them that makes it and them that takes it. I'm grateful to these and many other people who created the opportunities I have taken and to those who have shown faith by allowing me to take opportunities I wasn't entirely ready for.

Foreword

When I first heard that "yet another" Delphi programming book was in the works, I must admit I had some reservations about its chances of success in an already crowded field of Delphi programming titles. After all, how many different ways can one describe the intricate process of dropping a Delphi component on a form? What would this new book offer that hadn't already been through the mill a dozen times before? When I learned that this book was a skunkworks project by our own Danny Thorpe and would focus on advanced topics in component design and VCL system services, I knew immediately that this would be no ordinary Delphi paint-by-numbers cookbook. In Danny's six years on the Delphi (then Pascal) team, thoroughness and attention to detail have been his hallmark and made him one of our top information resources at Borland.

The chapters before you are essays on specific topics important to designing and implementing Delphi components. If you could sit down for a one-hour, one-on-one session with the Delphi R&D engineer who had a hand in designing or implementing some part of Delphi or VCL, you would receive the information contained in these chapters, as well as a lot of illegible whiteboard scribbles. In addition to describing the VCL classes and routines related to a topic, the chapters often provide background information about the task that the routines were designed to solve and notes on how the routines were intended to be used. This ambient information simply can't be gleaned from the source code alone.

While you can build components and applications without having complete knowledge of the VCL innards, you can build even better components and applications when you fully understand what's going on inside. I can think of no better person to bring you the Delphi inside story than Danny Thorpe.

Anders Hejlsberg
Delphi Chief Architect
August 1996

Introduction

This book has been a long time coming. About midway through Delphi 1.0's development, Borland's press relations people began quietly showing pieces of Delphi to authors and book publishers to drum up interest in Delphi and producing Delphi books. Judging from the number of Delphi titles that appeared scant weeks after Delphi 1.0's introduction, it would appear that few turned down the opportunity. Dozens more authors and publishers leapt into the fray once the viability of the Delphi book market was proven by several best-selling Delphi titles.

Since the Delphi publishing campaign began, I have been fortunate enough to participate in the technical editing of several superb Delphi programming books (and, yes, one or two real stinkers). Most of the books in the first wave were written for Delphi beginners, as you would expect for a new product release. As the Delphi customer base matured and the Delphi product approached its second major release (32-bit Delphi 2.0), more technical topics found their way into the second wave of Delphi books. Even so, I still found myself begging authors to dig deeper into VCL core topics: "This description is just the tip of the iceberg. Keep going! Don't stop! Don't stop!" A few authors made heroic efforts to accommodate such pleas in eleventh hour editing, but most responded with a perfectly valid point: "That level of detail is well beyond our target audience. We don't want to alienate our readers." Invariably, I'd sigh, and acquiesce: "OK, you're right of course. I just wish someone would write for the advanced Delphi crowd. *Delphi for Rocket Scientists. Delphi for Demigods.* Or *something.*"

Delphi Component Design is the result of repeating that wish once too often.

Intended Audience

This book is written for experienced Delphi programmers who seek a deeper understanding of the Delphi language, component model, and extensible tools interfaces and who aspire to build robust, professional components that take maximum advantage of Delphi's Visual Component Library (VCL). If you are already well into building Delphi components and have questions about which end goes up or if you are an accomplished Delphi application programmer interested in venturing into the realm of component design, this book is for you.

To get the most out of this book's facts, techniques, tips, and quips, you need to be familiar with the 32-bit Delphi 2.0 programming environment, general language syntax, and common component classes, and you need to have a working knowledge of object-oriented programming (OOP) principles. If you aren't sure what *encapsulation*, *inheritance*, and *polymorphism* mean or can't identify where they appear in everyday Delphi programs, spend some time reviewing the OOP tutorials in the Delphi product documentation or other Delphi primers before diving into this book.

With few exceptions, the topics in this book apply equally well to Delphi 2.0, Delphi 1.0, and the upcoming Delphi 3.0 release. The implementation details discussed here focus entirely on the Delphi 2.0 VCL code base. When reading such implementation details Delphi 1.0 readers will need to filter out the niceties of Win32 and Delphi 2.0, such as long strings and visual form inheritance; Delphi 3.0 readers will need to keep in mind that Delphi 3.0 will most likely have added to the Delphi 2.0 feature set and code base discussed here. While internal implementation details will vary from one version to the next, the interfaces of classes and subsystems you use to engage those implementations will not change dramatically. The design and programming techniques discussed here apply to all versions of Delphi.

This book is not an OOP tutorial; it's not a Delphi programming tutorial; it's not a treatise on general object-oriented design concepts. This book is about building Delphi components, from start to finish, from bird's-eye views of how a component fits into the system to nitty-gritty implementation details of how and why things work, from design-time support tools to run-time performance optimizations.

32-Bit Windows Programming: Big Pond, Big Fish

Writing Delphi components often requires working closely with the Windows Application Programming Interface (the Windows API). If you're not familiar with the use of window handles, window procedures, sending, posting, and receiving window messages, manipulating device contexts, dynamic link libraries (DLLs), pen handles, brush handles, font handles, bitmap handles, handles, handles, handles . . . , then you should be! Such experience is not required to understand the topics in this book, but it is foolish to write components without an awareness of the environment they must operate in: 32-bit Windows. Would you build and sail a boat with no knowledge of the sea? This isn't little old DOS. Win32 is an incredibly rich environment. Even seasoned Win3.1 programmers will find that Win32 is a much bigger pond, teeming with system services that 16-bit Windows programmers can only dream about. It is in your best interest to learn what Win32 can do for you, and to you, if only to avoid wasting time implementing features that are already provided by the operating system. The appendix summarizes a few of the major differences between 16-bit and 32-bit Windows programming.

How to Read This Book

This book is presented in three parts corresponding to the three phases of component creation: Analysis and Design, Implementation Details, and Design-Time Support Tools. Newcomers to Delphi or to OOP should read the chapters in order, front to back. Take your time going through Part II, Implementation Details. Just skim Part III, Design-Time Tools, until your component is actually ready to enter the design-time support phase of development.

Advanced Delphi component architects can probably read the chapters in any order, using the book as a reference or a collection of essays on specific topics. If you're like me, though, this will inevitably lead to reading the book from back to front, as you follow one intriguing reference after another back to their earlier chapters of origin. Nonlinear readers should check out the summaries at the end of each chapter for digests of the important topics covered in that chapter.

Somewhere in this book, I will probably use the terms *class* and *object* interchangeably. Strictly speaking, *class* refers to a type (a concept in your head), while *object* refers to an instance of a type (actual data in memory). When I must speak strictly, I'll use the terms carefully, but otherwise don't worry about it. Also, *object* could be misconstrued as a reference to the Borland Pascal 7.0 (BP7)-era object model. The DOS era has passed—you'll hear naught of BP7 objects in these pages.

Each chapter presents general recommendations along with specific techniques and detailed explanations. Some of the more detailed explanations may not sink in completely on the first read. There's no need to be concerned or frustrated by this unless the topic is still unfathomable in the fourth or fifth read. At that point, skip it, forget it, and get on with your project and the rest of the book. None of the advanced topics in this book are required knowledge to produce professional Delphi applications. The "Aha!" may strike you later when you're sizing up an odd problem in another project. Or, you can just have your kids explain it to you over video games and pizza (the hacker's muses).

Here Be Dragons

Many of the topics in this book delve deep into implementation details of Delphi's subsystems. Knowledge of how a feature is implemented is often key to understanding how it can be used most effectively. However, don't confuse awareness of implementation with indiscriminate reliance upon implementation details. Implementation awareness is knowing that, in the 2.0 version of Delphi, Integer and Longint types are the same size (4 bytes). Unhealthy implementation reliance would be writing code that *assumes* Sizeof(Integer) = Sizeof(Longint). Delphi implementation details are discussed in this book to provide background information so that you can better understand how your components interact with the rest of the system through the documented classes and functions.

The chapters of Part III document Delphi IDE design-time interfaces available to components and component writers that are probably not documented anywhere else. Borland reserves the right to change undocumented aspects of Delphi in future versions. However, given that much of the Delphi IDE depends on these interfaces, they aren't likely to change much without justifiable cause.

Many of these chapters refer to the VCL source code for examples of particular design or implementation techniques. It's neither practical nor appropriate for this book to print all the code associated with such references. Since you're interested in understanding the implementation of VCL, I assume you already have the VCL source code (included in the Delphi 2.0 Developer edition and Delphi 2.0 Client/Server Suite). This book will help you understand VCL details by summarizing and explaining aspects of the implementation, but the source code is always the ultimate authority. *Use the source, Luke!*

"Here be dragons" was a label cartographers of old inscribed in blank areas of the map, regions they knew little about or from which ships never returned. Technology has long since filled in most of the blank spaces on the old maps, but complete detail in modern charts has done little to diminish the power and wonders of the sea. Use this book to chart the deeper waters of Delphi, but take care to use this information responsibly. There still be dragons here, and, just as in days of yore, they feast on carelessness and poor judgment.

PART I

Analysis and Design

Chapter 1

The Delphi Programming Model

A model is a collection of patterns and rules that allows us to describe the behavior of a complex system without requiring complete knowledge of the system. You're constantly using models whether you realize it or not—modeling is a core function of the human mind, critical to memory, recognition, and analysis. The mind is not very good at retaining even small volumes of raw data, but it is fairly adept at recognizing and remembering relationships and patterns in data. Modeling is one of the mind's data compression and abstraction strategies that reduces difficult-to-store raw data into easier-to-store patterns, modifies existing patterns to accommodate new data, and synthesizes data from stored patterns. In data compression terms, modeling is a lossy compression. Modeling throws away much of the actual data after identifying patterns, and data synthesized from those patterns might not match the original data exactly. A mental model doesn't need to be exact; it just needs to be good enough to quickly distinguish between friend, foe, and food in a complex environment (like Windows).

A programming model is a collection of rules and guidelines that describes the interactions between subroutines and objects within a program, between the program and the operating system, and between the program and the end user. A programming model provides a basis for commonsense problem solving—quick, speculative solutions without an overload of details. Familiarity with a programming model gives you an intuitive sense of how things *should* work; familiarity with an implementation gives you a detailed sense of how things *actually* work.

Blueprints provide a model of a building's internal structure, but as any builder will tell you, what's on paper doesn't always translate directly into walls, wiring, and fixtures. The blueprints often aren't detailed enough to specify the placement of every nail in the building—this is usually left to the discretion and experience of the carpenter. Blueprints can contain errors (8-inch-diameter pipe in a 6-inch-thick wall), and construction can contain errors (6-inch pipe where

8-inch is specified and required for proper operation). In general, though, the two should be a close enough match that you can estimate costs of adding a room or removing a wall based on the blueprints and know where it is safe to begin knocking out plaster to gain access to electrical and water lines.

Even more important is the consistency that should accompany an overall design plan. As you're walking through the framed-up building, you want to be able to predict where electrical outlets will go and what kind they will be without having to continually refer back to the 40 pages of blueprints. Using a different kind of electrical outlet in every room severely compromises your ability to accurately guess which goes where. Your builder's ability to make ad hoc decisions goes down, the probability of error (due to lack of consistency) goes up, and the cost of implementing and maintaining the design rises dramatically.

As you have probably guessed by now, it is faster and easier to learn a programming model than to absorb the details of an entire implementation. If you know the model, you can learn the details on an as-needed basis, dictated by your works in progress. If you begin with the details, you can't really get anything started until you've assimilated enough details to invent your own mental model of how you *think* the system works.

This chapter describes the history, goals, and features of the Delphi programming model. The intent of this book is to help you develop an intuition for Delphi and its Visual Component Library (VCL). With that intuition, you can find your way around in Delphi's many components and subsystems as well as recognize and design components that fit naturally into the Delphi programming environment.

Delphi—10 Years in the Making

Despite the 1.0 version number on the box, Delphi is an evolutionary step in a long line of Borland Pascal compiler products. To better understand what and why Delphi is, let's take a quick trip through Mr. Peabody's Wayback Machine to look at the events that shaped Delphi's development.

In the Beginning

Borland's first commercial product, released in 1983, was Turbo Pascal 1.0, whose low price and blinding compile speed quickly put Borland on the software development tools map. Many an eyebrow was raised to ponder how a $49 compiler from an unknown upstart could run 10 times faster than $400 compilers made by the pros. Even more eyebrows went up when it was discovered that the upstart company was making a bundle—more than the pros, it seems—by selling at a low price in high volume.

Turbo Pascal 1.0 was also the debut of the Integrated Development Environment (IDE). The seamless integration of source code editor and compiler tools quickly became a Borland hallmark.

Turbo Pascal for the Mac introduced the notion of compiled unit modules, which found its way to the DOS world in Turbo Pascal 4.0 in 1987. Compiled units allow the compiler to load in one operation all the symbols and machine code previously compiled from a source code module, eliminating the need to recompile the source file over and over again. OBJ files emitted by traditional compilers contain machine code but hardly any symbol information—certainly not enough to stand in for source code. Eliminating redundant source code compilation improved compilation speed by orders of magnitude over compiled languages such as C that assume the compiler must see all the source code in the project. Header files in C are just a trick to make the compiler think it *has* seen the source code. Precompiled headers, developed years later in the C camps, are an approximation to the symbol information stored in Pascal units, but they still do not contain the machine code that corresponds to the source code program logic.

Turbo Pascal 5.0 saw the debut of integrated debugging in the IDE, a natural extension of the original integrated development environment idea. Never before had DOS programmers been able to change a line of source code, compile, link, and run the application to that point in the source code, and inspect the actual value of variables in the running program, all without leaving the development environment. Elapsed time for that entire exercise was about 3 seconds.

OOP Debut

In 1989, Turbo Pascal 5.5 introduced object oriented programming (OOP) language syntax and concepts. Many programmers were enchanted by the power and potential of OOP, but most (including me) didn't know quite what to do with it. Turbo Pascal 5.5 was criticized for its lack of ready-made objects—the compiler supported all the code reuse features promised by OOP, but the product didn't contain a library of objects ready for programmers to reuse.

In 1990, Turbo Pascal 6.0 answered that criticism with its Turbo Vision application framework, an extensive architecture of objects for building DOS applications with windowed text-mode user interfaces. While recognized as a technical triumph, Turbo Vision was criticized for being too complex, with a steep learning curve that put off many traditional DOS programmers. Much of that criticism was relative: Writing even moderately complex DOS programs using traditional structured programming techniques didn't require a great deal of effort or organization; at the same time, customer expectations for user interfaces in DOS apps were pretty low. So, compared to what DOS programmers were already accustomed to doing, Turbo Vision was more complicated and radically different. In many programmers' eyes, Turbo Vision's many automatic user interface and internal program structure benefits were not enough to justify making a radical shift in programming paradigms.

New Frontiers, New Challenges

In 1991, Turbo Pascal for Windows (TPW) hit the Windows 3.0 scene, complete with its Object Windows Library (OWL) application framework. OWL encapsulated the window and message management required in a Windows application. Using objects for this management allowed for more modular programming than was found in traditional Windows apps and took care of most of the gory details of keeping a Windows app afloat. Ironically, though OWL was not as sophisticated an application framework as Turbo Vision, OWL was more widely embraced than Turbo Vision primarily because it simplified the complex Windows programming environment. For DOS programmers, Turbo Vision was a step up in complexity. For Windows programmers, OWL was a step down in complexity. It was not uncommon to hear comments like "After writing an app with TPW OWL, you would be crazy to write Windows apps the old way."

Though used by most TPW programmers, OWL received criticisms on many fronts. It did not encapsulate or assist with graphics output or other Windows programming chores, forcing the programmer to grapple with the overwhelming Windows Application Programming Interface (API) on a daily basis. Object persistence, or storing the state of an object to disk for later retrieval, was no less complicated than in TP6's Turbo Vision. TPW included visual tools to design dialogs and menus, but these were difficult to synchronize with their corresponding OWL objects. Most display output required discrete code at great programming expense—and loss of hair. With the launch of Microsoft Visual Basic six months after TPW, these visual dialog and menu editing tools were quickly deemed inferior for what would later be called rapid application development.

The year 1992 saw the launch of Borland Pascal 7.0, a mammoth product that included tools for producing DOS apps, Windows apps, and protected-mode DOS apps. BP7 included incremental improvements to Turbo Vision, OWL, and the IDE, but its primary attractions were greatly improved compiler capacity for compiling very large projects and support for generating protected-mode DOS applications. Protected mode allowed DOS applications to break through DOS's inherent 640K memory limit and gain easy access to all available memory in 80286 or better machines—something Windows programmers already enjoyed.

A Time for Change

With the greatest (and possibly last) release of Borland Pascal for DOS development completed, the Pascal development team turned its full attention to "the Windows situation." Even though BP7 generated more revenue than all previous versions of the Pascal products combined, it was clear that the DOS development tools market was in rapid decline. About the same time as BP7's release, market analysts reported that sales of Windows applications and development tools had eclipsed sales of the same products for DOS, and Windows showed no signs of slowing down. Windows was clearly where the future growth opportunities for development tools lay, along with the stiffest competition. In DOS, Borland's Pascal products had enjoyed total dominance of a fairly well-defined niche—DOS Pascal programming—almost since inception. The Windows development tools market was far more volatile. TPW and BP7 were caught in a valley between the market-presence mountains of Visual Basic on the low end and C++ tools on the high end. The Pascal development team needed to design and build a product to break out of that dangerous squeeze play, either by going head-to-head with the competition or by redefining the product and its target market to put the competition at a disadvantage. In the end, Delphi did both.

Lessons Learned

The development team did a great deal of soul-searching throughout the development of Delphi, looking for issues small and large that plague the Windows software development process, in Borland tools and in competitors' tools. The following points are a condensation of the technical lessons gathered from Borland's previous 10 years of market experience in software development tools. These are the issues that shaped the development of the Delphi programming model and product.

- **OOP has many prerequisites.** Creating new objects from scratch and extending objects through inheritance require OOP skills and experience. Extending existing objects through inheritance requires knowledge of how the ancestor classes work and what opportunities they provide for overriding behavior.

Overriding virtual methods requires knowledge of what responses the methods must provide. Since most objects work in the context of a society of cooperating objects, extending objects also requires knowledge of the application framework that surrounds and supports the objects. All in all, extending objects requires a considerable amount of training and familiarity with the system.

- **Inheritance raises skill requirements.** In application frameworks such as Turbo Vision and OWL, you implemented most application-specific behavior by inheriting from and extending existing objects. In order to successfully build an application, you had to understand OOP principles, the nature of the objects you were inheriting from, and the framework around you. Relying almost solely on inheritance to build applications made the learning curve for these frameworks steeper than non-OOP tools.

- **Most programmers don't have the time to embrace an entire framework.** For most programmers, writing applications is not the objective, it is only a means to an end. The real job is to solve problems and implement solutions. Taking a few weeks off to learn the ins and outs of a new framework is a luxury few can afford, even if productivity would be enhanced after the hiatus. Programmers who ignore deadlines in favor of training may well find themselves highly trained unemployed programmers. An ideal development environment would allow the programmer to implement solutions with a minimum of retraining delay, and with minimal understanding of the environment and services being used.

- **Programming teams are internally segregated by experience and tools.** Few commercial or corporate programmers work alone. In any team, there will be a wide variety of experience among the team members. Most programming teams consist of a few highly skilled architects and a majority of less experienced implementors. Highly skilled programmers tend to favor either high-end object-oriented development tools or lowest-level machine code assemblers. Such tools have the power and flexibility to do exactly what the programmer wants, but they tend to be too complex and unwieldy for the rest of the team to use on a daily basis. Low-end, non-OOP development tools allow implementors to get their tasks done quickly, but they lack the power and flexibility demanded by the architects. Disparity in tools often leads to communication breakdowns within the team and problems integrating the many pieces of the application. The difference in tools also hampers the growth paths of implementors aspiring to build their experience up to architect levels. At some point in the path to enlightenment, they must abandon most of the practical experience they've accumulated with the low-end tools and start from scratch with the high-end tools.

- **Programmers loathe pointers and memory management chores.** Pointer manipulation, dynamic memory allocation, resource management, and lifetime analysis are usually considered advanced topics reserved for second-semester programming courses. Many professional programmers with years of experience loathe pointers and memory management even more than second-semester students do. Regardless of experience or predisposition, pointer manipulation and memory management are certainly among the leading sources of bugs in any software. Since pointers are critical to many powerful programming techniques, you still want and need pointer support in your tools, but anything that can be done to eliminate or hide the headaches of managing pointers from everyday code would go a long way toward making a programming tool more usable and the resulting programs more robust.

- **Most customized objects aren't reusable.** Creating applications with Turbo Vision and OWL always involved extending stock objects to perform specific tasks. Some of those customized objects were necessarily application specific, such as the application object or main window object. Many customized objects performed operations common to many apps, but these were often implemented in such a way that made the objects specific to a particular application. For example, it was common to create a custom button object type to perform a particular action when the button was clicked. The action might have been a generic operation, but the implementation of the object often referenced other parts of that particular application. Such references make it difficult to drop that custom button object into a different application.

    As we will see in Chapter 2, Designing Components, there will always be a need for application-specific code and classes. Part of the problem in Turbo Vision, OWL, and other OOP frameworks was that there was no clear distinction between creating application-specific code and creating application-portable code. A larger part of this issue was that inheritance was about the only way to implement application-specific behaviors in those programming models.

- **Most object customizations alter only a few kinds of behavior.** In OWL and Turbo Vision, custom button objects were frequently quite small, containing only code to respond to button clicks. Initialization, shutdown, and painting code were usually all that custom dialog objects contained. These kinds of flyweight objects were also usually application specific. Creating a substantially new object was far less common and, by definition, involved more than just a new button click response. Such new objects were much more likely to be autonomous application-portable code than the quick-and-dirty flyweights.

- **Objects were brittle across versions.** In Chapter 3, Virtual Methods and Polymorphism, we'll examine in detail why Turbo Pascal's original object model made it difficult to enhance base classes without breaking something in descendant classes. Once an object was released to customers, the author's options for enhancing the object were severely limited. Object persistence was also extremely version sensitive.

- **Object persistence was labor intensive and error prone.** Implementing persistent storage of an object's state (object streaming) was an involved process. The steps themselves weren't complicated, but they were far from obvious. If you added data fields to an object, you had to remember to write those fields to the stream in the object's Store method and read them from the stream in the object's Load constructor. When creating a new descendant, you had to remember to build a stream registration record for the new object type and register that record with the streaming system. You also had to choose a stream id number to uniquely identify your object type, which posed coordination problems for third-party developers of add-in object libraries. All of these chores added up to a lot of moaning and groaning from Pascal developers—including the members of the Pascal development team!

- **GUI applications need GUI development tools.** Using source code statements to arrange controls in a window leads to clunky interfaces and lots of development time lost to experimentation to get the controls lined up just right. In describing TPW, one observer noted, "It's a good thing the compiler's so fast, because you're going to have to modify, compile and run several times to get the controls situated." At the time, that comment was a compliment to the product's fast compile-and-test turnaround time because all development tools were pretty much in the same boat. As graphical user interface (GUI) design tools entered the Windows development market, though, that same comment picked up an unmistakable note of sarcasm.

- **Visual dialog resource editors are hard to integrate with source code.** The visual resource editors included in TPW made it much easier to place and position controls in dialogs and build menus than the code-only solution Turbo Vision programmers were used to. Still, the integration of source code and dialog template resources was far from perfect. There were many id numbers and names in the dialog and menu resources that had to match the source code exactly, or nothing would work. Maintenance of these links was largely a manual task and, as with any manual task, was easily broken.

- **Windows programming and resource management are complicated.** Since OWL encapsulated only the window management portion of a Windows application, programmers had to understand the rules and rituals of the Windows Graphics Device Interface (GDI) before any output could appear on the screen. Management of Windows resources—pens, brushes, bitmaps, device contexts, and so forth—was a constant hassle. The penalty for ignoring resource management was a resource leak that would eventually bring Windows to a screeching halt.

- **Most Windows applications use only a small subset of the Windows API.** Despite, or perhaps because of, the thousands of functions that make up the Windows API, most applications use only a handful of core routines for text output, graphics output, window management, and keyboard and mouse input. To simplify Windows application development, an ideal development tool wouldn't have to make all the Windows APIs easier to use. Making just the core subset of the most common Windows programming tasks easier to accomplish would be enough to make most Windows application development much simpler.

- **Error handling is complex, and poor error handling erodes program stability.** As discussed in detail in Chapter 4, Exceptions, traditional error-handling techniques are labor intensive and prone to failure. Proper handling of errors encountered in subroutine calls usually requires detailed knowledge of how the subroutines indicate error conditions and what action your code is expected to take to respond or relay that information elsewhere. Most Windows APIs return error codes, but because of the overhead traditional error checking adds to a program's source code, most programmers never check such error codes.

- **Integrated database support is needed everywhere.** Most programs exist to process data, and data seems to appear in ever-increasing volumes. Usually, when data and volume are used in the same breath, you need a database—a permanent data storage and retrieval system that may also provide data organization and analysis services. Borland offered a Paradox Engine development kit as an upsell for its DOS and Windows development tools, but this was far from the support needed to build full-featured database applications quickly and easily.

- **Existing OWL code is not easily portable to 32-bit Windows.** Even when Delphi was in its earliest phases of development, it was clear that 32-bit Windows would be an important platform down the road. Preliminary research showed that while it was possible to port the OWL architecture to 32-bit Windows, the port would require changes to the interfaces of many OWL objects. Interface changes meant that all OWL applications would have to be modified to match the new OWL to make the transition to 32 bits. After all that work, you would still be left with the same problems you faced in the original OWL—only bigger.

Delphi Solutions

Delphi's solutions to these issues involve all aspects of the programming process: language, OOP architecture, development environment, and programming model. Few development tools have enjoyed as much flexibility in tailoring all four of these facets to reach their goals as Delphi, and none before Delphi were native code compilers. In C and C++, language syntax is immutable and complex, which makes it difficult to achieve a clean, fast, unified source code and design environment model.

The following items summarize the key features of the Delphi programming model. These are Delphi's solutions to the issues identified in the previous section.

- **Custom behaviors through delegation instead of inheritance.** Delegation occurs when one object implements a special behavior for another object. Instead of creating a special button class just to make the button do something when it is clicked (the inheritance model), delegation allows a general-purpose button class to notify a delegate object when the button is clicked, and the delegate can then implement the specific behavior desired for the button click response. This solves the problem of having to create scores of trivial application-specific classes to implement application-specific behaviors. In Delphi, you still have application-specific classes, but these are almost exclusively forms. A form is the delegate for all components placed on the form. All application-specific behaviors of components are implemented in methods of the form that are called by the components through properties called *events* (pointers to methods in the form). This provides a clear distinction between application-specific code (events in the form) and application-portable code (component classes) and makes it easier to design components that are both highly reusable and easily customizable.

Using delegation to customize the behavior of an object has fewer prerequisites than inheritance. To use delegation (write an event handler), you don't need to understand objects or inheritance, or the syntax for declaring a descendant class and overriding virtual methods, or much about the application framework around you. To write an event handler, you really don't need to understand anything about the architecture of the component except when the component will fire the event. For most Delphi events, this is pretty obvious in the name of the event—OnClick, OnCreate, and OnPaint, for example.

- **Contractless programming.** When you override an inherited method, you must determine whether you are required to call the inherited method or not, whether the ancestor requires that your method perform some minimum task, and whether that method will be called when the object (or the system) is in a state that has special rules or limitations. For example, the WM_KILLFOCUS Windows message has the special limitation that you should not cause a focus change while processing that message. Failure to observe this rule will crash Windows. These rules, limitations, and requirements form a *contract* between the author of the base object and the author of the descendant object. For the object to operate correctly, the descendant's implementation of the overridden method must fulfill all requirements of the contract. To fulfill the contract, the implementor of the descendant must be familiar with the contract, which requires documentation, research, and retraining.

    Contractless programming places no limitations or special requirements on the implementation of a routine. In the interest of minimizing training and skill prerequisites to writing event handlers, Delphi component events should be contractless. A component should allow an event handler to do just about anything, within reason. A component must continue to work if an event handler is assigned but does nothing. Since you're allowing application writers to do anything in an event handler, exceptions are a very real possibility. A component should wrap calls to event handlers in `try` blocks to ensure that any temporary resources allocated by the component (written by you) are freed correctly if something goes wrong in the event handler (written by others). From a component's perspective, events are external calls where anything can and will happen.

If your component is in a partial state when an event needs to be fired, defer the event until the component is completely usable. For example, the OnExit event is fired when a control loses focus to another control in the same form. VCL implements its focus notifications such that the OnExit event does not execute in the context of a WM_KILLFOCUS message. Thus, OnExit is not subject to the restrictions or catastrophic consequences of WM_KILLFOCUS message—OnExit is contractless, even though its execution is linked (indirectly) to the very contractual WM_KILLFOCUS message.

Delphi's target entry-level user is someone who is already familiar with general programming principles (variables, loops, conditional statements) and one programming language. Contractless event handler programming combined with delegation enable these entry-level Delphi programmers to begin building useful applications with a minimum of retraining.

- **Visual program design seamlessly merged with programming environment.** Borland researched and built several visual design environment prototypes before arriving at the Delphi IDE visual design environment as we know it today. Some prototypes explored the possibility of pure visual programming, eliminating source code altogether. Other prototypes studied the feasibility of more traditional CASE tool approaches. Most of these prototypes were rejected either because they didn't solve the issues any better than existing development tools or because they introduced more problems than they solved.

    The visual design environment that emerged from this crucible is both a visual design tool and a source code editing and debugging tool. (Dessert topping and floor wax were given careful consideration but were eventually dropped to avoid market confusion.) The user can move freely from the visual representation of a component (in the form designer), to the Object Inspector to edit the initial run-time state of the component, to the source code editor to edit the execution logic of the component. Changing code-related properties in the Object Inspector, such as the name of an event handler, automatically changes the corresponding source code. Changing source code, such as renaming an event handler method in a form class declaration, is immediately reflected in the Object Inspector.

    Delphi's seamlessness between project management, code generation, and source code editing is unique in the industry. Most CASE tools maintain a database of project options and structural details and generate (copious!) source code based on that internal database. As soon as the source code file is generated, the internal database is obsolete—modifications to the generated source code may invalidate the data in the internal database. The process of capturing source code modifications and incorporating them back into the database is very difficult to accomplish reliably. Often, CASE tools either don't allow generated code to be edited or require that edits be restricted to specially commented zones in the source code. Failure to follow these rules usually results in the destruction of your source code modifications when the CASE tool regenerates the source code.

Unlike CASE tools, there is no opportunity for the source code to get out of sync with the Delphi IDE's internal representation of the project because the source *is* the Delphi IDE's sole representation of the project. This unity of source and environment is possible partly because of an extremely high-speed, lightweight parser in the IDE that rescans the current editor source file every time focus leaves the source code editor window. This "superparser" extracts the identifiers needed by the Delphi Project Manager to repopulate internal lists (such those used by event property editors) in far less than the blink of an eye, even if the source code is not in a compilable state. The unity of source and environment is also partly due to Delphi's relatively unencumbered Object Pascal syntax. Because the parser doesn't have to deal with unraveling macro substitutions, for example, valuable source code identifiers and syntax markers can be located with a minimum of processing overhead.

Though Delphi is technically a source code generator, it is not a program synthesizer. Delphi doesn't generate program logic; it simply helps with the housekeeping by generating empty event handler method bodies and fields and method declarations in the form's class type as needed. This makes adding components to the form as simple as drag and drop and adding an event handler for a component event as simple as a double click on the event property editor. It also helps ease programmers accustomed to interpreted or loosely typed languages into Delphi's strictly typed language.

The Delphi code generation and property streaming systems are completely open to inspection. There are no black boxes hiding information about the project. The contents of the form, all its properties, and all its components and their properties can be viewed—and edited—as text in the source code editor simply by selecting the View as Text option in the form designer's local menu. Also, complete source code is available for everything that winds up in your final EXE file—all the Delphi components and all of the VCL and RTL source code are available for your inspection, education, and (if you're really brazen) alteration. Everything that is a Delphi project is viewable and editable in the source code window.

The visual design environment doesn't stop with editing visual components. Nonvisual components can be configured and connected to other components and to event handlers using the Object Inspector, further streamlining the software development cycle. Many a fully functional Delphi application has been built without writing a single line of code. This is certainly a far cry from the TPW norm, where many a line of code was needed to get a program to load and use the dialog resources created with a visual design tool (resource editor)! Keep in mind, too, that TPW was revolutionary in its time: less than 100 lines of code were needed to produce a functional Windows application using the OWL application framework—far less than the available compiler tools of the day. The amount of code you must write to produce a Windows application with Delphi is orders of magnitude less than with TPW, and TPW's minimums were orders of magnitude less than traditional C tools.

- **Automatic object persistence through property streaming.** Published properties of components are the result of a marriage of compiler and VCL architecture support. In general, all you need to do to make a component streamable is make sure it has the TPersistent base class somewhere in its ancestry. All you need to do to make the data of your component streamable is declare properties in a published section of the component's class declaration. That's it! The declaration is all the compiler needs to generate internal Run-Time Type Information (RTTI) structures that describe how to read and write the published properties of your component class. RTTI, examined in Chapter 5, is all that VCL's streaming classes, discussed in Chapter 6, need in order to know what properties exist in a class, their data types, and how to read and write their data.

  More than 95% of the data carried by Delphi components is a simple type (string, ordinal, set, or float) and is handled automatically by the property streaming system. The other 5% (data in nonsimple types) is handled by the component author by overriding a component's DefineProperties virtual method and writing the special data more or less "the old-fashioned way."

  Automatic property streaming makes writing components far easier than in previous OOP architectures. Like delegation, property streaming reduces the need to override virtual methods, which reduces the training required to build a new persistent component. It also eliminates all the busywork steps required by other architectures to register various parts of an object with the system. In Delphi, the class declaration is all the registration that is needed for a component to be streamable. There are no mountains of table-generating macros or multiple-choice vtables to cross-wire or stream registration records to copy and link together.

- **Automatic design-time component editing.** RTTI and the streaming mechanism are critical to the Delphi IDE's design-time environment. The Object

Inspector uses RTTI the same way the streaming system does—to find out what properties exist in a class, their data types, and how to read and write their values—but for a different purpose. Where the streaming system uses RTTI to save property values to a file, the Object Inspector uses it to display property values at design time. Where the streaming system uses RTTI to assign file data to properties, the Object Inspector uses RTTI to edit property values. As covered in Chapter 12, the Object Inspector supports the use of custom editors for special properties, but the 95% coverage rule for automatic property streaming also applies to automatic design-time editing support. If a property is automatically streamable, it is also automatically editable in the Object Inspector.

- **Custom components easily incorporated into the visual design environment.** Some visual programming tools allow you to register custom controls, but they represent those custom controls with simulations, such as empty boxes. Some development tools don't support custom add-ins to the environment at all, while others, like Visual Basic, require that add-ins be written in a completely different language and programming model. Delphi is unique in that installing a new component into the development environment actually recompiles part of the IDE, making the new component an integral part of the IDE. When you drop a component onto a form, what you see is not a simulation of your component, but your actual component, executing as it would in any Delphi program.

    Many people find this amazing, almost supernatural. The amazement probably has less to do with the fact that their component is now sitting on a form at design time with all its properties available in the Object Inspector and more to do with how little they did to get it there. As with automatic property streaming and property editing, almost all components can be installed into the IDE component library with no special design-time coding considerations. The VCL architecture and RTTI take care of the details of making a component accessible to the design-time environment. Thus, the step from writing components to writing design-time editable components is negligible.

    For components with special design-time requirements or which must behave differently at design time than at runtime, there are a number of design-time interfaces available to components and component writers. The major Delphi design-time interfaces are covered in Part III of this book.

- **Memory allocation and pointers hidden but still readily available.** Delphi's class model allocates all object instances from the global heap. This gives up the option of storing object instance data on the stack or in the global data segment, but it provides a more consistent memory management and object-handling model. All objects are allocated from the heap, so all object variables are pointers to the heap. Since all object variables are pointers, explicit pointer dereferencing is redundant, and the compiler allows object variables to be used without an explicit dereference operator.

There is only one way to allocate an instance of a Delphi class: call the constructor. Memory allocation is implicit in the constructor call; deallocation, implicit in the destructor call. The VCL architecture defines component ownership rules, one of which is that when a component is destroyed, it also destroys all components it owns. Since all components manipulated with the visual design environment and most components created dynamically in program code are owned by another component (usually, the form), both memory allocation and deallocation of component instances are automatic.

Finally, Delphi 2.0's long-string support eliminates memory allocation chores commonly associated with managing large text buffers. Long strings are allocated from the global heap and managed by RTL and compiler-generated code, providing value semantics identical to the classic byte-length string (short strings).

These factors were all designed to pull memory allocation and pointer management out of the line of sight of Delphi programmers to address the issue that nobody enjoys wading through pointers. Pointer operations are, of course, still available, as they are a fundamental type critical to many data structures and high-performance algorithms, but allocating memory with GetMem is certainly much less common in Delphi 2.0 applications than in BP7 applications or even in Delphi 1.0 apps.

- **Structured exception handling for vastly improved program stability and reliability.** Delphi 1.0 introduced language support for structured exception handling, an automatic error response system that simplifies error-handling chores in most programs. Though often overlooked, structured exception handling is one of the critical enabling technologies in Delphi, right up there with RTTI and automatic property streaming. Exceptions and exception handling are covered in Chapter 4.

- **Graphics and control encapsulation to simplify programming techniques.** Delphi includes a set of classes that encapsulate the most commonly used aspects of the GDI—device contexts, fonts, brushes, bitmaps, pens, and so forth. The primary goal of this GDI encapsulation was to make Windows graphics output easier to program. A large part of that goal was to eliminate the resource management tasks associated with creating GDI handles, selecting handles into device contexts, and releasing the GDI resources when they are no longer needed. Delphi's graphics classes do this and more. To minimize resource use and improve performance, GDI resources are reference counted and shared among many VCL components. A typical Delphi application creates only a few GDI font handles, even though hundreds of components in the app have font objects. Components that have the same font attributes share the same GDI font handle. If a component modifies a property of its font object, the font object dissociates itself from any shared font handle group it subscribes to and creates its own GDI font handle with the altered property. All the reference-counted graphics objects use this copy-on-write scheme to ensure integrity. Chapter 8 discusses Delphi's graphics classes in more detail.

These VCL classes vastly reduce the complexity of drawing text, lines, and complex shapes on a window, as compared to using the raw Windows API. Most of the time, all you need to do is get a canvas object to draw on, set the current pen color, set the brush pattern (if needed), and draw on the canvas. There is no need to create GDI handles, or select handles into device contexts, or save handles for selection back into the device context later.

- **The 90% rule of Windows API feature encapsulation.** VCL does not attempt to encapsulate every nook and cranny of the Windows API. As noted earlier, most applications use a very small subset of the total Windows API. VCL's encapsulation goal was to cover most of the Windows features that most applications need. This became known as "the 90% rule." A related goal was to allow full access to the Windows API at all times and even to assist with "extracurricular" jaunts when possible. For example, the TFont object does not expose properties to control the dozens of Windows font creation options. However, if you use the Windows API to create a specially prepared font (say, rotated by 90 degrees), you can assign that font handle into a VCL font object and use that font like any other VCL font. VCL will even take care of destroying the font handle for you. Many VCL classes have writable Handle properties, which generally implies that you may create a handle manually and stuff it into the VCL class.

- **Comprehensive support for database operations, including client/server SQL database access.** Traditional development tools have a long history of poor support for high-performance database work. Sure, database code libraries have been around forever, but you had to write a lot of code to use them. More often than not, each library locked your application into a single file format and sometimes a proprietary format at that.

Database management and development tools also have a long history—a history of being terribly slow and having limited programming capabilities. Interpreted languages found a happy home in the database programming arena thanks to the widely held belief that it doesn't matter how fast the client program is since it will always be waiting for the server to provide the next piece of data. While it's true that you can't get data from a network server any more quickly in a compiled program, most database client applications do a lot more than just beg the server for more data. Client applications display, analyze, condense, and reformat data owned by the server, but full-featured applications tend to also provide a lot of less database-related program support—program options dialogs, client-side validation or filtering of user input, menus, buttons, toolbars, and so forth.

About midway through the product specification phase, the Delphi team realized (thanks to broad-spectrum market research) just how starved the database application development market was for high-performance client/server database application development tools and how comprehensive, integrated client/server database support could catapult Delphi out of the VB/C++ market squeeze play. Delphi's high-speed compiler, visual development tools, and component architecture positioned the product in direct competition with traditional Windows development tools, while Delphi's database component architecture and flexible database engine (BDE) redefined Delphi's target market to capitalize on competitors' weaknesses—Windows development tools' lack of database support and database tools' lack of Windows programming power.

Delphi's database architecture is component based, just like everything else in Delphi. Database components come in two flavors: nonvisual data access components for easy design-time setup of database connections, links, and options, plus data aware controls for viewing and editing the data managed by the nonvisual data access components. Through the use of the Borland Database Engine (BDE), the Delphi database architecture provides seamless and consistent access to data in a variety of file formats and from a variety of SQL database servers.

- **Continuous gradient of experience.** As we'll examine in detail in the next section, Delphi caters to two kinds of programmers: application writers and component writers. The skills and programming techniques required to build components are a superset of the skills needed to build Delphi applications. Delphi programmers can progress steadily from entry-level application writers to expert component writers and application architects without changing tools or world views. Development team members of all levels of experience (even managers!) can find a comfortable operating level in Delphi after a few hours of acclimation, and all members have an upward growth path they can pursue within Delphi.

While knowledge of OOP is not required to build Delphi applications, it certainly doesn't hurt. Thus begins the road to exploring Delphi, and OOP, and Windows programming.

The Delphi Application Writer—Component Consumer

Delphi programmers fall into two general categories: application writers and component writers. These classifications are rather arbitrary, and there are no clear lines distinguishing them. Application writers are primarily interested in building complete applications using whatever components are available. Component writers are typically more interested in building components to solve a specific application programming need. Advanced Delphi programmers often wear both hats, sometimes at the same time.

Since this book is geared toward component writing, you are probably more interested in finding out what it takes to be a component writer. The first step to writing great components is to understand your customer—the Delphi application writer. A component is useless if it is too complicated to be used by anyone but its creator. Components need to be application-portable to be cost-effective; they need to be programmer-portable to be used at all.

The Application Writer's Skill Set

Delphi is a programmer's tool, not a form-building tool for nonprogrammers. Delphi assumes an entry-level application writer is a programmer, familiar with some kind of programming language and with general programming concepts such as subroutines, program loops, variables, and data structures. The Delphi documentation and on-line help are designed to help programmers recognize the Delphi syntax or terms for programming concepts they are already familiar with. The Delphi documentation does not attempt to teach fundamental programming concepts (nor does this book).

Little or No OOP

Writing applications in Delphi requires little or no knowledge of OOP principles such as polymorphism and virtual methods. The application writer is exposed to inheritance through high-level design-time features such as form inheritance but otherwise doesn't give inheritance much thought. Encapsulation, the third stone in the OOP foundation, is a natural extension of using data structures, which we have assumed the application writer is already familiar with. Essentially, the fields or properties of a component can be used the same way you would use fields in a record structure.

Low Tolerance for Pointers

Application writers have a low tolerance for pointers and memory management chores. Components should not require the use of pointers (such as PChar null-terminated strings) or memory allocations as a normal part of using a component. For example, in Delphi 1.0, many components have a Text or Caption property of type String, which is adequate for almost all situations where a programmer wants to set the caption or text contents of a component. However, the 255-character limit on Delphi 1.0 strings can pose a problem for components that manage much larger bodies of text (like TMemo), so an alternate pair of component methods (GetTextBuf and SetTextBuf) exists to allow you to fetch or set larger text blocks using the less convenient PChar type. The string property is sufficient for most purposes and far simpler to use than the PChar routines. The PChar routines exist only to cover the remaining special cases. In Delphi 2.0, all string properties are long strings, which puts PChars in their proper place—a museum.

Mid-level application writers will be comfortable creating forms and components at run time. VCL's component ownership rules dictate that if you create a component with an owner, you don't have to worry about freeing that component—it will be freed by its owner. Sophisticated application writers will be adept at creating and destroying forms and components at run time, primarily to optimize memory use.

These last two points are mentioned mostly to remind you that components can and will be created on the fly at run time by your more adventurous application writers. Don't assume that a component will only be configured at design time—a component must be able to construct itself with reasonable default property values and must be fully configurable in code through its public properties and methods. Customized design-time editors can make a complex component easier to configure at design time, but don't neglect the component's programming interface.

Little Framework Knowledge

An application writer doesn't need to know much about the VCL framework to write Delphi applications. You need to be familiar with the handful of components that you actually use and how to use the design-time tools to modify properties and write event handlers, but you don't need to be aware of how VCL dispatches messages to components, for example. You need to have some idea of when a particular event handler will be called, but not how the call is actually made. You need to know how to use a string list property to access string values in some components, but you don't have to know how to create, populate, and manage list objects such as TList and TStringList.

No Windows API Knowledge

Most Delphi application development can be done with little or no awareness of the Windows operating system humming beneath VCL. Application writers rarely have need to write message-handling methods in forms or to use the Windows SendMessage or PostMessage functions. Sophisticated application writers, particularly those who have a background in traditional Windows programming, might dabble in Windows functions to create special effects with fonts or line styles, but almost all drawing code in an application is done using VCL graphics objects. I'm sure that the enchanting and frightfully powerful Win32 features available in Delphi 2.0, such as shared memory, multithreading, and events and semaphores will attract advanced application writers like ants to a picnic, but I do hope they will take the time to read up on the Win32 operating system architecture before dropping a wrench into the warp drive.

No Streaming Knowledge

Application writers may be aware of the existence of Delphi's automatic property-based streaming system, but not how it works or how component properties participate in the streaming system. Thanks to the View as Text option in the IDE, application writers can see—and edit—the information stored in a form's DFM file. How that information gets into the Object Inspector or the running program is not particularly important when writing applications.

Note that easy access to the text version of the DFM file means application writers will be aware of how a component streams its properties. A component that streams properties as an opaque binary blob is considerably less useful to form-as-text fans than a component that streams properties with self-documenting enumerated types, string values, or otherwise readable data. Easy access also means component writers should *not* assume stream data is inherently valid.

Characteristics of Application Writing

The driving issues and motivations in writing an application are different from writing components. When designing components, keep in mind that the application writer's goals and challenges are often very different from your component-writing goals and challenges.

App Completion and Maintenance More Important Than Reusable Internal Design

Application development is typically more concerned with producing results than with producing an internally consistent and reusable design. As we will explore in Chapter 2, you can abstract and generalize all you want, but eventually someone must commit a generalized design to a specific task. In Delphi, this is almost exclusively the job of the application writer—to match and tailor reusable components to solve a specific task. Certainly, larger applications or development teams will require more discipline and planning to coordinate the interlocking pieces of a large-scale endeavor, but in the end, an application is a solution to a specific task. Workgroup features like the Object Repository and form inheritance help bring reuse of application pieces into the application writer's vocabulary, but when push comes to shove, an application writer has more leeway to hard-code a temporary solution in an application than a component writer has in a component.

Lots of UI Design and Relatively Little Source Code

Most of the characteristics that determine an application's appearance and behavior are configured in Delphi's design-time environment. Relatively little of the program's behavior comes from source code written by the application writer. When program code is needed, it rarely exceeds a dozen or so lines per event handler or method. An application writer's program code is very focused and very specific—Button1Click does this, Button2Click does that, and never the twain shall meet.

Plug-n-Play Atmosphere—Contractless Programming

Application writers have the luxury of writing code in the contractless domain of Delphi event handlers. This is very easy to forget when you're up to your eyeballs in the intricate interdependencies and relationships of things inside the implementation of your component. The application writer doesn't care about and doesn't want to know how delicate the balance of internal stresses is in your component. Failing to deliver contractless events in your component will produce a lot of irritated (and possibly former) customers.

Event handlers rarely contain explicit error checking or error handling beyond the pervasive try...finally block. The application writer can reasonably assume that errors encountered in an event handler will raise an exception, which will be trapped by the default VCL exception handler for reporting to the end user. This means your component that calls the event handler must be prepared for all manner of exceptions to occur in the event handler. Your component should not block exceptions, particularly exceptions originating in application code. Chapter 4 explores exceptions in detail.

Performance Derived from Components More Than from Code Algorithms

Application writers tend to implement the most direct solution, rather than the most efficient solution. This is partly due to the skill set of the application writer and partly due to quantity-in-billing pressures of income management (i.e., get the job done). Finding an efficient solution usually requires knowledge of the implementation of the component properties or language features you're using and considerable programming experience to weigh the costs of alternate solutions. Neither of these is *required* to write successful Delphi applications.

It's up to the components to optimize their execution speed where possible by anticipating the most common ways they will be used and to provide performance-tuning options for more advanced application writers. For example, drawing graphics on the screen is one of the most time-consuming tasks most components will face. Changing a single property that affects the display of a component should cause a repaint of the component. How the component performs that repaint can make a world of difference in its perceived speed. If the property change forces an immediate repaint by calling Update, the component is redrawn immediately, before the property write method returns to its caller, and the component is redrawn every time the property is changed. If, instead, the property change forces an asynchronous repaint by calling Invalidate, multiple property changes can be rolled up into just one actual redraw operation. Changing the individual property is faster because it doesn't have to wait for the repaint, and the component flickers less due to the less frequent redrawing. This notion of procrastination is explored in Chapter 10, Optimization Techniques.

Component writers can provide a performance-tuning option for application writers in this scenario by providing a pair of methods (BeginUpdate and EndUpdate) to give the application writer control over when the component redraws itself in response to a property change. For example, if you are planning to modify all the strings in a listbox, you should call Listbox1.Items.BeginUpdate, then change all the strings, and then call Listbox1.Items.EndUpdate so that the listbox does not try to redraw itself with every string modification. The performance gains realized by this simple option can be astronomical: Modifying controls with screen updates disabled is often hundreds of times faster than with screen updates enabled. The same is true for the TDataset routines DisableControls and EnableControls, which control the automatic propagation of data from the dataset to its bound data aware controls.

Exception Handling by Rote

Application writers need to be familiar with the use of the try...finally statement to protect resource allocations like memory or files. This doesn't need to be particularly sophisticated. Just practicing the simple code sequence of allocate, try, operate, finally, free is all that's needed to ensure allocated resources are freed in all circumstances.

Application writers generally do not write try...except handlers. In code at the application level, try...except blocks are most often misused to trap an exception and report it to the user. This is unnecessary since VCL's default exception handler will report exceptions to the user anyway.

Application Writing Opportunities

While the preceding sections may have overemphasized the low skill requirements to writing Delphi applications, don't think for a minute that a highly skilled programmer is going to run out of interesting things to do and explore when writing applications in Delphi. There are plenty of opportunities for advanced programmers to take control of things managed by VCL or the Delphi IDE Project Manager to achieve special effects or to improve performance. And, as discussed in Chapter 2, customizing a component for a specific application (nonreusable) is an occasional task that should be in the repertoire of a sharp application writer.

High-Level Code Reuse Through Form Inheritance, Form Linking, and Data Modules

Delphi programmers can build a library of preconfigured forms ready to plop into new projects. In Delphi 1.0, this could be done with form or application templates that you copy into your new project. In Delphi 2.0, preconfigured forms can serve as the ancestors of new forms in your project. The inheritance model allows you to share common code and form layouts between projects and between similar forms within the same project. Inheritance realizes true code sharing—machine code sharing—at run time, as opposed to traditional copy-and-clone "sharing" of source code files.

Delphi 2.0 allows you to move nonvisual components and associated program logic out of your active display forms into nonvisual work areas, called data modules. These data modules can be accessed by components in visual forms and can be inherited from like normal forms.

These new features in Delphi 2.0 mean that application writers have a lot more flexibility in consolidating common code within and between projects without having to resort to writing custom components.

Direct Access to the Windows API for Specialized Operations

Windows features that are not commonly used in applications are generally not encapsulated by VCL components. For example, using rotated fonts to draw text at odd angles is not something that most apps need to do. However, if you're willing to drop down to the Windows API CreateFont to create a font handle with the desired rotation, you can still use that font handle in VCL. Just assign the custom-made font handle to the Handle property of a font object, and you can use that font object or its canvas to draw rotated text. When the font object is destroyed or when you change a font property that requires reconstructing the font handle from scratch, your custom font handle will be disposed of automatically.

Performance-Tuning Opportunities

Delphi's code generation model produces ready-to-run applications that make sure that global resources such as forms are available whenever your application code may need to use them. Basically, forms are created when the application starts up and remain in memory until the application shuts down. This is the simplest and the safest mode of operation for entry-level programmers. If you are willing to take responsibility for allocating and releasing secondary forms in your application, you can reduce your application's memory footprint and improve application start-up time. In addition to simply moving a secondary form from the left-hand listbox in the Project: Options: Forms dialog to the right-hand listbox, you have to consider what code refers to that secondary form, since that code will most likely crash if the secondary form's global variable is not initialized. When taking over lifetime management of Delphi forms, it's best to delete the form global variable generated by Delphi so that you know that the only references to the form will be in subroutines that declare their own local form variable, create the form, and destroy it in one step.

Rewards for More Sophisticated Programming Techniques

As you can see from these examples, Delphi's rewards for learning more advanced programming techniques and taking responsibility for certain resource management tasks are greater flexibility, greater precision, and greater performance in your Delphi applications. Delphi's programming model provides the ease-of-use and high-productivity tools needed for entry-level application programmers to be productive when writing normal Windows applications. The same tools enable advanced programmers to realize even greater productivity when writing complex Windows applications.

The Delphi Component Writer—Component Provider

Application writers use components like a driver uses a car: Turn the key, grab the wheel, stomp the gas, and the car moves. Component writers view components and VCL like a mechanic views a car: Explosive combustion and expansion of gases pushes the piston, which turns the crank, which turns the clutch, transmission, drive shaft, universal joints and differentials, which turns the wheel, and the car moves.

Let's now look at the skills needed to adopt this more mechanical view of the Delphi world, as well as the programming characteristics and opportunities that exist for component writers.

The Component Writer's Skill Set

Components exist to support application writers. In a very literal sense, application writers work *above* the component architecture, while component writers work *within* the component architecture. Application writers see only the exposed public and published properties and methods of components. Component writers have access to the less polished, more delicate protected properties and methods inside components and thus have greater opportunity to extend components to new heights—or shoot themselves in the foot.

Some OOP Knowledge—Polymorphism, Virtuals, Inheritance

To create components, you must create classes that inherit from one of the core VCL component classes. To override or change default behaviors, you must declare virtual method overrides and implement extension or replacement behaviors. These both require an understanding of inheritance and virtual methods. Knowledge of how polymorphism works is a plus, but it is not absolutely critical until you start implementing components composed of multiple internal classes (aggregation) or hierarchies of related components. Chapter 3 examines polymorphism and virtual methods.

Familiarity with the VCL Architecture

Knowing how to declare a descendant class or how to override a virtual method isn't very useful if you don't know which VCL class your component should inherit from or which virtual method you should override to change a specific behavior. A component writer needs to be familiar with the four principal VCL base classes (TPersistent, TComponent, TWinControl, and TGraphicControl) and must understand when to use each as the base for a new component class. A component writer also needs to be familiar with Delphi's noncomponent utility classes (such as TList and the TStrings and TStream families of classes) and how to use them to simplify the implementation of components. These are introduced in Chapter 2 and explored throughout the book.

There are several subsystems in VCL that a complete component should participate in, if appropriate. These include Assign/AssignTo for copying data between components, clipboard operations (primarily through Assign), interaction with database components and fields, keystroke and mouse message processing, general message handling, and, of course, property streaming. These topics are explored throughout the book.

Awareness of Property Streaming Relationships and Rules

A component that can't store its state isn't worth much in the Delphi design-time environment. A component writer must follow a few simple rules to get the VCL property streaming system to automatically handle the properties declared in a new component. Elaborate property data requires more detailed work in the component to store binary data or lists of data in the VCL streaming system. The VCL streaming system is covered in Chapter 6.

Some Resource Management Skills

Components exist to support the application writer, so components usually internalize responsibility for memory and resource management chores rather than expose raw pointers or put deallocation responsibilities on the application writer. This means the component writer has to think about resource allocation, ownership, lifetimes, and deallocation a lot more than an application writer. Contractless programming works for the application writer only because the component writer takes care of the dirty work. Most components can get by with an occasional TList of pointers or child components, but memory management can get as complicated as you wish. Problems caused by overly complicated designs can usually be filed under "self inflicted."

Some Windows API and Messaging Knowledge

Components can make use of the same VCL programming conveniences available to application programmers—VCL's graphics objects, string lists, event properties, and so forth. Some components, such as TSpeedButton, are completely implemented using only VCL native services. However, it's fairly rare for a complex component to not make some kind of direct use of the Windows API or respond directly to a Windows message. When writing a component, you must be aware of the environment around you, what it can do *for* you, and what it can do *to* you. If you're familiar with what VCL's graphics components support and if you have some idea of what the raw Windows GDI supports, you will be better able to blend the two to make use of some special Windows feature while retaining the conveniences of VCL.

Characteristics of Component Writing

Writing components requires more careful thought and preparation than writing a Delphi application. Many of the design-time environment and architectural features that reduce programming complexities for application writers don't provide the same degree of benefit to component writers. Certainly, writing components in Delphi is considerably easier than in other object-oriented languages or frameworks. However, application writers who have grown accustomed to the Delphi IDE's coddling may find component writing rather stark, perhaps even a bit "retro." Component writers spend most of their time writing *code* of all things!

Ease of Use and Reusability as the Highest Priorities for Component Design

Recall that one of the application writer's highest priorities is to complete the application as quickly as possible. Components contribute to rapid application development only if they can be used without a month's worth of planning (or training) and trial-and-error experimentation. Custom components specific to a particular application are not uncommon in Delphi 1.0 applications, but most of these will probably be replaced by form inheritance and data modules in Delphi

2.0. If you're going to go to all the trouble of an additional minute to create a custom component, you might as well invest a few minutes' worth of design planning to make it reusable so that you can spread its cost of development over multiple projects.

Ease of use often takes priority over even performance issues. Borland Pascal 7.0, for example, had a list class similar to TList that used a special callback function to iterate through the items in the list extremely quickly. The problem was that it was too complicated (or nonintuitive) for most programmers to use. Delphi's list classes gave up the high-speed iterator technique in favor of the more obvious loop-and-index list traversal model. As it turns out, the loop-and-index model is more portable between 16- and 32-bit platforms, and Delphi 2.0's 32-bit compiler optimizes the loop-and-index code down to a code sequence that is often faster than the iterator callback technique. (It's funny how things work out sometimes.)

Most Display Work Done in Code

A component's visual appearance is determined almost exclusively by program code. There is no visual designer where you can draw what your button component should look like in its disabled state, or its down state, and so on. Unlike application writing, implementing the display of a component is done with source code, usually using VCL graphics classes and occasional Windows API calls.

Larger Exception-Handling Repertoire

Since many components are middle layers of code managing some lower-level resource, components must take care to allow the higher-level application code to see exceptions originating in the lower-level code as a result of high-level actions. In addition to being the primary conduit of exceptions, components are also the primary source of exceptions. Components should raise exceptions when parameter data is unacceptable or inconsistent with the component's state or when a lower-level operation fails dramatically. Exception handling is covered in Chapter 4.

Component Writing Opportunities

Once a programmer gets into the groove of writing components, there are numerous opportunities to explore improvements in performance and/or ease of use through more sophisticated programming techniques.

Custom Design-Time Property Editors, Component Editors, and Experts

Building customized design-time tools to make configuring complex components easier is one of the most exciting opportunities for component writers. Custom property editors allow you to replace or extend the editors that the Object Inspector uses when displaying particular properties of your component.

Component editors manage the editing of some significant aspect of an entire component, such as viewing and editing the field objects in a TTable or editing the columns of a TDBGrid. Experts are dialogs, sometimes whole programs, devoted to building or configuring aspects of your project as a whole. The Database Form Expert builds a form with all the necessary controls to view and edit data in a particular table, for example.

Don't rely exclusively on design-time tools to solve ease-of-use issues, though. Your components still need an easy-to-use programming interface as well.

Direct Access to the Windows API at All Times

The opportunities here are primarily improved performance and enhanced capabilities for your components. Advanced Win32 GDI operations such as paths, advanced clipping regions, or custom stippled or mitered lines can allow you to implement features in your components that would otherwise be difficult to implement or would not be as fast. Components that deal with large files might realize speed improvements by using memory-mapped files instead of traditional buffered file I/O. Win32 threads allow components (and applications) to run true background operations for image rendering, printing, or database queries.

Opportunity to Encapsulate Anything Not Already Provided by VCL

Programmers who come to Delphi from other programming tools, particularly interpreted tools, often overlook one of Delphi's greatest strengths: If something you want isn't already provided in Delphi, you can implement it in Delphi. In most interpreted tools, if something isn't provided by or directly supported by the interpreted environment, it simply can't be done with that tool. Granted, some parts of Windows aren't particularly easy to write code for (say, OLE?), but as long as what you're after uses standard Dynamic Link Library (DLL) function exports or OLE/COM object interfaces, you can get there with Delphi.

What's more, there is no performance penalty for implementing solutions in Delphi. The Object Pascal code you write is compiled down to native machine code, with all the performance advantages that come with it. Would you write the

Visual Basic environment in VB's interpreted Basic? Not likely. Delphi, on the other hand, was built from the ground up in Delphi. Everything you see in the Delphi IDE is written in Delphi. (The nonvisual internals of the editor and debugger are implemented in DLLs with BC++ and TASM.)

Summary

The Delphi development environment and programming model are inseparable, born of evolution and revolution. With unprecedented synergy between compiled source code, visual design tools, reusable components, and a powerful database architecture, Delphi's programming model simultaneously lowers the barriers to writing Windows applications and raises the ceiling on programming opportunities, performance, and sophistication. Application writers use Delphi to build robust, full-featured Windows applications and Windows database applications in record time, with a minimum of retraining. Component writers use more advanced programming techniques to broaden the palette of tools available for Delphi application development, making Delphi applications ever more powerful and easier to build.

Chapter 2

Designing Components

Designing a component is like writing a play within a play. The component has its own inner world of variables, subroutines, and structure unique to itself, but the component is useless if it does not draw from, contribute to, and in many ways reflect the structure of the larger context in which it lives. There are many subsystems running through VCL that a component can draw from, and still others that the component can enhance by contribution. This chapter explores the subtexts, devices, and foils available in VCL, how to recognize them in the components you use, and how to use them in the components you write.

An efficient design needs to accommodate significant implementation issues, but without a design you don't know which implementation details are significant. Don't be alarmed by the number of forward references this chapter makes to the implementation chapters later in this book; they contain almost as many back references to design issues in this chapter. Such references are just a reminder that named but unexplained topics are fully explored elsewhere in the book.

> I've noticed some people have begun referring to their own Delphi components as "VCLs." VCL is short for Visual Component Library, the name of the collection of Borland-created units and components that form the foundation of the Delphi product and of Delphi applications. Saying "I built a VCL" sounds as silly as "I built a New York." Borland builds *the* VCL (noun). You build VCL (adjective) components.

Earth to Jargon Control

Balancing Design Priorities

The design of any component involves three primary factors: usability, extensibility, and abstraction. These factors compete for your attention and often work against one another, so it's important to prioritize them and set limits at the start of your design process if you intend to ever finish the component.

Usability

Components exist to support application writers. To that end, the component writer's highest priority at all times is to make components that are useful to the application writer, that are easy to use, and that have clear and bulletproof public interfaces. Everything else—extensibility, performance, reuse—is secondary. A brilliantly designed, cleverly implemented, highly extensible component that is too complicated for an application writer to use or that doesn't do anything significant for the application writer is a useless component. When designing a component, focus first on what it will do and how it will be used in application development, and tailor the design and implementation of the component to fit that use.

Extensibility

Extensible objects don't just happen. For an object to allow descendants to change aspects of its behavior, extensibility must be designed into the object and supported by the implementation of the object. Since extensibility is not of immediate value to the application writer and requires development time which could otherwise be devoted to the useful feature set of the component, extensibility is usually a much lower priority in a component's design and implementation. As you are designing and implementing the public feature set of your component, decide what sorts of things you will allow descendants to override or alter, and implement support for that in the protected interface of the component. As will be discussed later in this chapter, some aspects of any fully implemented object are inherently nonextensible, so you will always have to decide where extensibility ends.

Abstraction

Hand in hand with extensibility are issues of implementation abstraction—how much effort you invest in hiding the details of your component's implementation. Abstraction generally leads to more robust and extensible designs, but it can complicate an otherwise simple implementation of a simple feature set.

Abstraction requires development time, and while it may allow descendant classes more flexibility to change implementation details, it may also increase the "up close" complexity of your component's protected interface. Flexibility is good, but clarity is better.

Abstraction also affords you the flexibility of changing implementation details inside your component at some point in the future, without affecting the code that uses or inherits from your component. Implement a simple linear search now under extreme time constraints, and reserve the option to reimplement the search with a more efficient, more sophisticated implementation when you have more time in the future.

> **Perils of Abstraction: Physicists and Philosophers**
>
> Originally, physicists and philosophers had a great deal in common; they hypothesized about the universe, using the same logic and same set of knowledge. As time and technology advanced, physicists narrowed their view to study the smallest details of matter, while philosophers broadened their view by generalizing and abstracting so as to consider ever larger questions. Physicists learn more and more about less and less, until someday they'll know everything about nothing. Philosophers know less and less about more and more, until they'll know nothing about everything.

As with extensibility, you will always have to draw a line somewhere ending abstraction so that you can actually implement something. Many a great and wondrous architecture has abstracted everything and done nothing. (How they keep getting venture capital is a mystery.) For a simple component, it's usually adequate to hide the few implementation details from the public interface and expose them in the protected interface. A simple component by definition doesn't have much implementation to hide and has even less need to change that implementation in future revisions.

For a complex component, though, it's best to restrict all access to implementation details, even in the protected interface, since the probability of change in a complex system is fairly high and the implementation cost of exposing abstracted implementation details is equally high. Dole out access and privilege as you can afford to implement the necessary support for it. If you can afford the cost of abstracting your complex internals, that will buy you some extensibility, but at a pretty steep price. If you can't afford to abstract your complex internals, then you should cut back on your extensibility goals. Your component can still be extensible, but only within the implementation specifications you lay down in your component.

That's a key message of object-oriented design: Extensibility is not a given. You must decide how much extensibility of your object you are willing to support. And "support" doesn't mean changing static methods to virtual. An object full of virtual methods is no more extensible (and a lot more hazardous) than an object full of static methods. Sure, a virtual method can be overridden in a descendant class, but will that descendant class have access to sufficient information and control structures to actually do anything? Probably not, unless you take the time to research and implement support for such extensions when writing your component. Don't make a method virtual if you don't have the time to support it. It's better to have an inflexible component that works than a flexible component that doesn't.

Cost of Design Factors

One way to picture the relative cost and interactions of the primary design factors is in a cost equation:

$$\text{DesignEffort} = \text{FeatureSet} \cdot \text{Usability} \cdot \text{Abstraction} \cdot \text{Sqr}(\text{Extensibility} - \text{Abstraction})$$

where each of these variables is in the range 1...N, 1 being low priority and N being high priority, representing the relative importance of each factor in the design goals of your component. This formula is purely speculative and not derived from any empirical data.

FeatureSet represents the overall quantity or complexity of features in your component. Usability represents the degree of ease of use you want to achieve in the component. Abstraction represents the degree to which you want to expose abstractions of the implementation details of your component. Extensibility represents the degree to which you want your component to support extensions and implementation changes in descendant classes. Notice that Abstraction is a multiplier of FeatureSet (more features, more work to abstract their implementation, and more work to keep it usable) and that Abstraction reduces the cost of Extensibility. Also notice that Extensibility is squared—it's much easier to make an object that performs a task than to make an extensible object that performs a task and supports redefining the task.

Don't read too much into this equation. It's just one way to illustrate some of the dynamics of the primary design factors.

Reading a Class Declaration

Before you jump into designing a component, you should learn how to read a component class declaration. You have to pick an ancestor to derive your component from, and you need to understand what that ancestor expects of your descendant and what opportunities it provides for you. Much of this information can be gleaned from indicators in the component class declaration itself—it's all there in black and white or, occasionally, in the ether between the lines.

Published Sections

Properties that appear in the published section of a class declaration are streamable—the VCL property streaming system will read and write the property's data automatically (see Chapter 6, Streaming).

Published properties define the design-time interface of your component. If it isn't published, it doesn't show up in the Object Inspector at design time. There are other ways to configure components at design time (experts, component editors, and so forth), but the Object Inspector is the most visible and most common. You can implement custom property editors to assist with setting difficult properties, but don't forget that published properties can also be used by the component user's program code. Don't rely on custom property editors to hide overly complex or poorly thought-out properties. If you design your component so that its properties are easy to use in program code, you probably won't even need a custom property editor.

Methods that appear in a published section can be referenced by a published event property, and the reference will be streamable. You can assign a nonpublished method to an event property at run time, but if you try to store it to a stream, you'll get an exception reporting that the referenced method is not streamable. Fields that appear in a published section receive similar RTTI treatment as published methods but to a lesser degree. The specifics of how VCL uses published methods and fields are covered in Chapters 5 and 6.

Components should not publish methods or fields. The design environment doesn't support connecting events to published methods of components (only methods of the form), and component data should only be exposed through properties, not actual fields.

Anything appearing in a published section of a class is irrevocably exposed in that class and in all of its descendants to the component user, to the streaming system, and to the Object Inspector at design time. If a published property in a potential ancestor class conflicts with how you want to arrange your descendant component's interface, then that class is not a suitable ancestor. Published properties generally do not appear in classes that are intended to be used as general-purpose, extensible ancestor classes. You can certainly create descendants from classes with published properties, but this reduces your options to alter the component's exposed interface considerably.

Note that the default access directive in a class declaration is published. All the fields and methods at the top of a Delphi-generated form class declaration are published because they're inserted at the top of the class declaration. The Delphi-generated fields and methods need to be accessible to the streaming system so that component event properties can store references to them.

When changes are made to components between major versions, the published interface is the most precious section of the class declaration since the published interface largely determines the component's stream format. Remove a published property in version 2 of your component (or worse, change its type), and you will break not only source code but existing DFM form files as well. Such property changes are certainly recoverable (the errant property value in the DFM file can be ignored when you load the form into the IDE), but they are very disconcerting to your component users—the application writers.

The only penalty for adding a new property in version 2 of your component is reduced backwards compatibility. Version 2 can read version 1 streams, but version 1 won't read version 2 streams that include data for the new version 2 property.

Public Sections

Anything in a public section of a class is exposed to the component user, but not to the streaming system or Object Inspector. Items in public sections are generally methods that are useful to the component user to manipulate the component and properties that either don't need to be published, such as properties that return data synthesized from other persistent data, or cannot be published, such as array properties.

The *public interface* of a component is the combination of its public and published sections. Everything in a component's public interface should be "hardened" against misuse and error—all parameter data should be validated prior to use and, in most cases, should raise an exception describing the programmer transgression. The component should be designed so that properties and methods can be used at any time, in any order, within reason. The public interface of your component should be contractless and bulletproof.

Protected Sections

The protected interface of a class speaks directly to the component writer and only to the component writer. Protected items are accessible only to that class, descendants of that class, and anything in the unit that implements that class.

Properties declared in a protected section are usually found only in classes designed to be common ancestors. Descendants can promote an inherited protected property to published by redeclaring the property name (with no type) in their published sections. This allows a common ancestor to implement a property that can be shared by multiple descendants without forcing the property into the public interface of all descendants. The descendants that want the property can just expose it. Since these properties are simply promoted into the public interface of descendants, not reimplemented, the ancestor is responsible for making the properties contractless and bulletproof.

Protected methods provide descendants access to internal routines and data structures of the ancestor that are key to the operation of the component but that are too sensitive or volatile to expose to the component user. The intent is that descendants can use these routines to alter or enhance the feature set laid down by the ancestor. The risk is that descendants may misuse this internal access to corrupt the design of the component—twisting it into an abomination held together only by duct tape and blissful coincidence.

The protected interface is often contractual. A component may have internal states where some data is invalid or inaccessible for a time. These states should be hidden from the hardened public interface, but they might not be hidden from the protected interface. It is the responsibility of the ancestor component writer to express such contractual requirements that descendant classes must fulfill or situations they must avoid and to provide sufficient information in the protected interface so that descendants can detect and respond appropriately to such situations. It is the responsibility of the descendant component writer to seek out and understand the contractual requirements of the protected interfaces of the ancestor classes and to honor their terms and conditions.

The protected interface is not bulletproof. It is perfectly valid for an ancestor to assume or require that data be validated prior to calling into the protected interface, in the interest of speed and internal simplicity. Consequently, passing bad data to protected methods may cause access violations, floating-point exceptions, or even data corruption. It is clearly the responsibility of the descendant to honor and enforce the data integrity rules and assumptions of the ancestor when using methods in the ancestor's protected interface. If in doubt about some aspect of the protected interface, use the public interface instead.

Private Sections

The private sections of a class are off-limits to everything outside the class and the class's unit. Property read and write methods are usually shoved into a component's private section just to keep them out of the way, but everything else in a private section is solely devoted to the implementation of the component. Private sections are usually the only place where field declarations appear in a component—all external data access goes through exposed properties or methods. When scanning a class declaration for information on how it is implemented, go to the private sections. When scanning for things your descendants can use or override, ignore the private sections. You can't access what's in them, so just forget about them.

There's not much point in making private methods virtual since descendants can't access the private method to override it. If you want to allow descendants to override a property's read method, make it a protected virtual method, not private.

The main exception to private virtuals is when all possible or intended descendant classes are implemented in the same unit as their common ancestor. If you want a tightly knit cluster of related classes that share most of their code in a common ancestor, but you do not intend for others to create descendants of these classes, shoving most of the interface of the common ancestor into its private sections allows you to gain the code-sharing benefits of inheritance for your immediate needs while denying descendants outside the unit access to implementation details. This scenario may seem a bit contrived in the abstract, but in practice it's not uncommon for a component design to call for helper or internal building block classes that component users or other component writers have no business fooling around with. Internal building block classes are best hidden away inside the implementation section of a unit, but sometimes it's more convenient to declare the building block classes in the interface section of the unit. In the interface section, those internal building blocks are visible to outsiders, so making their contents private will minimize the risk of unwanted tampering.

The line between private and protected or between protected and public is rather arbitrary. A simple component can run fast and loose with every detail of its implementation exposed in its protected or public interfaces, but complex components are generally better off restricting all access to implementation details to very well-defined and safe areas, even in the protected interface. As will be discussed later in this chapter, access to implementation details is more of a hazard in the long run than a help, especially for large, complex systems. After all, one of the cornerstones of OOP is encapsulation, the isolation of implementation details from the rest of the system.

Virtual Methods

Both kinds of virtual methods (methods declared with a `virtual` or `dynamic` directive) scream, "Override me!" Except for the very rare case of using virtual methods to *reduce* the size of the EXE file (we'll get to that in Chapter 3), virtual methods are only provided where the component author has decided to allow descendants the option of overriding particular methods. As we'll see in the extensibility section later in this chapter, making a method virtual is not a decision to be taken lightly. As with private/protected/public exposure decisions, it's generally best to only make methods virtual when you see a reasonable need and after you have explored what additional support is required to fill that need.

Methods declared `virtual` carry a different message to the reader of the class declaration than methods declared `dynamic`: `virtual` indicates the component author expects the method to be overridden fairly often in descendant classes; `dynamic` indicates the author expects the method will almost never be overridden. The difference is in the storage characteristics of `virtual` and `dynamic` method tables; ancestor `virtual` methods consume space in every descendant class whether they are overridden or not; `dynamic` methods consume space only when overridden, but they use more space than a `virtual` when they are overridden. This, of course, assumes the author of that class is aware of the innuendos associated with each kind of virtual—or at least, has read Chapter 3!

Static Methods and Properties

Static methods are, well, static. Descendants can't change the behavior of inherited static methods. All property declarations are inherently static, though their read and write methods can be virtual. However, because each descendant class has its own name scope, descendants can declare their own static methods or properties that have the same name as static methods or properties in their ancestors. There is no actual relationship between the same-named static symbols in the ancestor and descendant, so the potential for confusion and error is very high, particularly when handling objects polymorphically with a base-class type variable. Polymorphism makes such hacks very hard to spot and therefore extremely dangerous, as illustrated in Chapter 3.

There are a few limited situations where "overriding" static methods or properties is warranted. TCollection is a container class that owns a homogeneous list of items. That is, the items are all the same type, or type-compatible. TList is also a list of items, but it carries no implications of uniformity. When extracting something from a TList, you almost always have to typecast the raw pointer stored in the TList to something more useful, such as a class. Anyway, because descendants of TCollection are designed to handle a particular kind of TCollectionItem descendant, it would be nice if each TCollection descendant had an array property that returned the class type used by that particular TCollection. Using virtual read and write methods for the array property won't help in this case because you can't change the parameter or return types of virtual methods when you override them. The simplest way to do this is to redeclare the array property in each TCollection descendant to return the appropriate class type. All the read and write methods for this array property do is call the inherited TCollection array property and typecast the result.

Note that overriding properties or static methods in this manner is only a syntactic convenience. The overriding static method *must not* introduce new behavior because there is no guarantee that this static method or property will be the only way the component is accessed. Using a variable of an ancestor type to manipulate your descendant instance (polymorphism) will not call the static methods or properties of your descendant. Specific examples are provided in Chapter 3.

In general, overriding properties by redeclaring them in descendants is a bad idea. The syntactic convenience just described is tolerable only because it does not change the behavior of the property. It doesn't matter to the component whether you use the ancestor's Items array property or the descendant's Items array property. Adding logic to the descendant's Items array property access methods (say, setting a flag in the component) would be going too far, since that flag would not be set if the descendant instance were accessed through a variable of the ancestor type.

Published Event Properties

Event properties store pointers to methods in other objects. Published event properties allow the component user to customize the execution of the component at design time. Published properties are almost exclusively reserved for the component user, and the methods they point to are almost always published methods of a form.

Never assign to published properties in component code. If you assign a method to an event property in your component's constructor, you may lose that assignment when the component's published property values are later read from a stream. If you assign to the event property after streaming is complete, you'll obliterate whatever the application writer had configured at design time. Sure, you could save the previous value of the event to a temporary variable before assigning your own method to the property, creating a chain of pointers much like hardware interrupt handlers, but you would be going about it the wrong way!

Presumably, the reason you're trying to assign your own method to a published event property is that you want to receive notification when that event is fired. There are two ways to receive that notification without tangling yourself up in chained event handlers:

1. Override the dynamic method corresponding to the event and that fires the event.

2. Eliminate the component user, design-time considerations, and property streaming from the picture by using aggregation (discussed later in this chapter). There can't be any conflict over the contents of the event property if you're the only one who has access to it.

Using Helper Methods to Fire Events

If the event you want to eavesdrop on is an event property in your own class inherited from some ancestor, then look in the ancestor for a dynamic method with a similar name to the event property. For example, TFont inherits a Changed procedure from its ancestor, TGraphic, as well as its OnChange event property. This Changed procedure does nothing more than call the OnChange event if it has been assigned. That in itself is helpful for component writers since it simplifies the code needed to fire the event. Instead of checking whether the OnChange property has been assigned and, if so, calling the event all over the implementation of a component, you can just call Changed to perform the check and call for you.

More importantly, though, Changed is a dynamic method, which means descendants can override it to listen in on those same notifications, without interfering with the actual event (don't forget to call the inherited method). This custom of providing a dynamic method to invoke each event gives event properties an added depth of polymorphism. Why dynamic? Because this isn't something you'll be overriding very often.

Isolating Helper Classes with Aggregation

The other scenario is that you want to respond to an event, not in your own class, but in a class that is used by your class. If the helper class you're using is completely exposed to the component user and streaming system, it will be difficult to maintain strict control over the published events. The solution is to hide the helper class from the component user and streaming system. To still allow design-time editing of selected properties of the helper class, declare those as published properties of your component and implement them to simply set or get the property values of the internal helper class instance. Once you have the helper class all to yourself, you can do whatever you want with its event properties.

Nonpublished Event Properties

Nonpublished event properties provide a callback notification mechanism for component writers. For example, consider again TFont's OnChange event, which is fired whenever the font is modified. This is not a published property because it is not intended to be exposed to the component user at design time, nor is it intended to point to a method of a form. It exists primarily so that the font can notify another object that it has changed. For example, TCanvas contains a font property. In the TCanvas constructor, it creates a TFont instance for its font property and it assigns a method within the canvas to that font object's OnChange event. When the font changes, it calls the canvas's method, which can make a note to itself that the font handle is no longer valid (the existing font handle, if any, no longer matches the font object's specifications). The font handle won't be recreated until the canvas actually performs an operation that needs the font, thus minimizing the number of times the font handle is recreated in response to font property changes.

As another example, TControl provides a protected font property ready for descendants to expose at their discretion. TControl automatically connects the font object's OnChange property to an internal method of the control. When the control's font changes, that internal method gets called, and it invalidates the control so that the control will automatically redraw itself to reflect the change in its font.

Nonpublished events are a very common notification mechanism seen throughout VCL. These notifications are what make so much of VCL automatic and simple to use.

Class Methods

Class methods are methods that can be called without an object instance. Class methods are often used to implement utility routines that are associated with a class but don't actually require instance data. Such utility functions could just as easily be implemented as stand-alone functions in the same unit as the class they're associated with, but putting them in the class declaration makes the relationship between the functions and the class unmistakable.

For example, the graphics unit supports the installation of additional file format handlers to allow TPicture to recognize and load images in other file formats, such as GIF or JPEG. The file format registration routines simply maintain a linked list of records containing file extensions and the TGraphic class types that can read them. This linked list is a global resource shared by all TPicture instances and useful only to TPicture instances, so the RegisterFileFormat routine is a class method of TPicture. Graphics file extensions are explored in more detail in Chapter 8.

Identifying Tasks and Parts

Since you're so determined to write a component, you probably already have a programming problem or task identified that you want a component to solve. Once you have a task in mind, you can brainstorm different ways of how that task might be solved. Once you have a solution strategy in mind, you can brainstorm what features a component will need to implement that solution strategy and how you will expose those features to the component user.

Note the use of the word *strategy* here. You don't need to have a complete implementation worked out in your head before you can proceed. You need to have a general idea of the goals and potential hazards you're up against to serve as a guide through the discovery process that is component design. If you hit a snag in design or implementation of the component, you back up a few steps, reassess your assumptions and goals, make adjustments, and start forward again. "Hitting a snag" may be discovering a flaw in the design during the formative stages of the design, during the implementation of the design, or during testing of the design with component users.

Spiral Development Process (Iterative Convergence)

Software design that goes through multiple design/implement/test cycles, with each iteration building upon the previous to converge on a goal, is characteristic of the *spiral design process*. This is in stark contrast to the classic *waterfall design process*, which dictates that all design aspects are completed prior to implementation and that implementation is completed prior to testing. This might be good enough for government work, but it's far too wasteful of development resources in the real world. The reality is that you usually don't fully understand the issues until you've begun to implement a solution and you encounter new issues not anticipated in the design phase. It's rare that an entire project can be designed and implemented in one fell swoop—projects are usually broken up into sections and designed and implemented in stages. You can realize greater economy of resources by starting software testing and documentation at those intermediate stages rather than waiting until the entire product is done (as in the waterfall model).

Decomposition (Finding the Atomic Parts)

Dissect the proposed feature set of your component into atomic (indivisible) behaviors, responsibilities, and data. If your component will need to keep track of multiple somethings, you'll probably need a list to hold them. Are those somethings of interest to the component user and bulletproof enough to expose? If yes, you'll probably need an array property to provide access to the internal list. Are the somethings text data? If yes, you can probably use a string list to store them.

A complete discussion of object decomposition techniques is beyond the scope of this book, but you can get a lot done just by asking yourself these kinds of exploratory questions, identifying and expressing your assumptions, questioning and justifying those assumptions, and tallying the survival of the fittest ideas on a notepad or whiteboard. It's important to keep track of decisions, assumptions, and alternatives throughout the design process not only for documentation purposes but also to make it easier to back up and head down a different path when one potential solution withers away under scrutiny.

Identification of IS and HAS Relationships

In the process of decomposing your task into implementable pieces, you'll often need to consider the relationship between atomic parts. These relationships fall into two camps: IS relations and HAS relations. If X is in need of a list to keep track of things, the questions are: IS X a list? Does X HAVE a list? The distinction is subtle, but valuable to your implementation decisions. The IS test helps you identify the lineage (inheritance) of items, whereas the HAS test helps identify supporting classes or properties (attributes) of items.

If an item fails the IS test because the item does not need all the capabilities of a candidate class, it will most likely pass the corresponding HAS test. That is, if you don't want to expose data using a string list object because the string list supports more data manipulations than you can allow on your data (data IS a string list = False), you can probably use a string list object internally (HAS a string list) but expose properties in your object to allow only the operations that make sense for your data.

For example, TDBGrid has a SelectedRows property of type TBookmarkList. The SelectedRows property indicates which rows in the database have been multiselected in the grid by the end user, and it allows a programmer to add, remove, or enumerate the list items programmatically. The contents of the list are database bookmarks. Bookmarks are stored as opaque string data, which means you're not supposed to manipulate or store the contents of the bookmark because the bookmark data is volatile and table dependent. Since the bookmarks are strings, it would appear that the list of bookmarks could be implemented using a TStrings or TStringList descendant. However, those string list classes include support routines such as SaveToFile that don't make sense for the volatile bookmark data. Rather than implement the bookmark list as a TStrings descendant and try to cut out standard features we don't want, we can create TBookmarkList as a new, independent class that *uses* a list object internally and exposes only the properties that make sense for volatile bookmark data.

Aggregation

Aggregation is the process of building a complex object by assembling multiple internal objects into a single functional unit. Each atomic behavior identified by decomposition analysis may be the responsibility of a different internal object. Aggregation plays a major role in code reuse in VCL: List properties are often implemented using internal TList or TStrings objects, and a variety of component properties, such as Font, Pen, Brush, and Canvas properties, are actually exposed aggregate objects. Virtually all visible components use these graphics classes, sharing their implementation code and realizing a significant savings in code size. The TBookmarkList scenario previously described is an example of using aggregation to reduce exposed features but still take advantage of existing classes to simplify implementation chores and reuse code again and again.

Choosing the Right Roots

OK, so you've spent some time studying your chosen task, explored various solution possibilities, and identified several major features or subtasks that the component needs to provide. Now the question is: What is your component? An incremental extension of an existing component or a completely new component blazing a path through uncharted territory?

One of the biggest mistakes you can make in writing a component is to pick the wrong ancestor. Whenever you find yourself spending more time disabling inherited behaviors than using and enhancing them, you're probably using the wrong ancestor. Take a step back to reevaluate what your component really IS, what your current ancestor really IS, and other IS and HAS relationships in your component. In many cases where choice of ancestor is in doubt, the component IS something much more primitive but HAS an internal aggregate class of the type you're mistakenly using as your ancestor.

Multiple Inheritance and Aggregation

Multiple inheritance (MI) is a language feature supported by C++ and other object-oriented languages that allows you to declare a new class as a hybrid descendant of multiple ancestor classes. Fans of multiple inheritance often praise Delphi for its elegant simplicity, clarity of source code, and blistering run-time performance, but they bemoan Delphi's exclusion of multiple inheritance. This exclusion is not accidental: The Delphi development team strongly believes that multiple inheritance creates more problems than it solves. Multiple inheritance may make it easier to specify solutions for certain kinds of design problems, but these conveniences are insignificant compared to the host of implementation and maintenance problems that ride on its coattails. The Delphi team is opposed, not to the idea of automatic aggregation support, but to the liabilities of multiple inheritance as implemented in C++ and related languages.

The upside of multiple inheritance is that it is a kind of automatic aggregation. You specify the ingredients and the compiler mashes them together for you. The downside of multiple inheritance is that for multiple classes to be merged together unambiguously, there cannot be any method names in common between the multiple ancestors anywhere in their ancestry. If two ancestor classes both have a Name function, you have a name collision: Which one of those Name functions will appear in the descendant class? The situation gets even hairier if the Name methods are virtual or if the ancestors share a common ancestor. Multiple inheritance encourages (almost requires) classes with similar functions to use dissimilar names. If a house were built using multiple inheritance to "mix in" a kitchen module, a living room module, and bath and bedroom modules, electrical outlets could be placed automatically in every room only if each room used outlets with a unique plug configuration.

Aggregation of classes is used to build just about every class and component in VCL, but without the ambiguities and implementation hazards of multiple inheritance. Nothing has been found that can be done with multiple inheritance that cannot also be done in Delphi without multiple inheritance. Delphi and multiple inheritance solutions require different approaches and programming techniques, but there is no real difference in capabilities.

TCustomxxx

If your component is primarily an extension to an existing component class, most of your design decisions have been made for you. Your design task is simply to understand the opportunities available in the component class you're trying to extend and make use of them with a minimum of fuss.

If your component is very similar to, but not completely like, an existing component, you may have to study the existing component very carefully to determine whether what you want to do can be done in that component. If the differences between your component idea and the existing component are primarily differences in exposed properties, you're in luck: Most components have an immediate ancestor whose class name begins with TCustomxxx. For example, TEdit has an immediate ancestor named TCustomEdit. If you look at the implementation of TEdit, you'll discover that there isn't any—the implementation is in the TCustomEdit class. All the TEdit class does is expose inherited protected properties as published. TCustomEdit defines most of those properties, but it keeps them in the protected section so that descendants can selectively expose the inherited properties they want and ignore the properties they don't want.

If your component design supports the use of your component as an ancestor class and your component needs to expose published properties for the application writer to use, you should follow this two-tier convention: Implement your component in a class named TCustomSomething, which declares and implements properties in its protected interface, and declare another class named TSomething, which inherits from TCustomSomething and promotes the appropriate inherited properties to published. Component writers who don't want all the published properties of your TSomething can step back to TCustomSomething and pick the properties they do want to expose in their descendants.

If your component is a new implementation, not just an extension of existing material, you'll need to decide which of the core VCL classes makes the most appropriate ancestor for your component. The following sections review the features and uses of the five core VCL base classes in order of increasing capabilities.

TObject

TObject is the base of the entire Delphi object hierarchy. All Delphi classes inherit directly or indirectly from TObject, even if they don't specify any ancestor at all. TObject provides very little functionality of its own: It defines utility and information methods, such as ClassName, a simple constructor, and a virtual destructor, Destroy. When implementing destructors in your components, always remember to specify `override` in your destructor declaration.

Classes derived directly from TObject are not components and are not streamable; they are usually support classes that are used as internal aggregates in the implementation of components. TList and the clan of TStream classes are examples of noncomponent, nonpersistent classes.

TPersistent

TPersistent is the foundation of Delphi's automatic property streaming support. All descendants of TPersistent get run-time type information for their published properties, fields, and methods, which the VCL streaming system uses to read and write data of published properties. TPersistent defines the DefineProperties virtual method, which descendants can override to implement streaming support for custom data types (such as lists).

Classes derived directly from TPersistent are not components, but their published properties are streamable. Such classes include TFont, TBrush, TPen, TStrings, TCollection, and TCollectionItem. These classes are most often used as exposed aggregates in the implementation of a component, such as a published Font property of a component or an Items string list property of a listbox.

Components that publish class-type properties must use class types that descend from TPersistent but not TComponent and must create instances for those properties when the component is created. For example, a component that declares its own SpecialFont: TFont published property must create an instance of TFont for this property in the component's constructor. When the component's properties are later read from a stream, the published properties of the nested class are read directly into the already existing instance. The streaming system does not create a new TFont instance for the SpecialFont property; it merely assigns data values to the existing SpecialFont instance's properties.

TComponent

TComponent is the foundation of all component classes in Delphi. Anything not derived from TComponent is just a class, not a component. Only TComponent descendants can be installed into the IDE's component palette and dropped onto a form at design time.

TComponent introduces the notion of ownership. A component can own multiple components. When we say component A owns component B, we mean that B appears in A's Components list (an array property) and that when A is destroyed, it will automatically destroy B.

TComponent introduces a virtual constructor, Create, that takes a single parameter, Owner. Any component that needs to add behavior to its constructor *must* do so by overriding the inherited Create constructor—using the `override` directive. You can define additional constructors for your components if you like, but you *must* support the virtual constructor defined by TComponent since that is the only constructor that will be called when the user drops your component onto a form at design time. Chapter 3's section on polymorphic construction with class references provides more details.

TComponent does not define any user interface or display capabilities, so it is the ancestor of choice for creating nonvisual components—that is, components that have no direct visual representation at run time. The database access components (TTable, TQuery, and so on) are all nonvisual components, as is TTimer. The common dialog components are considered nonvisual components, too: The common dialog component manages something that is visual (a dialog), but the component itself is not visual.

TGraphicControl

TGraphicControl is the base class for creating lightweight, visible controls that do not require keyboard input. TGraphicControls can own other components, but they cannot serve as the parent, or visual container, of other components. TGraphicControls do not use a window handle, so they consume fewer Windows resources and generally redraw more quickly than controls that have their own window handles. These lightweight controls receive mouse, paint, and other messages like TWinControls, but they do not receive keystroke messages or input focus. TGraphicControls also support true transparency, so you can achieve special effects by building up layers of overlapping TGraphicControls such as TBevel, TShape, and TLabel. TSpeedButton and TImage are examples of opaque TGraphicControls.

TWinControl

TWinControl is the base for most interactive components. Each TWinControl descendant class has its own window handle, so it can receive input focus, keystroke messages, and all other Windows messages, and its drawing area always obscures whatever is behind the control in z-order.

TWinControl introduces the notion of parentage. A parent is the visual container of its children. If you drop a panel on a form and a button on the panel, the button's owner is the form, and its parent is the panel. If you drag the button around, you'll find that it is literally inside the panel—the button is clipped to the display area of its parent, the panel. Similarly, the panel is clipped to its parent, the form. A TWinControl's Controls array property lists the child components of that TWinControl, and all the child components' parent properties refer back to that TWinControl.

A TWinControl can have a parent and can be a parent. A TGraphicControl can have a parent but cannot be a parent. (Or was that already apparent?)

For a component to be visible on the screen, it must have a visual context in which to display itself. That is, it must have a parent. Failure to assign to the parent property of a component that you create in program code will result in an exception when you try to make the component visible or otherwise refer to its window handle property.

If your component is a wrapper around an existing window implementation, perhaps a custom control DLL, you'll probably derive your component class directly from TWinControl. In such situations, your component class is a convenient facade hiding a raw window handle and DLL function call or window message programming interface. There are two entities at work here: the window implementation itself (whose machine code is probably not even in your application) and the Delphi class in your application that provides access to the features of that window implementation. Most of the standard components (TButton, TEdit, TMemo, TListbox, TCombobox, and so on) are TWinControl wrapper classes around controls that are implemented by Windows.

If you're implementing an entirely new component yourself, including painting logic, you should use TCustomControl as your ancestor. TCustomControl is a TWinControl descendant that adds some convenience routines to help with painting. To implement your own paint code, for example, just override the virtual Paint routine defined by TCustomControl. TWinControl doesn't define a paint routine because window handle wrappers usually leave painting logic to the window implementation they encapsulate.

Choosing the Right Implementation Tools

The second biggest mistake you can make in writing a component is to not take advantage of the tools available to you—to overimplement your component. Reinventing the wheel wastes your time, wastes space in your customer's EXE files, increases the risk of bugs, and increases the potential for confusion due to inconsistencies in redundant implementations.

Using common building blocks to construct your component makes the new-code contribution of your component very small. These common building blocks are most likely already being used by other parts of a Delphi application, so using them in your component adds very little new code to the application. Even if a particular building block seems like overkill for your simple needs, use what's available instead of writing a new class to do substantially the same thing. Using a large class that is already being used by something else in an application contributes less to the application size than creating a new, smaller class that is custom tailored to the immediate needs of your (and only your) component.

TList

Just about anywhere you find a plural in a component specification, you'll find a TList in the implementation of that component. TList is essentially a dynamically resizable array of pointers and is designed to be simple, flexible, and fast. TList assumes nothing about the 4-byte data items it stores. Consequently, the list does not destroy the data it contains. The upside to this is that the list can contain anything you want, from object instance pointers, to raw memory allocation pointers, to simply 4-byte integer or enumerated values.

You'll almost always wind up using a TList in a component, but you'll never create descendants of TList. TList is a worker drone, not a promiscuous ancestor class. If you want to create a list of a particular kind of item and that list is used only in the private or protected sections of your component implementation, then just use a plain TList and typecast the list's raw pointers into the type you put into the list to begin with.

If the list is exposed in the public interface of your component, typecasting is not an option. You cannot require a component user to typecast a list item appropriately in order to access it. You should create a simple wrapper class (derived from TObject, not TList) that exposes only the property and function equivalents of TList that you need and whose function return types and method parameter types match the type of the data that the list contains. The wrapper class then contains a TList instance internally and uses that for actual storage. Implement the functions and property access methods of this wrapper class with simple one-line calls to the corresponding methods or properties of the internal TList, wrapped in appropriate typecasts. This gives the component user the convenience and safety of the proper data type but makes use of the TList for actual implementation. This wrapper class can also add data ownership semantics, if appropriate—when the wrapper class is destroyed, it can free the items in its internal list.

For example, TComponent uses an internal TList to store the list of components that it owns. TComponent provides limited exposure of its internal list with its Components array property, ComponentCount property, and support methods such as InsertComponent and RemoveComponent. When the TComponent is destroyed, it first destroys all the components in its component list and then destroys the internal list object itself.

TStrings Derivatives

TStrings is the exact opposite of TList: TStrings is an abstract class that defines a string and object data storage interface but that does not actually implement any storage. You'll never create an instance of TStrings, but VCL defines many descendants of TStrings that implement their list storage in various ways. TStrings do not own the data that is placed in them. String allocations are taken care of automatically, but the data associated with each string (accessible through the Objects array property) is very much like a TList—no assumptions are made about the contents of the 4-byte data items.

The standard Windows listbox control, for example, already includes support for storing string and data items for each line in the listbox. TListbox encapsulates the standard Windows listbox control. TListbox exposes a published Strings property, of type TStrings, so that the component user can have easy access to the data in the listbox. TListbox implements that property using a TStrings descendant, TListboxStrings. TListboxStrings implements the abstract virtual methods defined in TStrings to set and fetch the string and object data to and from the Windows listbox control, using SendMessage and Windows-defined listbox messages. Using the listbox's data storage capabilities maintains consistency with Windows features since advanced Delphi programmers may want to use other listbox messages to reorder, sort, or change the data in the Windows listbox control. Even though there are two entities at work in the TListbox (the Delphi wrapper code around the Windows implementation), data is stored in only one place—in the Windows listbox control.

If your component manages multiple string data items and needs to expose these to the component user, you should declare your property with the type TStrings and internally create an instance of a TStrings descendant class of your own design or borrowed from elsewhere in VCL. Declaring the property with the TStrings abstract base type makes your property assignment compatible with any other string list property in VCL. You can copy the contents of a TMemo into a TListbox with the line

```
Listbox1.Items := Memo1.Lines;
```

or copy the contents of that same memo into a TQuery with

```
Query1.SQL := Memo1.Lines;
```

In these examples, Items, Lines, and SQL are all TStrings-type properties, and each is implemented internally using a different kind of TStrings descendant.

Assigning to Class-Type Properties

When implementing a property whose type is a class (like TFont or TStrings), it's perfectly valid to have the property read directly from the internal private instance variable in your class. For example, TListbox's Items property is declared to read directly from TListbox's FItems internal variable. In a statement like

```
X := Listbox1.Items.Count;
```

the Items object instance has already been created by the listbox, so there's no harm in reading directly from the listbox object's internal FItems variable so that the Count property can be accessed from the Items object instance.

However, you should not allow the property to write directly to your internal private instance variable. Writing over the instance variable will not free the instance it points to, and accepting a new instance from external sources can lead to problems such as multiple components referring to the same list or font object, which will cause access violations or heap exceptions when the multiple components try to delete the same list.

The solution is to declare a write method for the property. In the implementation of that write method, use the Assign method (inherited from TPersistent) to transfer data from the provided parameter object into the existing internal object, as shown in Listing 2.1. Chapter 8 examines the Assign method in more detail.

Listing 2.1 Write methods for class-type properties should copy data from the source to the internal object instance using Assign.

```
procedure TCustomListbox.SetItems(Value: TStrings);
begin
  FItems.Assign(Value);
end;
```

Helper classes exposed as properties should always have the same lifetime as their enclosing component. It's risky to destroy and recreate instances exposed as properties during normal operation of a component since a `with` statement is all that's needed to set up a single reference to a property that must be valid across multiple statements within the `with` block.

TStringList

TStringList is a generic implementation of TStrings that implements its own storage for its string and object data. This is the string list used by VCL components that need a string list but don't have any special storage capabilities of their own—that is, most components.

TStringList introduces two change notification events, OnChanging and OnChange, which are fired each time the string list is modified. A component that exposes a TStrings property implemented with TStringList should, at a minimum, plug into the string list's OnChange event. The component user can modify the exposed strings without touching anything else in your component. You need to know when such modifications occur so that you can redraw or update your component state based on the changed strings.

TCollection

A TCollection manages a homogeneous list of persistent objects. That is, all the items in the list are objects of the same or compatible types. The objects in the collection must be descendants of TCollectionItem, which is itself a descendant of TPersistent. A TCollection will dispose of the objects it contains when the collection is destroyed or emptied. Since TCollection knows what TCollectionItem class type it can contain, the collection can also create new items on demand. TCollection uses a TList internally to keep track of the collection items.

You would use a collection when you need to provide a list of lightweight, streamable objects of a uniform class type to the component user but don't really need (or want) the items in the list to be components. TStatusBar has a Panels property that is a collection of TStatusPanels, and TStatusPanel is a descendant of TCollectionItem. TDBGrid has a Columns collection of TColumn objects that store the display attributes of individual columns in the grid. THeader uses a collection of THeaderSections to keep track of the attributes of each header section. In all cases, the customized collection-item classes define several published properties. The collection object takes care of streaming the collection items and their published properties for you.

Most of the time, you'll use a collection in an exposed public or published property. As such, you will want the collection property to return data in the particular type managed by the collection. You can do this by creating a TCollection descendant class, implementing a new Add static method and Items array property to return the TCollectionItem descendant type your collection will use, and declaring the new Items property as the class's default array property. These new static methods simply call the corresponding methods inherited from TCollection and typecast the result. As mentioned earlier, overriding static methods in this situation is tolerable only because the descendant collection's static methods are not adding any functionality; they're merely performing a typecast service. The collection will operate correctly whether it is accessed as a simple TCollection or as your custom collection type.

Using a TCollection in a property almost always involves creating both TCollectionItem and TCollection descendant classes, designed to work together. Since the assumption is that you'll always create a descendant TCollection class, TCollection does not define an OnChange event. Instead, it just provides a virtual Update procedure that you can override to notify your enclosing component when the collection changes.

Graphics Classes (Fonts, Pens, and Brushes)

The graphic classes TFont, TPen, and TBrush are representative of how you can use helper classes to organize your component's public interface and compartmentalize features. The standard approach to using almost any helper class like TFont is as follows:

1. Declare a private instance variable in your component class declaration:

   ```
   FFont: TFont;
   ```

2. Declare a private FontChanged method in your component class, with a parameter list compatible with the TNotifyEvent method type:

   ```
   procedure FontChanged(Sender: TObject);
   ```

3. Declare a constructor and destructor in your component class, both overriding the inherited virtual constructor and destructor.

4. Declare a published property for the helper class, with the private instance variable as the property reader and a method for the property writer:

   ```
   property Font: TFont read FFont write SetFont;
   ```

5. Implement the component constructor to create an instance of the helper class and assign it to the private instance variable:

   ```
   FFont := TFont.Create;
   ```

6. Also in the constructor, assign the component's private change notification method to the helper class's OnChange event (if any):

   ```
   FFont.OnChange := FontChanged;
   ```

7. Implement the component destructor to free the helper class instance. (If you wear a belt and suspenders, assign `nil` to the private instance variable.)

8. Implement the private change notification procedure to do something appropriate in the component. In the case of a helper class like TFont that determines display characteristics of your component, the appropriate action is to invalidate the component's display area so that it will be redrawn with the changed font.

9. Implement the property writer method to call the Assign method of the internal helper class.

That's it! The helper class is now fully integrated into your component. All you need to do now is use it in the main logic of your component. It will be created when your component is created and destroyed when your component is destroyed, its properties will be written to and read from the stream when the component is streamed, and the property is assignment safe. A complete component, ready to install into your component library, is shown in Listing 2.2.

Listing 2.2 This complete component illustrates the minimum support needed to implement a published helper class property.

```
unit sample;
interface
uses Classes, Controls, Graphics;
type
  TSampleComponent = class(TCustomControl)
  private
    FHighlightFont: TFont;
    procedure HighlightFontChanged(Sender: TObject);
    procedure SetHighlightFont(Value: TFont);
  public
    constructor Create(Owner: TComponent); override;
    destructor Destroy; override;
    procedure Paint; override;
  published
    property Color; // expose inherited protected property
```

```
    property HighlightFont: TFont read FHighlightFont
      write SetHighlightFont;
  end;
procedure Register;
implementation
constructor TSampleComponent.Create(Owner: TComponent);
begin
  inherited Create(Owner);
  FHighlightFont := TFont.Create;
  FHighlightFont.OnChange := HighlightFontChanged;
end;
destructor TSampleComponent.Destroy;
begin
  FHighlightFont.Free;
  inherited Destroy;
end;
procedure TSampleComponent.HighlightFontChanged(Sender: TObject);
begin
  Invalidate;
end;
procedure TSampleComponent.SetHighlightFont(Value: TFont);
begin
  FHighlightFont.Assign(Value);
end;
procedure TSampleComponent.Paint;
begin
  // paint logic using HighlightFont goes here.
  Canvas.Font := HighlightFont;
  Canvas.Brush.Color := Color;
  Canvas.TextOut(10,10,'It works!');
end;
procedure Register;
begin
  RegisterComponents('Samples',[TSampleComponent]);
end;
end.
```

There are, of course, many variations on this theme. Depending on your needs and circumstances, you could make your helper class property read-only, you could not create the helper class instance until it was actually used (by implementing a Getxxx reader method for the property), and so on. Such variations should be done only if there is a strong reason to deviate from the norm. For example, there is little advantage to delaying the creation of the helper class instance unless creating the helper class is extraordinarily (and unavoidably) expensive in time or resources. Look first for ways to eliminate the expense of creating the helper class or, at least, to defer the expense to some time later when the helper class is actually used before carving away pieces of the property's standard support.

Operating Within the Implementation Bubble

Within the implementation of the private and protected methods of a class, you can operate under a number of simplifying assumptions of your own design. You can decide at what level parameter and data validation must be performed (public interface level, usually) and then assume data is valid and no longer needs continual checks in the lower levels of your implementation.

Within the implementation of your class, be careful of calls to an internal method that calls out of your class's implementation bubble. Firing an event property almost always calls end-user code or code in other components. That side trip into "external" code can raise exceptions, alter your class's properties, and change your internal state. Virtual method calls also have this potential. Be careful of bracketing outbound calls with state-sensitive code. That is, consider the ramifications of a state change during an outbound call on your internal code, as illustrated in Listing 2.3.

Listing 2.3 This internal routine contains state assumptions that may be invalidated by the external code in the FooChanged event.

```
procedure TMyComponent.InternalRoutine;
begin
  if HandleAllocated then
    PrepareFoo;
  try
    DoSomething;
    DoSomething;
    if HandleAllocated then
    begin
      ChangeFoo;
      FireFooChangedEvent;
    end;
    DoSomething;
  finally
    if HandleAllocated then
      ReleaseFoo;
  end;
end;
```

The code in Listing 2.3 correctly brackets the use of the Foo resource with a `try...finally` block, with the intent of freeing the Foo resource whether the routine exits normally or by exception. However, the dependence on the Handle-Allocated state is a problem. If HandleAllocated is True at the start of this internal routine, the Foo resource is allocated and modified, and FireFooChangedEvent is called. If that event does something that destroys and does not recreate the handle immediately, HandleAllocated will return False in the `finally` section of this internal routine, and the allocated Foo resource will not be released.

The opposite can happen, too. If HandleAllocated is False initially, the Foo resource will not be allocated. If one of the calls to DoSomething causes the component's window handle to be created, HandleAllocated will return True in this routine's `finally` section, and it will attempt to free a Foo resource that was never allocated.

While state changes such as the automatic creation of window handles can be controlled in your own internal methods, you cannot control them when execution leaves your implementation bubble. The solution for situations like this is to capture the state condition in a local Boolean variable so that your resource allocation, use, and deallocation are not affected by intermediate state changes, as shown in Listing 2.4.

Listing 2.4 Here's one way to eliminate the internal routine's sensitivity to changes in the component's state.

```
procedure TMyComponent.InternalRoutine;
var
  UseFoo: Boolean;
begin
  UseFoo := HandleAllocated;
  if UseFoo then
    PrepareFoo;
  try
    DoSomething;
    DoSomething;
    if UseFoo then
    begin
      ChangeFoo;
      FireFooChangedEvent;
    end;
    DoSomething;
  finally
    if UseFoo then
      ReleaseFoo;
  end;
end;
```

Setting the Degree of Extensibility

Extensibility is the degree to which the behavior or implementation of a class can be altered by descendant classes. Extensibility is not an absolute, any more than clarity of code. Some classes are designed to be used as base classes for a wide variety of purposes. Some classes are designed for a particular job but also provide a few specific opportunities for descendants to add or alter certain aspects of the class's behavior. Some classes are designed solely for a particular use and are not intended to be extended at all.

Maximum Extensibility = Minimum Functionality

Have you ever noticed that the more descendants a class has, the less the class does? Think about it. The most extensible class declaration you can write is an empty class declaration. Descendant classes can do absolutely anything they want. The second most extensible class declaration is an abstract virtual interface class—a class type that contains only abstract virtual methods. It defines intent, but no implementation.

What makes these two cases so very flexible for descendants is they don't define any implementation behaviors that would interfere with a descendant class changing the implementation. As you add functionality to a class, you reduce the number of options open to descendants. By the time you have built up a fully functional, useful class, you have so much momentum behind the design choices and behavior of that implementation that there are almost no real choices left for descendants. The only extensibility options remaining are the ones specifically identified and supported by the functional implementation.

In case you missed it earlier, this means that you have to deliberately consider and decide what opportunities you will provide for descendants of your component, if any, and then you must implement that support.

What Makes a Class Less Extensible?

Sets and Enumerated Types

These types cannot be expanded after the fact, so any set or enumerated type property or method parameter in a class cannot be altered by descendant classes. A poor alternative to an enumerated type is a list of integer constants; an even poorer alternative to a set is a list of integer constants arranged as bit flags. Sets and enumerated types score high on the ease-of-use scale, so they cannot be easily dismissed.

Instantiation of Aggregates

A class that constructs all its internal helper classes (aggregates) explicitly in its constructor leaves no opportunity for descendants to construct different or enhanced helper classes instead. A virtual method dedicated to instantiating a particular helper class allows descendants to change what kind of helper class is created, without having to circumvent the base class's constructor or program logic surrounding the creation of the helper class. (C++ converts puzzled by this last statement should note that Object Pascal allows polymorphic virtual method calls in constructors.) Class references are another way a base class can allow descendants to participate in the choice of helper class types that the base class instantiates. Grid components use the virtual method technique to allow descendant grids the opportunity to use their own TInPlaceEdit control descendant, even though all the in-place edit support code of the grid is implemented in the base TCustomGrid class. TCollection uses the class reference technique to determine which TCollectionItem descendant type the collection will accept and create instances of.

Access to Implementation Details

A component writer may expose implementation details of a class in its protected (or even public) sections with the intent of making the component more extensible, but if the implementation details themselves are invariant, the class is no more extensible than if the details were completely hidden. Unnecessary exposure to implementation details increases the risk that modifications to the base class implementation will break descendant code that relied on those implementation details. Don't expose details unless you have a specific use in mind.

Monolithic Methods

When 80% of the implementation of a base class is implemented in two or three methods, the reusability factor of the class is all or none. Making the monolithic methods virtual doesn't help a bit because you can't execute only *some* of an inherited method. To avoid this, split up the monolithic methods into groups of single-purpose subroutines in the base class's protected interface. These subroutines don't even need to be virtual; they just need to be accessible so that descendants have the opportunity to invoke specific features of the base class (in the subroutines) without having to reimplement all those behaviors. Make the kingpin (formerly monolithic) method(s) virtual to allow descendants to override the logic surrounding the calls to the specific subroutines while reusing the subroutines.

Published Properties

Descendants cannot "unpublish" inherited properties. Classes that you intend to be used as ancestor classes should not publish any properties. Implement your class in a TCustomxxx class type, with ready-to-use properties tucked away in the protected section. Then, declare the real class as a descendant of the TCustomxxx base class and promote the desired properties to published.

What Makes a Class More Extensible?

Planning

Take a step back and consider the features related to your component that a reasonable person might want to add to a descendant of your component. Consider where the addition of a virtual method opens up opportunities for descendants. Then surf those opportunities to make sure all the necessary resources are in some way accessible in the descendant. If an extensibility opportunity would require significant changes to your design, the person who suggested it will often suddenly appear much less reasonable. Whether that opportunity is worth the setback of a rewrite is something you'll have to decide for yourself.

Deferrable Decisions

Virtual methods allow a base class implementation to defer decisions or choices to descendant classes. Choice of helper class types to instantiate is one of the bigger decisions that descendants can benefit by deferral.

Simple, Clear Opportunities

Murphy's Law, paragraph 38, states, "Anything that's adjustable will eventually need adjustment and will probably be adjusted incorrectly." Rather than make a group of related utility methods all virtual, make one virtual method that the utility methods all use. For example, if a class has a virtual GetItem method, then there should be no need to make methods First and Last virtual as well. Too many options makes a class difficult to read and difficult to use.

Second Opinions

The author of a class is too close to the implementation to objectively critique the usability of the public interface or the extensibility of the protected interface. Get a fresh pair of eyes to go over the class declaration, use the component a bit, and finally review the implementation for trouble spots. When you've spent a lot of time running around inside a component, it is easy to lose track of which functions are private, protected, or public, so you will have trouble recognizing holes in your component's public and protected interfaces.

Access to Implementation Details

That's right. This was also listed as an extensibility inhibitor. Access to implementation details is a two-edged sword: You can't do much without it, and you often can't do much else when you have it. Abstraction of internal subsystems helps to provide the information descendants will need without making them fatally dependent upon implementation specifics. Abstraction of internal subsystems is one of the benefits of aggregation.

Providing Design-Time Support

Most components operate at design time pretty much as they do at run time. The form designer prevents components from receiving input focus at design time and orchestrates the variety of special services that the design-time environment provides around the component, but by and large the component doesn't have to do anything special to work at design time.

There are a few small behaviors that components perform differently when they realize they are operating in the design-time environment. For example, many controls display their component name on their person at design time, but not at run time. Controls ignore their Visible property at design time, too. (Have you ever tried to select an invisible component?) Some components allow direct manipulation of themselves at design time, such as clicking on the tabs of a TPageControl to switch pages or using the mouse to reorder the columns of a TDBGrid. All these examples require a line or two of code here and there in the component itself. Such design-time support code gets compiled into Delphi applications that use these components, so it's very important to keep such code to a bare minimum.

You can tell whether your component is operating in the design-time environment by testing

```
If csDesigning in ComponentState
```

Examples of controls that interact with the design time environment appear in Part III of this book.

Summary

Here are the rules of thumb covered in this chapter:

- Usability of the component is your top design priority.

- Extensibility must be designed into and implemented into a base class.

- Identify IS and HAS relationships in your component design process.

- Use aggregation to implement your component using common helper classes.

- Use aggregation to limit the exposed features of a class but still make use of common helper classes.

- Choose the right roots (TObject, TPersistent, TComponent, TGraphicControl, TWinControl, or TCustomxxx).

- Choose the right tools (TList, TStrings, TCollection, TFont, TPen, TBrush, and so on).

- Using a large class already used in an application adds less to the application size than creating a new, smaller, custom-tailored class.

- TList is used everywhere but is never inherited from.

- TStrings is never instantiated but is always inherited from.

- Create TCollection and TCollectionItem descendants in complementary pairs.

- All public and published component data should be exposed as properties, not raw data fields.

- Public and protected interfaces must be contractless and bulletproof.

- Protected interfaces are usually contractual and more trusting of data validation.

- Don't publish properties in intended ancestor classes; declare properties protected and let descendants publish them as needed.

- Fire event properties via protected dynamic methods (Click calls OnClick).

- Never assign to published event properties unless you have isolated the class internally.

- Prepare for exceptions and state changes when calling "out" to event handlers or virtual methods.

- Implement class-type property write methods using Assign to transfer attributes.

- Override Assign to copy data into your class from instances of your own or other class types.

PART II

Implementation Details

Chapter 3

Virtual Methods and Polymorphism

Polymorphism is perhaps *the* cornerstone of object-oriented programming. Without it, OOP would have only encapsulation and inheritance—data buckets and hierarchical families of data buckets—but no way to manipulate related objects uniformly. Polymorphism is the key to leveraging your code investments to enable a relatively small amount of code to drive a wide variety of behaviors without requiring carnal knowledge of the implementation details of those behaviors and without restricting the set of possible implementations to one. It is critical that you have a firm understanding of how polymorphism works and what opportunities it offers you before you can extend existing components or design new extensible component classes.

True to its name, polymorphism has "many forms" in Delphi, and a component writer typically uses a mix of all of them to implement a component. This chapter explores the implementation and use of `virtual` and `dynamic` methods and class reference types in detail, as well as some of the more peculiar sand traps and exotic uses of these language constructs. Message methods (methods declared with a `message` directive) are related to `dynamic` methods in implementation, but they are different enough to warrant their own chapter (see Chapter 7, Messaging.)

> **Note**
> In this chapter and the rest of the book, "virtual" denotes the *general* term that applies to all forms of virtual methods (methods declared with `virtual`, `dynamic`, or `override`), and "`virtual`" denotes the *specific* term that refers only to methods declared with the `virtual` directive. For example: Most polymorphism concepts and issues apply to all virtual methods, but there are a few noteworthy items that apply only to `virtual` methods.

This chapter assumes you are familiar with the Delphi class declaration syntax and OOP general principles. If you're feeling a little rusty, take a spin through the Delphi Language Reference.

Syntax Review

Let's review quickly the two kinds of virtual methods and four language directives used to declare them:

- Virtual methods come in two flavors: `virtual` and `dynamic`. The only difference between them is their internal implementations; they use different techniques to achieve the same results.

- Calls to `virtual` methods are dispatched more quickly than calls to `dynamic` methods.

- The compiler-generated tables for `virtual` methods require much more storage space than `dynamic` methods.

- Both `virtual` and `dynamic` always introduce a new method name into a class's name space.

- The `override` directive is used to redefine the implementation of a virtual method (`virtual` or `dynamic`) that a class inherits from an ancestor.

- An `override` method uses the same dispatch mechanism (`virtual` or `dynamic`) as the inherited virtual method it replaces.

- The `abstract` directive indicates that there is no method body associated with that virtual method declaration. Abstract declarations are useful for defining a purely conceptual interface, which, in turn, is useful for maintaining absolute separation between the user of a class and its implementation.

- The `abstract` directive can only be used in the declaration of new virtual (`virtual` or `dynamic`) methods; you can't make an implemented method abstract after the fact.

- A class type that contains one or more abstract methods is called an *abstract class*.

- A class type that contains nothing but abstract methods (no static methods, no virtual methods, no data fields) is called an *abstract interface* or, in C++ circles, a *pure virtual interface*.

Polymorphism in Action

What do `virtual` and `dynamic` do? In general, they allow a method call to be directed at run time to the appropriate piece of code, appropriate for the type of the object instance used to make the call. For this to be interesting, you have to have more than one class type, and the class types must be related by inheritance from a common ancestor.

Listing 3.1 contains three classes we'll use to explore the execution characteristics of polymorphism: the simple base class TBaseGadget, which defines the static method NotVirtual and the virtual method ThisIsVirtual, and two descendant classes, TKitchenGadget and TOfficeGadget, which both override the ThisIsVirtual method they inherit from TBaseGadget. TOfficeGadget also introduces the new static method NotVirtual and the new virtual method NewMethod.

Listing 3.1 Three classes used to explore polymorphism.

```
type
  TBaseGadget = class
    procedure NotVirtual(X: Integer);
    procedure ThisIsVirtual(Y: Integer); virtual;
  end;
  TKitchenGadget = class(TBaseGadget)
    procedure ThisIsVirtual(Y: Integer); override;
  end;
  TOfficeGadget = class(TBaseGadget);
    function  NewMethod: Longint;  virtual;
    procedure NotVirtual(X,Y,Z: Integer);
    procedure ThisIsVirtual(Y: Integer); override;
  end;
```

- **Identical names in different classes are not related.** Declaring a static method in a descendant which happens to have the same name as a static method in an ancestor is not an override, in the `override` sense. There is no relationship whatsoever between static methods declared in a descendant and static methods declared in an ancestor class other than the same-name similarity that your brain cells can't avoid noticing. The compiler makes no such association; TBaseGadget has a NotVirtual method, and TOfficeGadget has a completely different method, named NotVirtual.

In the next several pages, we'll be tracing execution paths through programs that use these classes. To make these paths crystal clear, you can implement the methods of these classes to write the class and method name to the screen in a bare-bones console app. For example:

```
procedure TBaseGadget.NotVirtual(X: Integer);
begin
   writeln('TBaseGadget.NotVirtual');
end;
procedure TBaseGadget.ThisIsVirtual(Y: Integer);
begin
   writeln('TBaseGadget.ThisIsVirtual');
end;
procedure TKitchenGadget.ThisIsVirtual(Y: Integer);
begin
   writeln('TKitchenGadget.ThisIsVirtual');
end;
{... etc.}
```

The best (and fastest) way to explore execution paths is to step through the source code using the debugger, but `writeln`s are easier to convey in print and make it easier to compare execution flow patterns.

If we start with a variable P of type TBaseGadget, we can assign to it an instance of a TBaseGadget or an instance of one of its descendants, such as a TKitchenGadget or TOfficeGadget. Recall that Delphi object instance variables are actually pointers to the instance data allocated from the global heap, and that pointers of a class type are type-compatible with all descendants of that type. We can then call methods using the instance variable P:

```
var
   P : TBaseGadget;
begin
   P := TBaseGadget.Create;
   P.NotVirtual(10);
   P.ThisIsVirtual(5);
   P.Free;
end;
```

When compiled as a console app (Project: Options: Linker: Console Application) and run, the program produces this output:

```
TBaseGadget.NotVirtual
TBaseGadget.ThisIsVirtual
```

In the interest of brevity, the execution traces are folded into comments in the source code. Pessimists are welcome to step through the sample code to verify the execution trace.

If P refers to an instance of TKitchenGadget, the execution trace would look something like Listing 3.2.

Listing 3.2 Execution with an instance of TKitchenGadget

```
var
  P : TBaseGadget;
begin
  P := TKitchenGadget.Create;
  P.NotVirtual(10);       { Call TBaseGadget.NotVirtual      }
  P.ThisIsVirtual(5);     { Call TKitchenGadget.ThisIsVirtual }
  P.Free;
end;
```

Nothing remarkable in Listing 3.2. We have one call to a static method going to the version defined in the ancestor type and one call to a virtual method going to the version of the method associated with the object instance type. One might deduce that the inherited static method (NotVirtual) is called because TKitchenGadget doesn't override it. The observations are correct, but the explanation is flawed, as the next example shows.

If P refers an instance of TOfficeGadget, you might be a little puzzled by the result in Listing 3.3.

Listing 3.3 Execution with an instance of TOfficeGadget.

```
var
  P : TBaseGadget;
begin
  P := TOfficeGadget.Create;
  P.NotVirtual(10);       { Call TBaseGadget.NotVirtual      }

{ The compiler will not allow the following two lines:
  P.NotVirtual(1,2,3);      "Too many parameters"
  P.NewMethod;              "Method identifier expected"     }

  P.ThisIsVirtual(5);     { Call TOfficeGadget.ThisIsVirtual }
  P.Free;
end;
```

- **Static method calls are resolved by variable type.** Even though TOfficeGadget has its own NotVirtual method and P refers to an instance of TOfficeGadget, why does TBaseGadget.NotVirtual get called instead? Because static (non-virtual) method calls are resolved at compile time according to the type of the *variable* used to make the call. For static methods, what the variable refers to is immaterial. In this case, P's type is TBaseGadget, which means the NotVirtual method associated with P's declared type is TBaseGadget.NotVirtual.

Notice that NewMethod defined in TOfficeGadget is out of reach of a TBaseGadget variable. P can only access fields and methods defined in its TBaseGadget class type.

- **New names obscure inherited names.** If P were instead declared as a variable of type TOfficeGadget, the method call P.NotVirtual(1,2,3) would be allowed and the method call P.NotVirtual(1) would not since TOfficeGadget.NotVirtual requires three parameters. TOfficeGadget.NotVirtual *obscures* the TBaseGadget.NotVirtual method name in all instances and descendants of TOfficeGadget. The inherited method is still a part of TOfficeGadget (proven by the code in Listing 3.3); you just can't get to it directly from TOfficeGadget and descendant types. The only way to get past this is to typecast the instance variable: TBaseGadget(P).NotVirtual(1).

If P were declared as a TOfficeGadget variable, P.NewMethod would also be allowed since the compiler can "see" NewMethod in a TOfficeGadget variable.

- **Descendant >= Ancestor.** An instance of a descendant type could be greater than its ancestor type in both services and data, but the descendant-type instance can never be less than what its ancestors define. Because a descendant must be at least everything that its ancestors are, type compatibility rules can exist that allow a variable of an ancestral type (TBaseGadget) to refer to an instance of a descendant type without loss of information.

- **Inheritance is a one-way street.** With a variable of a particular class type you can access any public symbol (field, property, or method) defined in any of that class's ancestors. You can assign an instance of a descendant class into that variable, but you cannot access any new fields or methods defined by the descendant class. The fields of the descendant class are certainly in the instance data that the variable refers to, but those new fields are "out past the end" of where the variable's declared type says the base class instance data ends.

There are two ways around this nearsightedness of ancestral class types:

1. Typecasting—The programmer assumes a lot and forces the compiler to treat the variable as a descendant type.

2. Virtual methods— The magic of polymorphism will call the method appropriate to the type of the associated *instance*, determined at run time.

- **Ancestors define the standard.** Why do we care about the nearsightedness of ancestral classes? Why not just use the matching variable type when you create or manipulate an object instance? Sometimes, that is the simplest thing to do, but as soon as you start talking about manipulating multiple classes that do almost the same things, that simplest solution falls apart. Ancestral class types set the minimum interface standard through which we can access a set of related objects. *Polymorphism* is the use of virtual methods to make one verb (method name) produce one of many possible actions depending upon the instance. To have multiple possible actions, you have to have multiple class types (like TKitchenGadget and TOfficeGadget), each potentially defining a different implementation of a particular method. To be able to make one call that could cover those multiple class types, the method has to be defined in a class from which all the multiple class types descend—an ancestral class (like TBaseGadget). The ancestral class, then, is the least common denominator for behavior common to a set of related classes.

    For polymorphism to work, all the actions that are common to the group of classes need to at least be named in a common ancestor. If every descendant is required to override the ancestor's method, the ancestral method doesn't need to do anything at all—it can be declared `abstract`. If there is a behavior that is common to most of the classes in the group, the ancestor class can pick up that default behavior and leave the descendants to override the defaults only when necessary. This consolidates code higher in the class hierarchy for greater code reuse and smaller total code size. However, providing default behaviors in an ancestor class can also complicate the design issues of creating flexible, extensible classes, as was discussed in Chapter 2.

- **Polymorphism lets ancestors reach into descendants.** Another aspect of polymorphism doesn't appear to involve instance pointer types at all—at least not explicitly. Consider the code fragment in Listing 3.4.

Listing 3.4 Polymorphism allows ancestors to call into descendants.

```
procedure TBaseGadget.NotVirtual;
begin
  ThisIsVirtual(17);
end;
var
  P: TBaseGadget;
begin
  P := TKitchenGadget.Create;
  P.NotVirtual(10);         { Call TBaseGadget.NotVirtual          }
  P.Free;
end.
```

TBaseGadget.NotVirtual method's code contains an unqualified call to ThisIsVirtual. When P refers to an instance of TKitchenGadget, P.NotVirtual will call TBaseGadget.NotVirtual. (So far, nothing new.) When that code calls ThisIsVirtual, it will execute TKitchenGadget.ThisIsVirtual (surprise!). Even within the depths of TBaseGadget, in a nonvirtual method, a virtual method call is directed to the appropriate code! How can this be? Answer: Resolution of virtual method calls depends upon the object *instance* associated with the call. A pointer to the object instance is secretly passed into all method calls, surfacing inside methods as the Self identifier. Inside TBaseGadget.NotVirtual, a call to ThisIsVirtual is really a call to Self.ThisIsVirtual. Self in this context operates like a variable of type TBaseGadget that refers to an instance of type TKitchenGadget. Thus, when the instance type is TKitchenGadget, the virtual method call resolves to TKitchenGadget.ThisIsVirtual.

How is this useful? It means an ancestral method, virtual or not, can call a sequence of virtual methods. The descendants can determine the specific behavior of one or more of those virtual methods. The ancestor determines the sequence in which the methods are called, plus miscellaneous setup and cleanup code, but does not completely determine the final behavior of the descendants. The descendants inherit the sequence logic from the ancestor and have the opportunity to override one or more of the steps in that sequence, but they don't have to reproduce the entire sequence logic themselves. This is how OOP promotes code reuse.

- **Fully qualified method calls are reduced to static calls.** As a footnote, consider what happens if TBaseGadget.NotVirtual contains a qualified call to TBaseGadget.ThisIsVirtual, as shown in Listing 3.5.

Listing 3.5 This fully qualified method call is compiled as a static call.

```
procedure TBaseGadget.NotVirtual;
begin
  TBaseGadget.ThisIsVirtual(17);
end;
```

Even though ThisIsVirtual is a virtual method, a fully qualified method call will compile down to a regular static method call. You've made it clear that you want only the TBaseGadget.ThisIsVirtual method called, so the compiler does just what you tell it. Dispatching this as a virtual method call might call some other version of that method, which would violate your very explicit instructions. Except in very special circumstances, you do not want this in your code! This defeats the whole purpose of making ThisIsVirtual virtual.

- **Dynamic behaves the same as virtual.** If you replace all the `virtual`s in the sample program with `dynamic`, the behavior of the program will be exactly the same. The only differences between `virtual` and `dynamic` are their internal storage and dispatch technique, which should be considered when creating a new virtual method. First, we'll look at the internal implementation of `virtual` methods; then, `dynamic` methods.

The Virtual Method Table

A Virtual Method Table (VMT) is an array of pointers to all the `virtual` methods defined in a class *and* all the `virtual` methods the class inherits from its ancestors. A VMT is created by the compiler for every class type because all classes descend from TObject and TObject has a `virtual` destructor Destroy. In Delphi, VMTs are stored in the program's code space. There is only one VMT per class type: Multiple instances of the same class type refer to the same VMT. At run time, the VMT is a read-only lookup table.

Structure of the VMT

As shown in Figure 3.1, the first 4 bytes of data in an object instance are a pointer to that class type's VMT. The VMT pointer points to the first entry in the VMT's list of 4-byte pointers to the entry points of the class's `virtual` methods. Since methods can never be deleted in descendant classes, the location of a `virtual` method in the VMT is the same throughout all descendant classes. Thus, the compiler can view a `virtual` method simply as a unique entry in the class's VMT. As we will see shortly, this is exactly how `virtual` method calls are dispatched. Thinking of `virtual` methods as indexes into an array of code pointers will also help us visualize how method name conflicts are resolved by the compiler.

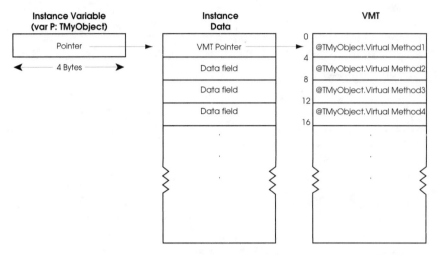

Figure 3.1 The structure of the Virtual Method Table and its relationship to the object instance.

There is no information in the VMT indicating how many `virtual` methods are stored in it or where the VMT ends. The VMT is constructed by the compiler and accessed by compiler-generated code, so the compiler doesn't need to make notes to itself about size or number of entries. (This does make it difficult for BASM code to call `virtual` methods, though.)

Optimization Note
> A descendant of a class with `virtual` methods gets a whole new copy of the ancestor's VMT. The descendant can then add new `virtual` methods or override inherited `virtual` methods without affecting the ancestor's VMT. If the ancestor has a 12-entry VMT, the descendant has at least a 12-entry VMT. *Every* descendant class type of that ancestor and all descendants of those descendants will have at least 12 entries in their own VMT. All these VMTs occupy memory. For most programs, this will not be a problem, but extraordinarily large class types with thousands of `virtual` methods and/or thousands of descendants could consume quite a bit of memory, both in RAM and in EXE file size; `dynamic` methods are much more space efficient, but at a slight execution speed penalty.

Inside a Virtual Method Call

Now we'll examine the mechanics behind the magic of `virtual` method calls.

When the compiler is compiling your source code and encounters a call to a `virtual` method identifier, it generates a special sequence of machine instructions that will unravel the appropriate call destination at run time. The machine code snippets in Listing 3.6 assume compiler optimizations are enabled and stack frames are disabled.

Listing 3.6 The machine instructions for a `virtual` method call.

```
// machine code for statement P.SomeVirtualMethod;
  MOV    EAX, [EBP+4]   { move instance data address (P^) into EAX }
  MOV    ECX, [EAX]     { move instance's VMT address into ECX }
  CALL   [ECX + 08]     { call address stored at VMT index 2 }
```

The VMT pointer is always stored at offset 0 in the instance data. In this example, the method being called is the third `virtual` method of a class, including inherited `virtual` methods. The first `virtual` method is at offset 0, the second at offset 4, and the third at offset 8.

That's it! All the magic of `virtual` methods and polymorphism boils down to the fact that the indicator of which `virtual` method to invoke on the instance data is stored in the instance data itself!

The Dynamic Method Table

The compiler creates a Dynamic Method Table (DMT) for every class type that declares new `dynamic` methods or overrides inherited `dynamic` methods. The format of the DMT is radically different from the VMT. Where the VMT stores a complete snapshot of all `virtual` methods available to a particular class type, a DMT stores only how a particular class type's `dynamic` methods *differ* from its immediate ancestor. Since DMTs only contain information about what's new or what's changed, DMTs are typically much smaller than VMTs for large class types with lots of descendants in deep class hierarchies.

Similar in concept to `virtual` methods, the compiler assigns `dynamic` methods a unique id number. Unlike `virtual` methods, though, this id is not a direct index into an array of code pointers. Instead, it is a token that identifies which `dynamic` method addresses are stored in a class's DMT.

Structure of the DMT

As illustrated in Figure 3.2, a DMT consists of a word-sized count of the entries in the table, an array of word-sized ids of the `dynamic` methods contained in the DMT, and a matching array of 4-byte pointers to the code of those `dynamic` methods.

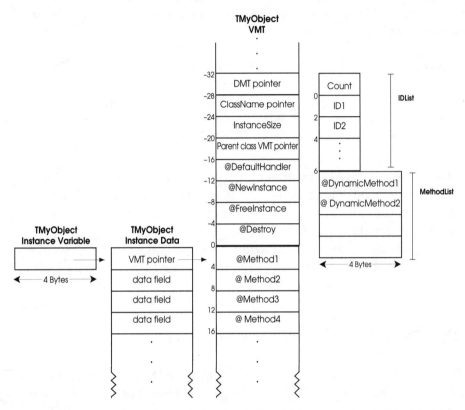

Figure 3.2 The structure of the Dynamic Method Table and its relationship to the object instance and VMT.

Inside a Dynamic Method Call

To call a `dynamic` method, the compiler generates machine code to call an internal dispatch subroutine, passing the `dynamic` method's internal id number as a parameter. The internal dispatch routine locates the class's DMT by grabbing a pointer located 32 bytes *above* the start of the VMT. The VMT pointer in the object instance data points to the first VMT entry, but there is a lot more class information stored just above the first VMT entry—at negative offsets from the VMT pointer.

THE DYNAMIC METHOD TABLE

The internal dispatch routine searches the DMT's array of id numbers for a match. If the desired dynamic method id does not appear in that class's DMT (because that dynamic method is not overridden or introduced in that class), the dispatch routine looks in the class's immediate ancestor's DMT, and so on, until a matching id number is found. Since the dispatch of dynamic methods is completely compiler controlled, a match will eventually be found—the compiler won't allow you to call a dynamic method that doesn't exist in your class or its ancestors. When a matching id is found, the dispatch routine notes its index in the current DMT's array of ids and calls the code address at that index in the current DMT's array of code pointers. Figure 3.3 illustrates the DMT dispatch process.

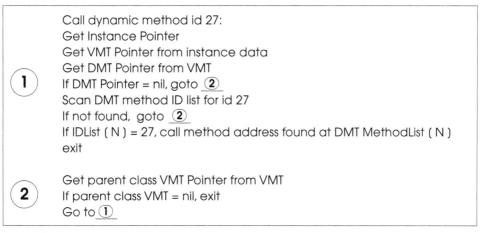

Figure 3.3 The steps involved in the DMT dispatch process.

Since the search for a matching dynamic method id starts at the instance's class type and works its way up the inheritance tree, the first matching id is guaranteed to be the most recent override of the method in the class's ancestry or the original declaration of the dynamic method if nothing overrides it. The same id may appear multiple times in a class hierarchy, each time the same dynamic method is overridden.

It should be obvious that this active search will take more CPU cycles than the single-pointer lookup required for a virtual method call. The extra time required to dispatch a dynamic method call is negligible to your end users in all but the most time critical programming situations.

Just as with virtual methods, a call to a dynamic method using a fully qualified type identifier will be compiled as a static method call, defeating the dynamic method id search and its polymorphic behavior.

Redeclaring Virtual Methods

Whenever you declare a method using the `virtual` or `dynamic` directive you are *always* creating a new identifier, independent of any same-named methods declared in ancestor classes: `virtual` always tells the compiler to append a new slot to the class's VMT; `dynamic` always tells the compiler to create a new unique `dynamic` method id. Since the internal ids of these new methods are different from the ids of similarly named methods in ancestor classes, these new methods cannot participate in the polymorphism set up by the ancestors' methods. Since these new methods are completely new, you are free to declare any parameter list or function return type you wish—further evidence that these new methods cannot participate in polymorphism through their ancestor types. For example, let's return to the gadget classes used in earlier examples and change the TOfficeGadget.ThisIsVirtual declaration from `override` to `virtual`, as shown in Listing 3.7.

Listing 3.7 TOfficeGadget declares its own ThisIsVirtual method, which makes it difficult to see what the code really does.

```
type
  TBaseGadget = class
    procedure NotVirtual(X: Integer);
    procedure ThisIsVirtual(Y: Integer); virtual;
  end;
  TOfficeGadget = class(TBaseGadget);
    function  NewMethod: Longint;  virtual;
    procedure NotVirtual(X,Y,Z: Integer);
    procedure ThisIsVirtual(Y: Integer); virtual; //!!
  end;
{...}
var
  P : TBaseGadget;
begin
  P := TOfficeGadget.Create;
  P.NotVirtual(10);            { Calls TBaseGadget.NotVirtual     }
  P.ThisIsVirtual(5);          { Calls TBaseGadget.ThisIsVirtual!! }
  P.Free;
end;
```

With this minor change, TOfficeGadget.ThisIsVirtual is in the same fix as TOfficeGadget.NewMethod: It cannot be accessed from a TBaseGadget variable.

However, since the names of the methods are the same, it can be extremely difficult to figure out why the simple code in Listing 3.7 does not perform as you would expect. Everything looks fine in the code that calls the methods, and in the implementation of the virtual methods (not shown in Listing 3.7), and even (superficially) in the declaration of the class types. And yet, this code does not behave "correctly." The program does not call TOfficeGadget.ThisIsVirtual. The only thing that is wrong is that in order for this code to behave correctly, TOfficeGadget.ThisIsVirtual must override the original version of ThisIsVirtual by declaring the method as `override` instead of `virtual`.

For this reason alone, you should *never* use this virtual method redeclaration capability deliberately. Compile your source code with compiler warnings enabled, and the compiler will scold you bitterly should you ever accidentally redeclare a virtual method instead of overriding it.

Why Delphi Supports Redeclaring Virtuals

If redeclaring virtuals is something you should never do, why does Delphi allow it? Simple—source code version resiliency. Redeclaring virtuals was deliberately built into Delphi's Object Pascal syntax so that new virtual methods can be added to ancestor classes in subsequent releases without breaking existing descendant classes that happen to have their own virtual methods by the same name. In previous versions of Borland's Pascal product line and in other compiled languages, adding virtual methods to a widely used base class will invariably break somebody's descendant class.

For example, suppose for a moment that descendant classes were only allowed to override inherited virtual methods (requiring exactly the same parameter lists and return types as the ancestor methods they override), along with declaring new virtual method names that don't already exist in their ancestors. Now suppose we upgrade our TBaseGadget class to version 2.0, and this new version sports a shiny new virtual method called NewMethod, a function returning a string. TOfficeGadget already had its own NewMethod virtual method prior to the upgrade of the base class. In this situation, we would not be able to recompile our TOfficeGadget class since its own NewMethod's function result type does not match the same-named ancestor method's result type. Thus, adding functionality to the base class has broken a descendant class through no fault of the descendant class. Delphi solves this problem by allowing descendant classes to have their own name scopes that take precedence over inherited names.

The Effect—Still Compiles, Still Runs *Correctly*

When descendant classes have their own name scopes, new virtual methods can be added to base classes without the constant fear of breaking descendant classes. Note that this is more than just a recompilation issue: Not only are descendant classes still compilable after the introduction of name collisions in a base class, but they also continue to run and operate normally. Continuing with the TOfficeGadget example, in version 1.0 of your class library, the only way to access TOfficeGadget's NewMethod method is with a variable of type TOfficeGadget or by typecasting a variable to TOfficeGadget. When version 2.0 of the class library introduces a different NewMethod in an ancestor class, it won't affect any of your existing (1.0-based) code because the 1.0-based ancestor didn't have a NewMethod method for your existing code to call and because the 1.0-based code that does call NewMethod must do so through an explicit TOfficeGadget variable or typecast. Since redeclaring a virtual method in a descendant severs all ties with similarly named methods in the ancestor, none of the version 2.0 ancestor code that calls the new NewMethod has any knowledge of TOfficeGadget.NewMethod. Thus, the spheres of influence (scopes) of the ancestor's NewMethod and the descendant's preexisting NewMethod do not overlap, so the program can compile and run normally.

Redeclaring virtuals is a lifesaver for getting code up and running in transition situations, but that doesn't make it a desirable programming technique by any stretch of the imagination. Automobile airbags are lifesavers, too, but you don't drive around with them inflated. Compile your projects with warnings enabled and eliminate redeclared virtuals (by renaming the descendant method) immediately.

Abstract Interfaces

An abstract interface is a class type that contains no implementation and no data—only abstract virtual methods. Abstract interfaces allow you to *completely* separate the user of the interface from the implementation of the interface. With abstract interfaces, you can have an object implemented in a DLL and used by routines in an EXE just as if the object were implemented in the EXE itself. Abstract interfaces can bridge conceptual barriers within an application, logistical barriers between an application and a DLL, language barriers between applications written in different programming languages, and address space barriers that separate Win32 processes. In all cases, the client application uses the interface class just as it would any class it implemented itself.

Let's now take a closer look at how an abstract interface class can bridge the gap between an application and a DLL. Abstract interfaces are also critical to object linking and embedding (OLE), which we'll examine in Chapter 9.

ABSTRACT INTERFACES

Importing Objects from DLLs—The Hard Way

If you want an application to use a function in a DLL, you have to create a "fake" function declaration that tells the compiler what it needs to know about the parameter list and result type of the function. Instead of a method body, this fake function declaration contains a reference to a DLL and function name. The compiler sees these and knows what code to generate to call the proper address in the DLL at run time.

If you want an application to use an object that is implemented in a DLL, you could do essentially the same thing, declaring a separate function for each object method in the DLL. As the number of methods in the DLL object increases, though, keeping track of all those functions will become a chore. To make things a little easier to manage, you could set up the DLL to give you (the client app) an array of function pointers that you would use to call any of the DLL functions associated with a particular DLL class type.

Perhaps you can see where this is headed. A VMT is precisely an array of function pointers. Why do things the hard way when the compiler can do the dirty work for you?

Importing Objects from DLLs—The Smart Way

What the client module (the application) needs is a class declaration that will make the compiler visualize a VMT that matches the desired DLL's array of function pointers. Enter the abstract interface class. The class contains a hoard of `virtual; abstract;` method declarations in the exact same order as the functions in the DLL's array of function pointers. Of course, the abstract method declarations need parameter lists that match the DLL's functions exactly, too.

Now, you can fetch the array of function pointers from the DLL and *typecast* a pointer to that array into your application's abstract interface class type. (OK, it actually needs to be a pointer to a pointer to an array of function addresses. The first pointer simulates the object instance, the second pointer simulates the VMT pointer embedded in the instance data—but who's counting?) With this typecast in place, the compiler will think you have an instance of that class type. When the compiler sees a method call on that typecast pointer, it will generate code to push the parameters on the stack, then look up the Nth virtual method address in the "instance's VMT" (the pointer to the function table provided by the DLL), and then call that address. Voila! Your application is using an "object" that lives in a DLL as easily as one of its own classes.

Exporting Objects from DLLs

Now for the flip side. Where did the DLL get that array of function pointers? From the compiler, of course! (Who, me work?) On the DLL side, create a class type with `virtual` methods with the same order and parameter lists as defined by the "red-herring" array of function pointers, and implement those methods to perform the tasks of that class. Implement and export a simple function from the DLL that creates an instance of the DLL's class and returns a pointer to it. Again, voila! Your DLL is now exporting an object that can be used by any application that can handle pointers to arrays of function addresses—also known as objects!

Abstract Interfaces Linking User and Implementor

Here's the clincher. How do you guarantee that the order and parameter lists of the methods in the application's abstract interface class exactly match the methods implemented in the DLL? Simple. Declare the DLL class as a *descendant* of the abstract interface class used by the application, and override all the abstract virtual methods. The abstract interface is shared between the application and the DLL; the implementation is contained entirely within the DLL.

Abstract Interfaces Crossing Language Boundaries

This can also be done between modules written in different languages. The Microsoft Common Object Model (COM) is a language-independent specification that allows different programming languages to share objects as just described. At its core, COM is just a specification for how an array of function pointers should be arranged and used. COM is what all of OLE is built upon. Since Delphi's native class type implementation conforms to COM specs, there is no conversion required for Delphi applications to use COM objects, nor any conversion required for Delphi applications to expose COM objects for other modules to use.

Of course, when dealing with multiple languages, you won't have the luxury of sharing the abstract interface class between the modules. You'll have to translate the abstract interface class into each language, but that is a small price to pay for the ability to share the implementation.

The Delphi IDE is built entirely upon abstract interfaces, allowing the IDE main module to communicate with the editor and debugger kernel DLLs (implemented in BC++) and with the multitude of component design-time tools that live in the component library (CMPLIB32.DCL) and installable expert modules. Part III of this book explores the IDE's design-time interfaces in detail.

Virtuals Defeat Smart Linking

When the Delphi compiler/linker produces an EXE file, the procedures, variables, and static methods that are not referenced by "live" code (code that is actually used) will be left out of the EXE file. This process is called *smart linking* and is a great improvement over normal linkers that merely copy all code into the EXE file whether it is actually needed or not. The result of smart linking is a smaller EXE file on disk that requires less memory to run.

> If the type information of a class is touched (for example, by constructing an instance) by live code, then all the virtual methods of the class and its ancestors will be linked into the executable file, regardless of whether the program actually uses the virtual methods.

Smart linking rule for virtuals

For the compiler, keeping track of whether an individual procedure is ever used in a program is relatively simple; figuring out whether a virtual method is actually used requires a great deal more analysis of the descendants and ancestors of the class. While it is not impossible to devise a scheme to determine whether a particular virtual method is never used in any descendants of a class type, such a scheme would certainly require a lot more CPU cycles than normal smart linking, and the resulting reduction in code size would rarely be dramatic. For these reasons (lots of work, greatly reduced compile/link speed, and diminishing returns), adding smart linking of virtual methods to the Delphi linker has not been a high priority for Borland.

If your class has a number of utility methods that you don't expect to use all the time, leaving them static will allow the smart linker to omit them from the final EXE if they are not actually used by your program.

Note that inclusion of virtual methods involves more than just the bytes of code in the method bodies. Anything that a virtual method uses or calls must also be linked into the EXE, and anything those routines use, and so on. Through this cascade effect, one method could potentially drag hundreds of other routines into the executable file, sometimes at a cost of hundreds of thousands of bytes of additional code and data. If most of these support routines are used only by your unused virtual method, you have a lot of deadwood in your EXE file.

The best general strategy to keep unused virtual methods and their associated deadwood under control is to declare virtual methods sparingly. It's easier to promote an existing static method to virtual when a clear need arises than to try to demote virtual down to static at some late stage of your development cycle.

Virtuals Enhance Smart Linking

Smart linking of virtuals is a two-edged sword: What is so often cursed for bloating EXEs with unused code can also be exploited to greatly reduce the amount of code in an EXE in certain circumstances, even beyond what smart linking could normally achieve with plain old static methods and procedures. The key is to turn the smart linking rule for virtuals inside out.

> Inverse smart linking rule for virtuals
>
> If the type information of a class is *not* touched by live code, then *none* of the virtual methods of the class will be linked into the executable file, *even if* those virtual methods are called polymorphically by live code.

In a `virtual` method call, the compiler emits machine code to grab the VMT pointer from the instance data and to call an address stored at a particular offset in the VMT. The compiler can't know exactly which method body will be called at run time, so the act of calling a `virtual` method does not cause the smart linker to pull any method bodies corresponding to that `virtual` method identifier into the final executable file. The same is true for `dynamic` methods. The act of constructing an instance of the class is what cues the linker to pull in the virtual methods of that particular class and its ancestors. This saves the program from the painful death that would surely result from calling virtual methods that were not linked into the program. After all, how could you possibly call a virtual method of an object instance defined and implemented in your program if you did not first construct said instance? Answer: You can't. If you obtained the object instance from some external source (like a DLL), then the virtual methods of that instance are in the DLL, not your program.

So, if you have code that calls virtual methods of a class that is never constructed by routines used in the current project, none of the code associated with those virtual methods will be linked into the final EXE. Consider the code in Listing 3.8.

Listing 3.8 Inverse virtual smart linking: TOfficeGadget.Whirr will not be linked into this program, even though Whirr is touched by the live method TOfficeManager.OperateGadget.

```
type
  TBaseGadget = class
    constructor Create;
    procedure Whirr; virtual;   { linked in: YES }
```

```
    end;
    TOfficeGadget = class(TBaseGadget)
      procedure Whirr; override;  { linked in: NO }
      procedure Buzz;             { linked in: NO }
      procedure Pop; virtual;     { linked in: NO }
    end;
    TKitchenGadget = class(TBaseGadget)
      procedure Whirr; override;  { linked in: YES }
    end;
    TOfficeManager = class
    private
      FOfficeGadget: TOfficeGadget;
    public
      procedure InstantiateGadget; { linked in: NO }
      procedure Operate(AGadget: TOfficeGadget); virtual;
                                  { linked in: YES }
    end;
{... nonessential code omitted...}
procedure TOfficeManager.InstantiateGadget;
begin   { Dead code, never called }
  FOfficeGadget := TOfficeGadget.Create;
end;
procedure TOfficeManager.Operate(AGadget: TOfficeGadget);
begin   { live code, virtual method of a constructed class }
  AGadget.Whirr
end;
var
  X: TBaseGadget;
  M: TOfficeManager;
begin
  X := TKitchenGadget.Create;
  M := TOfficeManager.Create;
  X.Free; M.Free;
end.
```

The code in Listing 3.8 will cause the linker to pull in all the virtual methods of TKitchenGadget and TOfficeManager because those classes are constructed in live code (the main program block) as well as all the virtual methods of TBaseGadget because it is the ancestor of TKitchenGadget. Since TOfficeManager.Operate is virtual, its method body is all live code (even though Operate is never called), so the call to AGadget.Whirr is a live reference to the virtual method Whirr. However, TOfficeGadget is not constructed in live code in this example—TOfficeManager.InstantiateGadget is never used. Nothing of TOfficeGadget will be linked into this program, even though a live routine contains a call to Whirr through a variable of type TOfficeGadget.

Variations on a Theme

Let's see how the scenario changes with a few slight code modifications. Listing 3.9 adds a call to AGadget.Buzz in the TOfficeManager.Operate method. Notice that the body of TOfficeGadget.Buzz is now linked in, but TOfficeGadget.Whirr is still not. Buzz is a static method, so any live reference to it will link in the corresponding code, even if the class is never constructed.

Listing 3.9 Notice how the addition of a call to the static Buzz method affects its linked-in status, but TOfficeGadget.Whirr is still not included.

```
type
  TBaseGadget = class
    constructor Create;
    procedure Whirr; virtual;    { linked in: YES }
  end;
  TOfficeGadget = class(TBaseGadget)
    procedure Whirr; override;   { linked in: NO }
    procedure Buzz;              { linked in: YES }
    procedure Pop; virtual;      { linked in: NO }
  end;
  TKitchenGadget = class(TBaseGadget)
    procedure Whirr; override;   { linked in: YES }
  end;
  TOfficeManager = class
  private
    FOfficeGadget: TOfficeGadget;
  public
    procedure InstantiateGadget; { linked in: NO }
    procedure Operate(AGadget: TOfficeGadget); virtual;
                                 { linked in: YES }
  end;
{... nonessential code omitted...}
procedure TOfficeManager.InstantiateGadget;
begin   { Dead code, never called }
  FOfficeGadget := TOfficeGadget.Create;
end;
procedure TOfficeManager.Operate(AGadget: TOfficeGadget);
begin   { live code, virtual method of a constructed class }
  AGadget.Whirr;
  AGadget.Buzz;   { this touches the static method body }
end;
var
  X: TBaseGadget;
  M: TOfficeManager;
begin
```

```
    X := TKitchenGadget.Create;
    M := TOfficeManager.Create;
    X.Free; M.Free;
end.
```

Listing 3.10 adds a call to the static method TOfficeManager.InstantiateGadget. This brings the construction of the TOfficeGadget class into the live code of the program, which brings in all the virtual methods of TOfficeGadget, including TOfficeGadget.Whirr (which is called by live code) and TOfficeGadget.Pop (which isn't). If you were to delete the call to AGadget.Buzz, the TOfficeGadget.Buzz method would become dead code again. Static methods are linked in only if they are used in live code, regardless of whether their class type is used.

Listing 3.10 With a call to InstantiateGadget, the construction of TOfficeGadget becomes live and all of TOfficeGadget's virtual methods are linked in.

```
type
  TBaseGadget = class
    constructor Create;
    procedure Whirr; virtual;    { linked in: YES }
  end;
  TOfficeGadget = class(TBaseGadget)
    procedure Whirr; override;   { linked in: YES }
    procedure Buzz;              { linked in: YES }
    procedure Pop; virtual;      { linked in: YES }
  end;
  TKitchenGadget = class(TBaseGadget)
    procedure Whirr; override;   { linked in: YES }
  end;
  TOfficeManager = class
  private
    FOfficeGadget: TOfficeGadget;
  public
    procedure InstantiateGadget; { linked in: YES }
    procedure Operate(AGadget: TOfficeGadget); virtual;
                                 { linked in: YES }
  end;
{... nonessential code omitted...}
procedure TOfficeManager.InstantiateGadget;
begin    { live code }
  FOfficeGadget := TOfficeGadget.Create;
end;
procedure TOfficeManager.Operate(AGadget: TOfficeGadget);
begin    { live code, virtual method of a constructed class }
  AGadget.Whirr;
```

```
      AGadget.Buzz;    { this touches the static method body }
    end;
var
  X: TBaseGadget;
  M: TOfficeManager;
begin
  X := TKitchenGadget.Create;
  M := TOfficeManager.Create;
  M.InstantiateGadget;
  X.Free; M.Free;
end.
```

Life in the Real World

Let's take a look at a slightly more complicated (and more interesting) example of this virtual smart linking technique inside VCL. The Delphi streaming system, discussed in detail in Chapter 6, has two parts: TReader and TWriter, which descend from a common ancestor, TFiler. TReader contains all the code needed to load components from a stream. TWriter contains everything you need to write components to a stream. These classes were split apart because many Delphi applications never need to write components to a stream; most apps only read forms from resource streams at program start-up. If the streaming system were implemented in one class, you would wind up carrying around all the stream output code in all your applications even though many don't need it.

So, splitting the streaming system into two classes improved smart linking. End of story? Not quite. In careful examination of the code linked into a typical Delphi application, the Delphi team noticed that bits of TWriter were being linked into the EXE. This seemed odd because TWriter was definitely never instantiated in the test program. Some of those TWriter bits touched a lot of other bits that piled up rather quickly into a lot of unused code. Let's backtrack a little to see what led up to this code getting into the EXE and its surprising solution.

Delphi's TComponent class defines virtual methods that are responsible for reading and writing the component's state in a stream, using TReaders for reading and TWriters for writing. Since TComponent is the ancestor of just about everything of importance in Delphi, TComponent is almost always linked into your Delphi programs, along with all the virtual methods of TComponent. Some of TComponent's virtual methods use TWriter methods to write the component's properties to the stream. Those TWriter methods were static methods. So, we have the following: TComponent virtual methods are always included in Delphi form-based apps, and some of those virtual methods (like TComponent.WriteState) call static methods of TWriter (like TWriter.WriteData), so those static method bodies of

TWriter were being linked into the executable file. TWriter.WriteData is the kingpin method that drives nearly the entire stream output system, so when it gets linked in, almost all the rest of TWriter tags along—everything, ironically, except TWriter.Create.

The easiest way to eliminate the unneeded TWriter code was to make more methods of TWriter virtual! The all-or-none clumping of virtual methods that we curse for working against the smart linker can be used to our advantage so that TWriter methods that must be called by live code are not actually included unless TWriter itself is instantiated in the program.

Reviewing What's Really in Your Executables

The simplest way to find out whether a particular routine is linked into a particular project is to set a breakpoint in the body of that routine and run the program in the debugger. If the routine is not linked into the EXE, the debugger will complain that you have set an invalid breakpoint.

To get a complete picture of what's in your EXE or DLL, configure the linker options to emit a detailed map file (Project: Options: Linker: Detailed map file) and then recompile your project. The map file will contain a list of the names of all the routines (from units compiled with $D+ debug info) that were linked into the executable file. Since the 32-bit Delphi Compiled Unit (DCU) file has none of the capacity limitations associated with earlier 16-bit versions of the Borland Pascal product line, there is little reason to ever turn off debug symbol information storage in the DCU. Leave the $D, $L, and $Y compiler switches enabled all the time so that the information will be available when you need it in the integrated debugger, the map file, or the object browser.

Novelty of Inverse Virtual Smart Linking

This technique of using virtual methods to improve smart linking is not unique to Delphi, but because Delphi's smart linker has a much finer granularity than other compiler products, this technique is much more effective in Delphi than in other development products.

Most compilers produce intermediate code and limited symbol information in an OBJ format, and most linkers' atom of granularity for smart linking is the OBJ file. If you touch something inside a library of routines stored in one OBJ module, the entire OBJ module is linked into the EXE. Thus, C and C++ libraries are often broken into swarms of little OBJ modules in the hope of minimizing dead code in the EXE.

Delphi's linker granularity is much finer—down to individual variables, procedures, and classes. If you touch one routine in a Delphi unit that contains lots of routines, only the thing you touch (and whatever it uses) gets linked into the EXE. Thus, there is no penalty for creating large libraries of topically related routines in one Delphi unit. What you don't use will be left out of the executable file.

Developing clever techniques to avoid touching individual routines or classes is generally more rewarding in Delphi than in most other compiled languages. In other products, the routines you so carefully avoided will probably be linked into the EXE anyway because you are still using one of the other routines in the same module. (Measuring with a micrometer is futile when your only cutting tool is a chainsaw.)

Class Reference Types

Class references are variables that point to a class *type*, instead of a class instance. Since there is no instance data associated with a class reference, you might at first question the usefulness of class references. So you can point to a class type, so what? What can you do with it?

The answer may send you for a loop: You can use class references to achieve polymorphic *creation* of objects. Normally, when you want to create a new instance of a class type, you have to call a constructor of the class using the fully qualified constructor name, like TKitchenGadget.Create. The class type is hard-coded into the constructor call.

With a class reference variable, you can assign a class type into the variable, pass the variable to a subroutine, and have the subroutine create instances of whatever class type you put in the class reference variable. The one subroutine can create instances of a variety of classes, without knowing exactly which types it's manipulating: It creates instances polymorphically.

The trick to all of this is in the declaration of the constructor. In order to call a constructor polymorphically, the constructor itself must be declared `virtual`. Since normal construction of an instance requires a fully qualified constructor name and fully qualified references to virtual methods compile down into direct static calls, virtual constructors are useful only in the context of class references.

To see an example of polymorphic object instantiation, just look at the Delphi component palette. When components are compiled into the Delphi IDE's component library, the component's type is added to a list of component class references. When you click on a component icon in the component palette and drop it on a form, an instance of that component type is created and inserted into the form. Creating component instances in a drag-n-drop fashion is as simple as this:

```
ComponentClassList[Palette.SelectedIndex].Create(SelectedForm);
```

Another example of class references in use is Delphi's TCollection class. TCollection is a homogeneous list of objects that are owned and freed by the collection object. TCollection's constructor takes a class reference as a parameter, which the collection uses to create new object instances in TCollection.Add and to validate the type compatibility of items inserted into the collection. Thus, multiple instances of a single, small TCollection class can each manage lists of very different objects.

You can also call *class methods* using class reference variables, but these just don't have the same capacity to boggle the mind as polymorphic instantiation. Calling class methods without needing an instance is nice, but it's not something that will dramatically affect your programming habits. To compare the relative significance of language features, consider how much effort would be required to solve the same kinds of problems without that language feature. Class methods can easily be replaced with normal procedures and functions declared in the same unit as the classes they support. Class references, though, would be very difficult to implement without compiler support.

Class Reference Mechanics

The requirements for polymorphic instantiation with class references are the same as for polymorphic method calls with virtuals. You need to have multiple class types related to one another through a common ancestor class, and the ancestor class must define the virtual constructor(s) that can be used polymorphically with all the descendant classes. The extra bit that class references require is that you must declare a class reference type and a variable of that class reference type, as shown in Listing 3.11.

Listing 3.11 Creating instances polymorphically with class references.

```
type
  TBaseGadget = class
    constructor CreateMe; virtual;
  end;
  TKitchenGadget = class(TBaseGadget)
    constructor CreateMe; override;
  end;
  TOfficeGadget = class(TBaseGadget);
```

VIRTUAL METHODS AND POLYMORPHISM

```
    constructor CreateMe; override;
  end;
  TBaseGadgetClass = class of TBaseGadget;
function WhatsBehindDoorNumber3Monty: TBaseGadgetClass;
begin
  Result := TOfficeGadget;
end;
var
  GadgetType: TBaseGadgetClass;
  P: TBaseGadget;
begin
  GadgetType := TKitchenGadget;
  P := GadgetType.CreateMe;    { calls TKitchenGadget.CreateMe }
  P.Free;
  GadgetType := WhatsBehindDoorNumber3Monty;
  P := GadgetType.CreateMe;    { calls TOfficeGadget.CreateMe }
  P.Free;
end;
```

The class reference variable GadgetType works with types much like the instance variable P works with instances. You can assign any class type that descends from the specified ancestor class to that class reference variable. Virtual constructor(s) and virtual class methods defined in the ancestor class that are called using the class reference variable will be resolved at run time according to the type information stored in the class reference variable.

The actual data stored in the class reference variable is a 4-byte pointer to the VMT of the class type that was assigned to the variable.

Note that assigning a class type to a class reference variable in live program code touches the class's type information, which will cause the smart linker to pull in all the virtual methods of that class. In the smart linking rules described in the previous section, constructing an instance of a class in live code was named as one way to touch the type information of a class. Assigning a class type to a class reference is the other way to touch the class type.

As mentioned in Chapter 2, class references are great for building highly flexible, extensible classes that do a lot of dirty work for their descendants but don't lock themselves into allowing only one kind of internal data item class—TCollection, for example.

Type information that can be manipulated at run time is sometimes called *metadata*. Class references are a form of metadata. Since class references combine polymorphism with metadata, does that make them polymetamorphicdata?

Summary

Here are the important points covered in this chapter:

- Declaring a new class creates a complete copy of the Virtual Method Table (VMT) of the ancestor class.

- Declaring a new `virtual` method appends new entries to the end of the new class's VMT.

- Declaring an `override` of an inherited `virtual` method replaces that method's VMT entry with the address of the new class's method. Thus, when the compiler generates code to call VMT entry number 34 (the VMT slot allocated to a `virtual` method declared in an ancestor class), the object instance data's VMT pointer points to the new class's VMT, and the new class's VMT slot 34 contains the address of the new class's replacement implementation (`override`) of that method, so the call jumps to the new class's implementation of that method.

- The polymorphic behavior of `dynamic` methods is identical to `virtual` methods, though the internal implementation is different.

- Dynamic Method Tables (DMTs) are only created when a class overrides an inherited `dynamic` method or declares a new `dynamic` method and only contain information about how the class differs from its immediate ancestor.

- Calling a `dynamic` method involves an active search at run time through the DMTs associated with a class and its ancestors.

- The compiler-generated tables for `dynamic` methods are much more space efficient than for `virtual` methods, but `dynamic` methods take a little longer to call.

- Use `dynamic` when you need a method to be polymorphic, you expect your class to have many descendants, and you expect that descendant classes will override this method only rarely. If you expect that descendant classes will almost always override the method, then they'll almost all be consuming 4 bytes each for the method anyway, so you might as well use the faster `virtual` method declaration.

- Descendant classes define their own name scopes, which allows them to declare virtual methods independent of similarly named methods defined in their ancestors. This provides a high degree of source code version resiliency when the ancestor classes are enhanced in future versions. Redeclaring virtual methods should be avoided (or corrected when discovered) because it compromises source code readability.

- Abstract interface classes allow complete separation of user and implementor of a class, spanning the gap between applications and DLLs and between modules written in different programming languages.

- Abstract interface classes allow DLLs to easily export the classes they implement and allow applications (or DLLs) to easily import classes implemented in DLLs.

- Abstract interface classes are the foundation of the Microsoft Common Object Model (COM), which, in turn, is the foundation of all OLE interface classes.

- All virtual methods of a class and its ancestors are linked into a program only if the class's type information is touched in live code, regardless of whether live code contains polymorphic references to the virtual methods. This is usually cursed for pulling unused virtual methods into a project, but it can be used to improve smart linking and reduce EXE size dramatically in some cases.

- Constructing an instance of a class touches the class's type information.

- Assigning a class type to a class reference variable touches the class's type information.

- A static method of a class is linked into a program only if it is referenced by live code, regardless of whether its class's type information is referenced by live code.

- Fully qualified references to virtual methods are treated as static references for the purposes of call dispatching and smart linking.

- Delphi's smart linker has finer granularity than most other development environments, which means Delphi is more responsive to programming techniques that minimize references to unnecessary code.

- Class references allow you to manipulate types at run time at a level of abstraction higher than polymorphic method calls (polymorphic object instantiation).

Chapter 4

Exceptions

One of the most significant Object Pascal language features introduced in Delphi 1.0 was *structured exception handling*. Delphi has been heralded as the next generation of rapid application development tools (RAD), with an arsenal of visual design tools, experts, and customizable components, all of which changed the way you build Windows programs. Visual tools help you configure and arrange components. Components provide prepackaged code to reduce the amount of code you have to write. These and other aspects of Delphi can change the way you organize source code and think about programming, but as we'll see in this chapter, nothing changes your mental model of the program execution space as radically as structured exception handling.

An Exceptional Communication System

Structured exception handling is a system by which you can communicate error notifications from the code that detects the error to code that is prepared to handle such an error. This requires using language constructs to "guard" areas of source code and define error handlers to recover gracefully should something go wrong in those guarded code blocks. Exceptions are supported by the Win32 operating system, making them independent of hardware, programming language, and module boundaries. Simply put, exceptions communicate "exceptional" conditions that a subroutine is not prepared to deal with. Though we'll often refer to exceptions as error conditions, it's important to keep in mind that an exception is only a notification, not necessarily an indication of an error.

The Fire Brigade

In traditional error handling, errors encountered in a subroutine are typically communicated outward (to the caller of the subroutine) through function results, parameters, or global flags. Every caller of a subroutine is responsible for checking for the error result and performing some appropriate action, which often is simply to exit to the next outward caller, and so forth. That is, function A calls B, B calls C, C encounters an error and returns an error code to B, B checks the return code and discovers C's error, B returns an error to A, and A checks the return code and reports an error or decides to try something else since the first effort didn't work.

This "fire brigade" error-handling system is laborious and code intensive. It's easily broken and difficult to maintain. A single oversight in the chain of result checks could prevent vast areas of your program from communicating error conditions to the outside world, resulting in strange behavior, lost data or resources, or crashes. Maintenance is a particularly thorny problem when different subroutines in your libraries return error codes through different channels (function results, parameters, or global variables) or by using different values—lack of consistency increases the chances of programming error. This method of error reporting often interleaves error codes and data values in the same variable or function result, further complicating matters. For example: If function XYZ succeeds, it returns an integer greater than zero. If the function fails, it returns a negative number indicating the error condition.

Automatic Notification

Structured exception handling replaces the manually built and maintained fire brigade error-handling system with an automated, compiler-generated notification system. In the preceding ABC example, A would set up a guarded code block with associated error handlers and call B within that guarded section. B wouldn't set up any guarded code sections; it would simply call C. When C detected the error condition, it would *raise* an exception. Special code generated by the compiler and built into the Run-Time Library (RTL) would begin an active search for an exception handler appropriate for the particular exception type that C raised.

The search uses information stored on the stack to locate guarded code sections. Let's say C doesn't contain any guarded sections and B doesn't contain any guarded sections, but A does. If the exception handlers that A registered for its guarded section match the exception type that C raised, execution jumps to the exception handler in A. The stack frames (local variables, passed parameters, and return address) of C and B are removed from the stack; those functions are abandoned in mid stride.

If the search for an exception handler does not find a match in A's exception handlers, the search continues outward to A's caller, and so on, until either a suitable handler is found for the raised exception or the search reaches the RTL's default exception handler. Any exception that finds its way into the RTL default exception handler will terminate your application.

> **Unhandled Exceptions**
>
> VCL has its own default exception handler at a level higher than the RTL default exception handler. Embedded in VCL's message-processing routines, the VCL default exception handler traps unhandled exceptions and allows the application to continue running. This is an important distinction: In VCL form-based Delphi applications, unhandled exceptions are generally nonfatal; in raw console-based Delphi applications, unhandled exceptions are generally fatal. Since console applications are not the focus of Delphi or this book, we will operate under the assumption that unhandled exceptions are nonfatal.

Without all the error checks after every subroutine call, your source code should be less cluttered and easier to read, and the compiled code should execute faster. With exceptions, subroutine B doesn't have to contain additional machine code to test the result of calling C. If B can assume that C will raise an exception in an error condition, then B doesn't have to do anything for C's exception to migrate out beyond B's scope into A's scope—the built-in exception system does all the work.

We call this *structured* exception handling because the error handling is determined by the execution scope of the guarded sections, which can be nested within one another and/or spread across nested function calls. The search for an exception handler starts in the current scope looking for a handler suitable for the raised exception; if none is found, the search moves to the next outward scope on the stack. Execution cannot jump to any arbitrary piece of code. Execution can only jump to an exception handler in an active routine on the stack—that is, a routine through which execution has passed and which is awaiting the return of a subroutine call.

The Delphi exception model is a *nonresumable* exception model. Once an exception has been raised, you cannot return to the instruction that raised the exception to resume execution (as resumable exception systems allow). Non-resumable exceptions destroy the stack as they wander outward in search of a handler; resumable exceptions have to preserve the stack and the state of the CPU registers at the point of the exception and perform the handler search and execution of exception handlers on a separate stack, among other things. Resumable exceptions are useful for low-level services such as handling page faults (loading the missing page into memory and restarting the instruction that caused the fault), but they make application-level exception handling more complicated than nonresumable exception systems do.

Exception Syntax

Now that we've reviewed what exceptions are, let's briefly review Delphi's Object Pascal exception syntax. Listing 4.1 contains the A, B, and C routines mentioned earlier, and Listing 4.2 contains the output of this test program.

Listing 4.1 Simple example of exception syntax and execution.

```
type
  ESampleError = class(Exception);
var
  ErrorCondition: Boolean;
procedure C;
begin
  writeln('Enter C');
  if (ErrorCondition) then
  begin
    writeln('Raising exception in C');
    raise ESampleError.Create;
  end;
  writeln('Exit C');
end;

procedure B;
begin
  writeln('Enter B');
  C;
  writeln('Exit B');
end;

procedure A;
begin
  writeln('Enter A');
  try
    writeln('Enter A''s try block');
    B;
    writeln('After B call');
  except
  on ESampleError do
    writeln('Inside A''s ESampleError handler');
  on ESomethingElse do
```

```
      writeln('Inside A''s ESomethingElse handler');
    end;
    writeln('Exit A');
  end;

begin
  writeln('Begin main');
  ErrorCondition := True;
  A;
  writeln('End main');
end.
```

Listing 4.2 The output of Listing 4.1, when ErrorCondition = True.

```
Begin main
Enter A
Enter A's try block
Enter B
Enter C
Raising exception in C
Inside A's ESampleError handler
Exit A
End main
```

Procedure C checks for an error condition (in this case, a global variable mockup), and, if ErrorCondition is True, raises an exception of class ESampleError.

Procedure A sets up a guarded section of source code in a `try...except` block. The first part of a `try...except` block is a source code statement block, just like a `begin...end` block. The `try` statement block is terminated with the keyword `except`, followed by zero or more on clauses, followed by an optional `else` block, followed by a terminating `end;`. Each on clause specifies which exception class type that clause is for. If the raised exception is compatible with the on clause's type, execution jumps into that on clause's statement block. The raised exception is compatible with the on clause type if the raised exception is the same type or is a descendant of the on clause type. Therefore, an on clause could opt to handle all exceptions related to integer arithmetic, for example, by using the generic EIntError exception type or could opt to handle only one specific kind of integer math error, ERangeError, which is a descendant of EIntError. An `except` block `else` clause and an `except` block with no on clauses match any kind of exception.

You can gain access to the currently raised exception object by placing an identifier in the on clause of the `except` block, like this:

```
on E: EIOError do.
```

Within such an on clause, you can use the identifier to access data fields or methods of the exception object.

The example procedures in Listing 4.1 use `writeln` statements to indicate the execution path through these routines. When C raises an exception, execution jumps to A's error handler, completely jumping out of procedure C and procedure B in one step. Consequently, neither `'Exit C'` nor `'Exit B'` nor `'After B call'` `writeln` statements are executed. Regardless of how many lines of code follow the `raise` in procedure C, or follow the C call in procedure B, none of them will be executed if C raises an exception. It doesn't matter how many function calls like B exist between A and C; it doesn't matter whether B and C are even code that you wrote—procedure A will still get the exception notification.

The search for an exception handler ends when it finds a suitable handler. After the handler's code block executes, execution resumes at the first statement following the exception handler's end statement—in this case, the `writeln("Exit A')`.

If you want to have an exception handler perform some action for some particular exception and then pass control to the next outward exception handler, you can simply put `raise;` in the exception handler code block with no parameters. This will reraise the current exception and resume the search for a matching handler in the next outward scope.

The `try...except` blocks are good when you know what kind of exceptions you want to handle in a particular situation, but what if you need to perform some action in any case, error or not? That's where another try block comes in: `try...finally`. Consider the modified B procedure shown in Listing 4.3.

Listing 4.3 Unprotected memory allocation: What if procedure C raises an exception?

```
procedure NewB;
var
  P: Pointer;
begin
  writeln('Enter B');
  GetMem(P, 1000);
  C;
  FreeMem(P, 1000);
  writeln('Exit B');
end;
```

When C raises its exception, execution flies right past procedure NewB, never to return. What about that 1000 bytes of memory that NewB allocated? Because of C's exception, NewB's `FreeMem(P, 1000)` never gets called, so you've lost a chunk of memory. How can this be fixed? Insert NewB nonintrusively into the exception process with a `try...finally` block, as shown in Listing 4.4.

Listing 4.4 Use `try...finally` blocks to ensure allocated resources are freed regardless of how execution leaves a routine.

```
procedure NewB;
var
  P: Pointer;
begin
  writeln('Enter NewB');
  GetMem(P, 1000);
  try
    writeln('Enter NewB''s try block');
    C;
    writeln('End of NewB''s try block');
  finally
    writeln('Inside NewB''s finally block');
    FreeMem(P, 1000);
  end;
  writeln('Exit NewB');
end;
```

Listing 4.5 shows the output of the test program if you replace A's call to B with a call to NewB and ErrorCondition is True.

Listing 4.5 Output of test program when procedure A calls NewB.

```
Begin main
Enter A
Enter A's try block
Enter NewB
Enter NewB's try block
Enter C
Raising exception in C
Inside NewB's finally block
Inside A's ESampleError handler
Exit A
End main
```

The code in the `finally` block will be called if any exception occurs in the associated `try` block. The `finally` block will also be called if no exception occurs. Either way, NewB gets to release its memory properly. If the `finally` block were called as part of an exception, the search for a real handler would continue outward when execution reaches the end of the `finally` block. If the `finally` block were called as part of normal program execution, execution would continue with the next statement after the end of the `finally` block.

Why isn't the GetMem call in Listing 4.4 inside the `try` block? GetMem could fail, raising an EOutOfMemory exception. If it did and it was inside NewB's `try` block, execution would jump to the `finally` block, where Free-Mem would attempt to free a pointer that was never successfully allocated. Releasing resources should only be done *after* the resources have been successfully allocated. By placing the GetMem in an unguarded section of NewB, the author of NewB is telling us that NewB assumes it can allocate that memory, and if it can't, NewB will let the EOutOfMemory exception notify NewB's caller of the failure.

What if NewB needs to allocate four pointers, in an all-or-nothing manner? If the first allocation succeeds and the second fails, how do you free the pieces that have been allocated? One technique is to simply nest four `try` blocks inside each other, as shown in Listing 4.6. A less nested and slightly more efficient technique appears in Listing 4.7.

Listing 4.6 Using nested `try` blocks to manage deallocation of multiple resources.

```
procedure NewB;
var
  p,q,r,s: Pointer;
begin
  writeln('Enter B');
  GetMem(P, 1000);
  try
    GetMem(Q, 1000);
    try
      GetMem(R, 1000);
      try
        GetMem(S, 1000);
        try
          writeln('Enter B''s innermost try block');
          C;
          writeln('End of B''s innermost try block');
        finally
          FreeMem(S, 1000);
        end;
```

```
    finally
      FreeMem(R, 1000);
    end;
  finally
    FreeMem(Q, 1000);
  end;
finally
  FreeMem(P, 1000);
end;
writeln('Exit B');
end;
```

Listing 4.7 Initializing variables so that only one `try` block is needed to handle multiple resources.

```
procedure NewB;
var
  p,q,r,s: Pointer;
begin
  writeln('Enter B');
  P := nil;
  Q := nil;
  R := nil;
  S := nil;
  try
    writeln('Enter B''s try block');
    GetMem(P, 1000);
    GetMem(Q, 1000);
    GetMem(R, 1000);
    GetMem(S, 1000);
    C;
    writeln('end of B''s try block');
  finally
    writeln('inside B''s finally block');
    if P <> nil then FreeMem(P, 1000);
    if Q <> nil then FreeMem(Q, 1000);
    if R <> nil then FreeMem(R, 1000);
    if S <> nil then FreeMem(S, 1000);
  end;
  writeln('exit B');
end;
```

By first setting the variables to `nil`, and then performing the allocations inside a `try` block, you can determine which pointers were successfully allocated and therefore need to be freed. Since each `try` block requires a few bytes of stack space and as many machine instructions to initialize those stack fields, having one `try` block is slightly more efficient (in execution speed and code size) than having many `try` blocks. The actual performance difference is negligible, though, so as long as the cleanup code has no risk of raising exceptions, the choice between these styles is just a matter of personal preference. If there is the possibility that the cleanup code could fail with an exception, you should use nested `try` blocks to ensure that every cleanup item gets a chance to execute.

Remember, if the call to GetMem fails because of low memory, GetMem will raise an exception. The variable passed to GetMem will not be changed, so the `nil` test is valid even on the variable where the allocation failure occurred.

The `try...except` and `try...finally` blocks can be used anywhere a statement block is allowed, including nested within one another in any combination to any depth. Exceptions can be raised in exception handlers, and `try` blocks can be used in exception handlers.

Exceptions Change Your Assumptions

In the fire brigade style of traditional error handling, you can assume nothing about the subroutines your code calls except that you are completely responsible for handling error codes returned by every subroutine. You are responsible for handling all errors, all of the time, for every subroutine call, even if the routine you're writing is a middle-layer routine that neither originates nor has the authority to resolve error conditions. Failure on your part to process any error code returned by the subroutines you call compromises the stability and error reporting of the entire routine. Since most routines call other subroutines and processing error codes for every subroutine call is tedious at best, it is very common for programmers to ignore error codes returned by most subroutines and just hope nothing goes wrong.

In an exception-based environment, you have a universal error notification system that will inform code that cares about particular kinds of exceptions that occur in their scope. Code that doesn't care about exceptions doesn't have to do anything to allow the system to work. In an exception driven environment, you can assume that subroutines that encounter significant errors will raise an exception. You are not responsible for handling any error conditions except the ones you specifically express an interest in through the use of on clauses in `try...except` blocks.

Assumptions Simplify Source Code

The assumption that errors will raise exceptions translates into subroutines that return only valid data—if they are unable to return valid data, they don't return at all, but raise an exception instead. When writing code with exceptions in mind, you continually remind yourself, *"If program execution reaches here, everything before must have succeeded."* If anything in prior statements and subroutine calls had gone wrong, it should have raised an exception, and therefore execution could not have reached "here."

For example, in the sample code listed earlier, procedure NewB allocated memory for a pointer and immediately used the pointer, with no explicit checks to see whether the allocation succeeded. In traditional code, you (should) always follow calls to GetMem with a check to see whether the pointer variable actually received a memory allocation. With exceptions, you can assume that GetMem will raise an exception if it cannot fill the memory request, so there is no need to check the pointer after the call. The exception model allows you to eliminate most of the continual result checks required by fire brigade error handling, greatly simplifying your source code and improving its clarity.

A related benefit of exceptions is that you don't have to invent schemes to interleave error codes in your function result data. Data is data, and errors raise exceptions. Neat and tidy.

Simplification Improves Performance

Simplifying source code is more than just an aesthetic issue. If checking the pointer after GetMem requires, say, 6 bytes of machine instructions (load, compare, and jump), and your program contains 1000 such calls to GetMem, exception assumptions can allow you to shave 6000 bytes of machine code from your EXE. Reducing machine instructions also improves execution speed, particularly when you can avoid conditional branches (`if` statements) that stall the instruction pipelines of CPUs like the Intel 80486 and Pentium processors.

However, there is a performance cost associated with raising an exception and searching for an appropriate handler that should be weighed against its too-frequent use. Raising an exception to escape from a tight loop might simplify and speed up the loop exit logic, but you would probably lose much of that performance gain when the exception is raised. Raising an exception as the primary means to exit a loop is almost certainly wasteful. Raising an exception to exit a loop under unusual/infrequent circumstances (which, by definition, makes a performance hit acceptable) is more reasonable. Similarly, raising an exception to exit a stack of recursive function calls could save you some time testing for and relaying the recursion exit condition back up through the recursion stack, but you had better perform some benchmark tests to confirm that use of the exception provides a net gain. When weighing performance factors, consider raising and handling a single exception to take 100 times longer than a single test for an error or exit condition. Using exceptions as an exit optimization doesn't pay off until you're faced with thousands of simple exit tests or scores of computationally expensive exit tests.

Exceptions Allow Separation of Tasks

Exceptions allow you to separate error-detection code from error-handling code, with an automatic and consistent line of control between the two points. Some would argue that this separation is a bad thing; it's true that overuse or poor organization of exception handlers in a routine can make as much a mess of source code as the original fire brigade, but on the whole, exceptions should lead to a reduction of source code and more consistent and reliable error handling system-wide. Most programs already separate error detection from error handling; the weakest part is the communications link between the two.

Exceptions reduce the need for continual error checking in middle- and high-level routines, but they do not reduce the need for error checking in the low-level routines that provide data to the rest of the program. Low-level routines that convert data between formats, that import or export data files, or that have specific data requirements must still perform `if` statement checks to validate the data they use. In fact, since exceptions encourage the assumption that all is well unless interrupted by an exception, it is *critical* that subroutines validate the data they return. Error detection doesn't go away; it stays pretty much where it has been all along—in the code that produces the data.

Exceptions do not reduce your need to deal with errors, but they do let you choose what code will deal with which errors. If you're writing a library routine that opens a file, you must decide whether your routine should handle file open errors internally or leave them for your caller to sort out. If the caller gives you a file name that you're supposed to open, let the caller deal with any file open errors that occur. (Caller's data, caller's problem.) If, on the other hand, you are opening an internal temporary file that the caller knows nothing about, you should probably handle that error internally. (Your data, your problem.) "Handling internally" might mean trapping a file-related RTL exception and simply raising a different exception class specific to your library and current operation so that the caller can distinguish your errors from errors from other sources.

Error handling doesn't disappear with exceptions—it just moves out of the main line of execution. Within a single routine, the code that performs the primary task of the routine goes inside a `try` block, resource cleanup code goes in `finally` blocks, and code that responds to failures or abnormal deviations from the primary task goes in `except` blocks, if the routine needs to respond to specific errors at all. On an application-wide scale, low-level and middle-level routines detect errors and raise exceptions, while error reporting is generally reserved for application-specific high-level routines. There's nothing more frustrating than an error message box you can't get rid of because it's displayed by a black-box low-level subroutine.

Rules of Thumb for Implementing Exception Handlers

As with any powerful tool, there are many ways to use exceptions, and many more ways to *mis*use exceptions. Here are some rules of thumb to help you get the most benefit from exception handlers without disrupting the necessary flow of exceptions through your app.

- **Trap only the exception types you are prepared to deal with.** Keep in mind that an exception handler is always a link in a chain. If you write an exception handler that is too broad in its definition of the exception types it handles, it will trap exceptions that you aren't really interested in. That could lead to inappropriate responses to errors or, even worse, prevent vital exceptions from reaching the caller.

- **Avoid unqualified exception handlers.** An *unqualified exception handler* is an `except` block with no on clauses, or with an `else` clause, or with a very generic on clause, like on `Exception do`. Unqualified exception handlers are useful for implementing a response to any kind of error that is executed *only* in an error situation. For example, a subroutine that is responsible for creating a list object, populating the list with data, and returning the list object as the function result could use an unqualified `except` block to ensure that the list object and its contents were freed if an exception were encountered after the list object was allocated but before the list was fully populated (see Listing 4.8). You must be very careful to reraise the exception in such situations, though, or you will block *all* exceptions from passing through your subroutine.

Listing 4.8 Legitimate use of an unqualified exception handler, complete with reraise of the exception.

```
function GetXYZList: TList;
var
  I: Integer;
begin
  Result := TList.Create;
  try
    { allocate and add items to Result list }
    for I := 0 to XYZCount-1 do
      Result.Add(New(XYZ));
  except
    for I := 0 to Result.Count-1 do
      Dispose(PXYZ(Result[I]));
    Result.Free;
    Raise;    {!! critical !!}
  end;
end;
```

- **Think twice before killing an exception.** An `except` block traps qualifying exceptions and kills them (prevents the exception from propagating outward to the caller) unless you explicitly reraise the exception. In killing an exception, you are assuming full responsibility for the proper and complete response to that exception—and all descendants of that exception class, past, present, and future.

- **Application-specific code has greater license to kill exceptions than generic subroutines.** Subroutines should steer clear of user interface decisions as much as possible to maximize their reusability in other projects. How to report errors and which errors to report to the user are definitely user interface decisions that each application will want to control independently. You can control the how and which of error reporting application-wide by hooking into the Application.OnException event. The default VCL exception handler passes all exceptions it traps to this event.

- **Never use exception-killing unqualified exception handlers.** If you combine the observations in the last few points, writing an unqualified exception handler that kills the exception means you are taking full responsibility for the correct and complete handling of all exceptions that could potentially pass through your routine—including all exceptions types that may be defined *in the future!* Exceptions have a bright future. Don't kill that future with a shortsighted exception handler.

The only time an exception-killing unqualified exception handler is justified is when you must set up a firewall in a callback function or DLL exported function to prevent any exception from escaping from your module. Such exception firewalls are required in 16-bit Delphi 1.0 DLLs (because exceptions aren't supported by the OS and therefore can't reliably cross module boundaries), and they typically convert the exception to some kind of function result status code or call Application.HandleException to let the application report the exception as it sees fit.

Since exceptions are supported by the Win32 operating system, such firewalls are generally unnecessary in Delphi 2.0. It's possible that someone is still producing Win32 apps that aren't exception aware. If you have to write a DLL in Delphi for use by one of these, let's call them, "distinguished applications," you'll have to resort to 16-bit firewall tactics to trap all exceptions and convert them to something the app can handle.

- **Favor `try...finally` over `try...except`.** The `try...finally` blocks outnumber the `try...except` blocks by a very consistent 3-to-1 margin across the entire code base of Delphi 2.0—the VCL, IDE, and component library (form designer and component and property editors) source code files. This is primarily because `try...finally` blocks are used to ensure that resources are freed wherever they are allocated. The `try...except` blocks are rarer because they are used when processing must be done *only* in an error condition—a much more specialized situation than `try...finally`. Most Delphi applications are not as complex or low-level as the Delphi IDE and VCL internals, so most Delphi apps should have an even wider spread between `try...finally` and `try...except` blocks—on the order of 10 to 1.

- **Let the default VCL exception handler notify the user of error conditions.** If most of your exception handlers do little more than show an error message to the user, you've missed the point. The beauty of exception classes is that they can carry all the information needed to describe the exception condition, and exceptions that go unhandled in a VCL app will be trapped and displayed by the VCL default handler (using Application.OnException). Thus, if you take the time to explain the situation when you raise the exception (see the next section), you don't need to write exception handlers all over your application to explain yourself after the fact.

- **Don't be afraid to let exceptions fly.** Exceptions are supposed to be rare events, usually caused by invalid or inconsistent data. Since bad data is often directly attributable to the user's most recent actions, let users see the exceptions they caused. If you want to change the wording or explanation text associated with an exception when it is encountered in a particular context, it's better to raise a new exception to replace the original (see Listing 4.9) than to display an error message dialog right there in the exception handler, especially in middle- and low-level subroutines and classes. Converting exceptions lets you alter the explanation text without interfering with the user interface of the application or the caller's ability to handle the exception after you.

Listing 4.9 Converting an exception to a context-specific class and text description.

```
unit LogFile;
interface
type
  ELogFileError = class(Exception);
procedure OpenLogFile(const FileName: String);
implementation
procedure OpenLogFile(const FileName: String);
begin
  try
    { ... open log file here ... }
  except
  on EIOError do
    raise ELogFileError.CreateFmt(
       'Can''t open log file %s',[FileName]);
  end;
end;
end;
```

Rules of Thumb for Raising Exceptions

The previous section was primarily concerned with avoiding exception handlers that cripple the automatic exception notification system. This section provides tips for raising exceptions without making a nuisance of yourself.

- **Raise exceptions only when you have no other recourse.** Exceptions should be, well, exceptional: they should be statistically rare events. Abusing your right to `raise` will erode performance (the performance cost of initializing the exception object and finding a handler is considerable), annoy the end user with swarms of insignificant error messages, and complicate the programming chores of your customer, the Delphi application writer.

- **Raise exceptions when well-defined requirements are violated.** Receiving invalid parameters in a function is sufficient grounds to raise an exception, as is calling a function before the object or program has met all its prerequisite conditions. When a routine has well-defined requirements that are easy to determine and fulfill in code, such a breach of protocol can only be described as programmer error. For example: Item 43 is requested from a list that has only 40 items, when the list count is readily available.

- **Avoid exceptions when requirements are ambiguous or difficult to obtain.** When it's difficult to pass guaranteed valid parameters to a function or guarantee use of a function in the proper context due to a lack of information or cost to obtain it, it's harder to justify raising an exception. For example: In a SQL query, you don't know how many rows are in the result set, so you can't know that you're looking at the last row until you try to fetch the next row and fail. In this context, it would be counterproductive to raise an ESeekPastEndOfFile exception when the TQuery.Next is called and you were already at the end of the result set. Instead, Next sets the TQuery.EOF property to True when Next discovers the end of file condition.

- **Assume that end users will see your exception messages.** If that is a disturbing prospect, then perhaps raising an exception is not the best way to deal with the situation at hand. Raising exceptions with unintelligible messages ("Error 51.") only places additional burdens on the application writer to trap your gibberish and convert it into something less embarrassing.

  To allow your error messages to be translated into other end user languages along with the rest of the application, exception text should be loaded from string resources. The base exception class includes many constructor variations to support creating an exception with a predefined string resource message. For example, Exception.CreateRes takes an integer resource id parameter, which it uses to load a corresponding error message string from the application's string resource table. Similarly, Exception.CreateResFmt uses the resource id parameter to load a format control string from the application's string resource table and then calls Format to merge the additional parameter data into that control string.

- **Exception object and message should describe the situation completely.** Don't worry about the additional time it will take to compose a complete statement of the problem. Performance is not an issue in code that is rarely used, as should be the case for raising and handling exceptions. If you have a choice, favor small code size over fast techniques when collecting the information needed to raise the exception with sufficient description. Use the handy CreateFmt and CreateRes constructors of the Exception base class to format data into the exception message string or load a message string from the resource string table, respectively, in one fell swoop.

- **Provide "hard" and "soft" versions of some routines.** When a subroutine can be used for experimental queries (for example, to find out whether valid data is available), it would be wrong to raise an exception just because the experimental query failed. If the same routine will be used frequently in a well-defined, deterministic manner, though, you would like the conveniences associated with an exception-raising routine. This is easily resolved by providing two versions of the subroutine: one defined as always returning valid data or raising an exception ("hard" requirements), and another defined as possibly returning data but not raising an exception ("soft" requirements). TDataset has an example of such a pair: FindField and FieldByName. FieldByName will raise an exception if the dataset does not contain the requested field name; FindField will simply return `nil`. The programming assumptions allowed by each of these methods are quite different. You can use FieldByName anywhere you are confident that the field name you are requesting is in the dataset, and you don't want to have to check for `nil` after every call. You can use the function result of FieldByName (it returns a TField object) with confidence, directly calling methods of the returned object:

    ```
    Caption := Table1.FieldByName('Lastname').Value
    ```

    With FindField, you can be less careful with the input, but you have to be more careful with the output, remembering to check the result for `nil` before using it. FieldByName is actually implemented as a call to FindField, followed by a `nil` check.

    Adding a Boolean parameter to a subroutine to control whether it raises exceptions or not is a bad idea. An additional parameter complicates the parameter list (the fewer parameters the better), and it skates precariously near the old problem of mixing real data with nondata, as mentioned at the start of this chapter.

- **Provide a family of exception classes.** A base exception class unique to your component or unit allows exception handlers to trap any and only exceptions raised by your particular component or unit. Descendant exception classes allow exception handlers to zero-in on one specific kind of error without having to examine the exception object instance carefully to figure out whether the exception is the kind it's interested in. It's nice to have specific exception classes for common error conditions that may need a specific response, such as EDivByZero, a descendant of EIntError, the base exception class for integer arithmetic errors.

Summary

Structured exception handling provides a powerful automatic communication system between code that detects errors and code that is prepared to deal with those errors. The automatic nature of the system makes it more reliable than traditional fire brigade error-handling systems. The two kinds of exception handlers allow you to specify code that executes only in error situations, or that will be executed in all situations error or not. Exception classes allow for a full range of hierarchical categorization of related errors and handlers and provide transport of detailed information about the error situation. The separation of exception notifications from the main line of execution simplifies the source code and improves performance where it matters most—in the code that executes most frequently.

Most of all, exceptions allow you to operate under nearly ideal assumptions:

- If execution reaches "here," then everything prior to this point must have succeeded.

- Subroutines return only valid data, or they don't return at all.

- Errors that your code is not prepared for will be reported to the user automatically.

In traditional fire brigade error-handling systems, the programmer must take an active role to ensure that error codes are checked, decoded, and relayed to the caller in order for the application to run smoothly. Exceptions are almost the opposite: The programmer must resist the urge to meddle with, and perhaps defeat, the automatic systems. When writing exception handlers, take care not to lobotomize the automatic systems by carelessly blocking exceptions you are not prepared to deal with. When raising exceptions, avoid making a nuisance of yourself with frivolous exceptions. The secret to unleashing the full power of structured exception handling is learning to let it do its job.

Chapter 5

Run-Time Type Information

Programs compiled into native machine code generally have no knowledge of the names used for types and identifiers in the original source code. The machine cares only about numbers, not what your chosen names for those numbers are. Run-Time Type Information (RTTI) is a mechanism by which the Delphi compiler can embed type information details into the compiled executable file for the program to use at run time. RTTI gives names to the numbers and memory addresses that the running program normally deals with. That name association is what makes Delphi's streaming system automatic.

The compiler generates lists of information describing each published property of a component and stores that information in the program EXE file. Since the RTTI data is stored in the code portion of the EXE file, it is always read-only. Special routines in the TypInfo unit decode the compiler's shorthand to provide the running program with information such as what published properties a class has, the types of those properties, how each property is read and written, and a host of other information. When writing components to a stream (discussed in Chapter 6), the VCL streaming class TWriter uses TypInfo routines to enumerate the published properties of a component and to write their data values to the stream in a manner appropriate to each property's type. When reading components from a stream, the TReader class uses TypInfo routines to locate component properties named in the stream and to assign the stream data to those properties.

The TypInfo Unit

The TypInfo unit is a shadowy figure lurking just beyond the lamplight cast by the Delphi product documentation. The reason for its exclusion from official coverage is simple: The data structures exposed in TypInfo are too closely tied to the innards of the compiler to guarantee their migration from one version of the compiler to the next. Borland reserves the right to make any modification to the

TypInfo unit necessary to accommodate internal changes in the compiler regardless of the implications to code which uses the TypInfo unit. Documenting the TypInfo structures and functions alongside the normal VCL routines would give the false impression that the TypInfo structures were as safe to use as normal VCL routines and classes—they aren't. Thus, TypInfo is excluded from the normal Delphi user's documentation, and its source code is very clearly marked as exposing volatile implementation details that will change (and already have) between Delphi versions.

Plan for change: Isolate use of TypInfo into one area of your code so that it will be easy to locate and modify when TypInfo changes in the future. The TypInfo data structures and field-encoding techniques are more likely to change than the TypInfo helper routines. The helper routines exist to isolate you from changes in the data structures. Use the TypInfo functions with discretion and restraint, and avoid using fields of TypInfo data structures except when absolutely necessary.

> **Fün mit Pronünciätion**
>
> *TypInfo* is usually pronounced "type info" by the unwashed masses, but the unit has acquired the nickname "tip info" within the Delphi team to mark (mock) the absence of the letter *e* in the unit's name. *TypInfo* is an intrinsic function in the Object Pascal language, and unit names always lose identifier conflicts.
>
> One of the more subtle ways to irk your northern European friends (particularly Danes) is to pronounce the unit "tÿp info," where "tÿp" is pronounced somewhere between "turp" and "toop" depending on how well you can change your nasal resonance to resemble a kazoo (kazü?). The gag will require some explanation (and spelling) after the first attempt, but it's a guaranteed grimace for each use thereafter. If you can deliver a European "ÿ" with an American drawl, you'll really have 'em howling in anguish.

The RTTI Fountainhead

The compiler emits run time type information for all published properties, methods, and fields of a class declared under the influence of the $M+ compiler directive, as well as any descendant of such a class. The Classes unit declares the TPersistent with $M+. All VCL components are descendants of TPersistent, so all VCL components automatically get RTTI for their published symbols. Helper classes such as TFont and TCollection are not components but do need to be streamable, so they, too, are descendants of TPersistent.

You can declare your own class (not related to TPersistent) with $M+ and then use RTTI routines to query the published properties of that class and its descendants. You can think of this as an *illuminated class* since it contains lavish detail about its contents but doesn't actually do anything with that information. An illuminated class is not streamable. The VCL streaming system can only handle descendants of TPersistent. A class derived from TObject declared within a $M+ block is an illuminated class. A class derived from TPersistent is illuminated and streamable (persistent).

RTTI is not limited to just classes. RTTI is also generated for every type used by a published property. The RTTI for an enumerated type, for example, is the text names of the elements in the enumeration.

You can also illuminate your own types, even if they aren't used by a published property of an illuminated class. How? Declare the type in a $M+ block. For example, look at the source code fragment in Listing 5.1, which contains an enumerated type, TChessPiece, and a form with a button and a listbox. When you click the button, the listbox is filled with the names of the elements of the TChessPiece enumerated type. We'll examine the TypeInfo and GetEnumName functions later.

Listing 5.1 This button click method lists the names of the elements of an enumerated type, using RTTI.

```
{$M+}
type
  TChessPiece = (Pawn, Rook, Knight, Bishop, Queen, King);
{$M-}
procedure TForm1.Button1Click(Sender: TObject);
var
  I: Integer;
begin
  for I := 0 to Ord(High(TChessPiece)) do
    Listbox1.Items.Add( GetEnumName(TypeInfo(TChessPiece), I));
end;
```

The significance of this example may not be immediately apparent. You see, when the compiler compiles your source code into machine code, none of the symbol names wind up in the machine code. The machine doesn't care what your text names for things are; all it cares about is where those things are in memory—addresses and numerical data. Of course, any string constants must be placed in the final EXE, but those are data, not program identifiers. There is no way to get the name of an element in an enumerated type, for example, because the compiler compiles enumerations down to a list of numbers (the first element has ordinal value 0, the second has ordinal value 1, and so on). The compiled program deals only with concrete numbers, not with the abstract names that you deal with in the source code.

With RTTI, you can create illuminated types that a program can use to describe its internal state in words instead of numeric codes with very little support code written by you. When you change the names of the elements in the enumeration in the source code and recompile, the program will use the new names automatically.

RTTI Advantages

The advantage of using RTTI in this manner is that it can allow you to consolidate resources and reduce maintenance chores. The traditional solution to naming the elements of an enumeration is to declare an array of strings and manually populate the array with string constants yourself. If you modify the enumerated type, you also have to modify the array of names to match. This is clearly a source code maintenance risk.

If the enumerated type is already being used as the type of a published property, the compiler is already generating RTTI for that type, so there are two lists of string names in your final EXE: the RTTI generated by the compiler (which is always up-to-date), and the array of strings you maintain manually. Changing your code to fetch the element names from the RTTI spring allows you to eliminate that redundant data in your EXE and eliminate the manual maintenance headaches associated with it. For a dozen enumerations each having dozens of elements, the size and time savings can be significant—thousands of bytes.

RTTI Disadvantages

- **Symbol names are meaningless to end users.** There are significant disadvantages to using RTTI in the manner just described. First and foremost, it exposes parts of your program source code to the end user. Symbol names that may be meaningful to a programmer in the context of a particular module's source code will probably not be as meaningful to end users as names created specifically for the end user. Having text in a program change automatically when the source code changes may be a boon to programmers, but it's usually a liability for the end user and documentation. Most people use computers by rote (rather than by thinking), so changing any aspect of your program after it's deployed is likely to confuse your end users.

- **Source code symbol names aren't translatable.** Using RTTI to provide names for numeric values is also bad for translation. To translate an application into other spoken languages or cultural markets with a minimum of effort, you should discipline yourself to externalize all displayed strings—to move string constants out of source code modules and into string table resources. This way, the display strings of the app (in string tables and in DFM form resources) can be translated to the needs of a particular locale, but the program itself does not need to be recompiled (just relinked with replacement resources). RTTI is just another form of the evil source code string constant—it's beyond the reach of your translators. Don't even think about modifying the source code for each locale so that the RTTI names will be appropriate. There are lots of non-English characters (accents, umlauts, and so on) that are not allowed in Pascal identifiers, so RTTI cannot express names containing those characters.

- **RTTI symbol names are visible to EXE snoopers.** Even if you don't display RTTI-derived strings to the end user, RTTI strings will still be in your executable file. Class names, published property names, and portions of the types of published properties are all easily accessible to snoopers armed with a simple hex-dump file viewer. Since a program's data types, class names, and enumeration values tend to be self-descriptive so that the programmer can remember what each does, they are also descriptive to snoopers. A surprising amount of information about how a program is organized can be gleaned from studying its embedded strings. Most embedded strings in Delphi EXEs and DLLs come from RTTI. If you have secrets to hide in your program, you should avoid referring to them in class names, published properties, or enumerated types used by published properties. If you have secrets whose implementations must be streamable, you can choose between using meaningless names in published properties (and your source code) or meaningful names in nonpublished properties that are streamed using custom defined properties with meaningless names (more on custom-defined properties in Chapter 6). Note that class names are always stored in the executable file, regardless of whether the class contains published properties. If you're prone to using rude language in your program identifiers, you should consider switching to ALGOL.

  RTTI adds to the size of your executable file and to the memory required to run your program. To keep RTTI info under control, always leave the $M compiler switch in the off state ($M–) except where you specifically need it, which is almost never. Similarly, since the default visibility attribute of a class declaration is `published`, you should get into the habit of explicitly declaring the visibility of declarations in your class types (usually, `protected` and `public`) so that you don't litter your EXE with unnecessary RTTI symbol information.

As mentioned earlier, the TypInfo unit is subject to change in each revision of Delphi. An advantage of using RTTI is that it may reduce your day-to-day source code maintenance chores. The disadvantage is that RTTI may add to your upgrading chores when you migrate your app up to some future version of Delphi with a slightly different TypInfo unit. C'est la vie.

RTTI Supported Types

The Delphi compiler generates RTTI for the following Object Pascal simple types:

Ordinals—char, byte, word, integer, longint, and enumerated types

Set types with up to 32 elements (up to 16 in Delphi 1.0)

Strings

Class types

Method pointers

Floats—Single, Double, Extended, Comp, and Currency

Variants

Non-RTTI Types

RTTI does not support the following types. Declaring a published property with one of these types will cause a compile error:

Compound types, such as array or record types

Array properties

Sets containing more than 32 elements (16 in Delphi 1.0)

File types (Text, File of Integer, and so forth)

Old-style objects

Pointer types

RTTI Data Structures and Pseudostructures

The TypInfo unit defines several record types used by or returned by the TypInfo routines. You may notice that several of these record types contain field declarations in comment blocks. The RTTI data structures are stored in a tightly packed format, placing the next field or record immediately after the last data character of a string field, for example. Since string data lengths vary, the location of the field or record following such a string can't be expressed as a static location or offset, so the field can't be expressed in a type declaration.

Such record types are called *pseudostructures* because they're only an approximation of the actual data's structure. RTTI data is stored as hierarchical trees of type descriptors, and these TypInfo record types are simply typecasting conveniences that can be overlaid on the RTTI data to gain access to parts of the type descriptors. The commented-out pseudofields of the TypInfo structures are always at the end of the record, and their mock definitions are always some sort of array of substructures.

Let's now take a quick look at each of the major data types defined in TypInfo.

TPropInfo

First, consider the TPropInfo structure:

```
type
  PPropInfo = ^TPropInfo;
  TPropInfo = packed record
    PropType: PTypeInfo;
    GetProc: Pointer;
    SetProc: Pointer;
    StoredProc: Pointer;
    Index: Integer;
    Default: Longint;
    NameIndex: Smallint;
    Name: ShortString;
  end;
```

On the rare occasions that you'll need to tap into RTTI with TypInfo routines, you'll almost always use the TPropInfo structure. TypInfo's routines reflect this as well: Almost all operate on or return pointers to TPropInfo data. Once you have a PropInfo pointer, you can get the data type of the property (PropType), get the name of the property (Name), determine how the property is read and written (GetProc, SetProc), and find out what the property's declared default value is, if any (Default).

TPropInfo exists primarily to support automatic property streaming at run time and at design time. In this one structure, you have all the information you need to identify the property and to read and write the property's data.

The easiest way to explore this information is to write a program. Listing 5.2 shows the complete source code for RTTI1.DPR, a simple console application that extracts and displays the TPropInfo data fields for various published properties in a test class. Listing 5.3 shows the output of this program.

Listing 5.2 Surf the TPropInfo data with a simple console application, RTTI1.

```
program rtti1;
uses  Sysutils, Classes, TypInfo;
type
  TRTTITest = class(TPersistent)
  private
    FTest: Integer;
    FString: String;
    procedure SetTest(X: Integer);
    procedure SetIndexedProp(I, X:Integer);
    function  GetInt: Integer; virtual;
    function  IsStored: Boolean;
    function  IsStored2: Boolean; virtual;
  published
    property TestProp: Integer read FTest write SetTest
      stored False;
    property IndexedProp: Integer index 20 read FTest
      write SetIndexedProp default 10;
    property VirtualProp: Integer read GetInt
      write FTest stored IsStored;
    property test2: string read FString stored IsStored2;
  end;

procedure TRTTITest.SetTest;
begin
end;

procedure TRTTITest.SetIndexedProp;
begin
end;

function TRTTITest.GetInt: Integer;
begin
```

```
end;

function TRTTITest.IsStored: Boolean;
begin
end;

function TRTTITest.IsStored2: Boolean;
begin
end;

procedure Display(const PropName: String);
var
  P: PPropInfo;
begin
  P := GetPropInfo(TRTTITest.ClassInfo, PropName);
  if P = nil then
  begin
    Writeln(PropName,' is not a published property of this
class');
    Exit;
  end;
  Writeln(P.Name, ': ', P.PropType.Name);
  Writeln(Format('GetProc: $%p', [P.GetProc]));
  Writeln(Format('SetProc: $%p', [P.SetProc]));
  Writeln(Format('StoredProc: $%p', [P.StoredProc]));
  Writeln(Format('Index: $%.4x', [P.Index]));
  Writeln(Format('Default: $%.4x', [P.Default]));
  Writeln(Format('NameIndex: $%.4x', [P.NameIndex]));
  Writeln;
end;

begin
  Display('TestProp');
  Display('IndexedProp');
  Display('VirtualProp');
  Display('test2');
  Display('foobar');
end.
```

Listing 5.3 The output of the RTTI1 program reveals several data-encoding variations.

```
TestProp: Integer
GetProc: $FF000004
SetProc: $00407F24
StoredProc: $00000000
```

```
           Index: $80000000
           Default: $80000000
           NameIndex: $0000

           IndexedProp: Integer
           GetProc: $FF000004
           SetProc: $00407F28
           StoredProc: $00000001
           Index: $0014
           Default: $000A
           NameIndex: $0001

           VirtualProp: Integer
           GetProc: $FE00000C
           SetProc: $FF000004
           StoredProc: $00407F30
           Index: $80000000
           Default: $80000000
           NameIndex: $0002

           test2: string
           GetProc: $FF000008
           SetProc: $00000000
           StoredProc: $FE000010
           Index: $80000000
           Default: $80000000
           NameIndex: $0003

           foobar is not a published property of this class
```

The TRTTITest class in Listing 5.2 inherits from TPersistent, so the compiler will automatically generate RTTI for the published properties of the class. The class contains a few private data fields and property access methods and four published properties arranged to provide a representative sample of Delphi's property declaration variations. Take a minute or two to study the declaration and the program output for each property. What you should notice in comparing the property declarations with the program output is that many of the fields of the TPropInfo record have multiple data encodings, corresponding to the multiple syntax variations supported by Delphi.

PropType and Name

The PropType and Name fields of the TPropInfo record are the fields you'll use most often. Name is the property's identifier, exactly as it appears in the source code declaration (case preserved). PropType points to a TTypeInfo structure from which

RTTI DATA STRUCTURES AND PSEUDOSTRUCTURES

you can determine the type of the property, among other things. The TTypeInfo record is described in the next section.

GetProc/SetProc

Properties can read and write data in three ways: by a static method call, by a `virtual` method call, or by direct field access. (Property read and write methods cannot be `dynamic` methods.) Consequently, the GetProc and SetProc fields of TPropInfo have three encodings. For static methods, the field value is positive and contains the address of the method body (see IndexProp.SetProc). For virtual methods, the high byte of the field value is $FE and the lower bytes are the method's VMT offset in the class's VMT (see VirtualProp.GetProc). For properties that access a field of the instance directly, the high byte of the TPropInfo Get/SetProc field is $FF and the lower bytes are the offset of the field in the instance data block (see TestProp.GetProc). A read-only property declares no property writer; its SetProc is `nil` (see Test2.SetProc). Similarly, a write-only property's GetProc is `nil`.

You should never really need this information to directly call a property read or write method. The TypInfo helper routines will do all the work of decoding, calling, and returning property data for you.

StoredProc

Properties can be declared with an optional `stored` directive, which can take a Boolean value, refer to a Boolean field of the class, or refer to a Boolean function of the class. A `stored` directive of False sets StoredProc to 0, a `stored` directive of True sets StoredProc to 1, and a reference to a static or virtual function or to a field uses the same encoding rules as GetProc and SetProc. You know that StoredProc contains a static method address if its value is positive *and* greater than 1. If a property declaration doesn't specify a `stored` directive, StoredProc defaults to 1 (True).

Index

The Index field of TPropInfo gets the value of a property's `index` directive, if any (see IndexedProp.Index). TPropInfo.Index defaults to $80000000, indicating no value (see VirtualProp.Index).

Default

The Default field of TPropInfo gets the value of a property's `default` directive, if any (see IndexedProp.Default). TPropInfo.Default defaults to $80000000, indicating no value.

NameIndex

The NameIndex field associates a number with the property name that is guaranteed to be unique within the class and its ancestors. If a descendant class redeclares a property to obscure an inherited property having the same name, the name index of the descendant property is still the same as the inherited property. Since PropInfo.Name preserves the case of the source code identifier and since Pascal is a case-insensitive language, you would have to convert the string to upper (or lower) case in order to compare it to other Pascal identifiers. For the sake of performance, you definitely don't want to do that. You can use NameIndex as a precalculated, perfect hash value to check the equality of TPropInfo records instead of comparing the TPropInfo.Name strings. Comparing two integers is many times faster than case-shifting and comparing two strings.

TTypeKind and TTypeInfo

Next, consider TTypeKind and TTypeInfo.

```
type
  TTypeKind = (tkUnknown, tkInteger, tkChar, tkEnumeration,
    tkFloat, tkString, tkSet, tkClass, tkMethod, tkWChar,
    tkLString, tkLWString, tkVariant);
  PTypeInfo = ^TTypeInfo;
  TTypeInfo = record
    Kind: TTypeKind;
    Name: ShortString;
    {TypeData: TTypeData}
  end;
```

When you're working with TPropInfo structures, you'll often tap into its PropType field to find out what the type of the property is. PropType is a pointer to a simple TTypeInfo structure containing just the Kind and Name of the property's type identifier.

Kind uses the TTypeKind enumeration, which lists all the types that RTTI supports, as well as a few that it doesn't—tkUnknown and tkLWString. tkUnknown is never generated by the compiler, but it can be used for error checking. If you find yourself looking at a tkUnknown TypeInfo record, you've definitely bungled one of your PropInfo pointers somewhere along the way. tkLWString is a placeholder for the WideString Unicode string type that has been proposed for future versions of Delphi. WideString is not implemented in Delphi 2.0.

TTypeData

TTypeInfo is actually a header for a much more complicated type descriptor record, TTypeData, shown in Listing 5.4. TTypeData lies at the heart of the RTTI system. It contains the most detailed information, but it is also the structure most likely to change in future versions of Delphi. Study Listing 5.4 for a moment, before we hit the high points of this structure.

Listing 5.4 TTypeData, the heart of the RTTI system.

```
type
  TOrdType = (otSByte, otUByte, otSWord, otUWord, otSLong);
  TFloatType = (ftSingle, ftDouble, ftExtended, ftComp, ftCurr);
  TMethodKind = (mkProcedure, mkFunction);
  TParamFlags = set of (pfVar, pfConst, pfArray);

  PTypeData = ^TTypeData;
  TTypeData = packed record
    case TTypeKind of
      tkUnknown, tkLString, tkLWString, tkVariant: ();
      tkInteger, tkChar, tkEnumeration, tkSet, tkWChar: (
        OrdType: TOrdType;
        case TTypeKind of
          tkInteger, tkChar, tkEnumeration, tkWChar: (
            MinValue: Longint;
            MaxValue: Longint;
            case TTypeKind of
              tkInteger, tkChar, tkWChar: ();
              tkEnumeration: (
                BaseType: PTypeInfo;
                NameList: ShortString));
          tkSet: (CompType: PTypeInfo));
      tkFloat: (FloatType: TFloatType);
      tkString: (MaxLength: Byte);
      tkClass: (
        ClassType: TClass;
        ParentInfo: PTypeInfo;
        PropCount: SmallInt;
        UnitName: ShortString
        {PropData: TPropData});
      tkMethod: (
        MethodKind: TMethodKind;
        ParamCount: Byte;
        ParamList: array[0..1023] of Char
        {ParamList: array[1..ParamCount] of
          record
```

RUN-TIME TYPE INFORMATION

```
            Flags: TParamFlags;
            ParamName: ShortString;
            TypeName: ShortString;
          end;
       ResultType: ShortString});
  end;
```

Like TPropInfo, TTypeData exists to support run-time property streaming. However, TTypeData also includes information that is really only useful at design time—trivia such as the maximum storage length of a string property, the unit name of a class type, or the parameter list of a method pointer type. Where TPropInfo is primarily concerned with *how* to access property data, TTypeData deals with *what* the property data is—its type and size.

Here are the highlights of the TTypeData structure:

- **Long strings and variants.** These require no special information in the TTypeData structure because their size in the object instance is constant—4-byte pointer for long strings and 16-byte data block for variants.

- **OrdType.** This field indicates the number of significant bits in an ordinal or set type and whether the ordinal type uses signed or unsigned values. Since publishable set types must have 32 or fewer elements in their base type, sets can be lumped together with ordinals, and published sets can store default values in the 32-bit TPropInfo.Default field. Sets with less than 8 elements are stored in a single byte; sets with between 8 and 15 elements are stored in a 2-byte word.

- **CompType.** This is a pointer to a TTypeInfo structure describing the set's base type, which could be a simple ordinal type, an ordinal subrange type, or an enumerated type.

- **MinValue and MaxValue.** These indicate the minimum and maximum data values allowed by the type definition. This is primarily useful for subrange types (type Teens = 13..19;) and the range-checking property editors they ride in on.

- **NameList.** For enumerated types, this is a packed list of short strings containing the names of each item in the enumeration. Don't bother with decoding this packed list. Just call TypInfo's GetEnumName or GetEnumValue routines.

- **FloatType.** This indicates which kind of floating-point representation the property uses. From this, you can extrapolate the size of the data (Simple = 4 bytes, Double = 8 bytes, and so on). Note the omission of the 6-byte Real type from the TFloatType enumeration. The Real type is an anachronism dating back to the earliest days of Turbo Pascal, long before IEEE floating-point encoding standards like Single and Double were widely supported in CPU hardware. Delphi continues to support Pascal source code that uses the old 6-byte Real data format by promoting Real variables to Double for the purposes of calculation, and then lopping off a few bits to cram the result back into the 6-byte variable. Delphi doesn't allow you to publish Real-type properties because the Real type itself is just a compiler trick.

- **MaxLength.** This indicates the maximum declared length of a short string type. For type MyString = String[80], MaxLength is 80.

- **Class types.** The ClassType field is a class reference to the actual class type of the property. From this class reference, you can call class methods such as ClassName (ClassType.ClassName) and InstanceSize or even create an instance of the class. ParentInfo is a shortcut to the RTTI info of the class's immediate ancestor. The scenic route to the parent's RTTI is Self.ClassType.ClassParent.ClassInfo. UnitName is the name of the unit containing the class type declaration. The IDE form designer uses this to generate the `uses` list in a form unit based on the components dropped into the form. PropCount indicates how many published properties that class type contains. The PropData pseudofield contains an array of that class's TPropInfo structures.

- **Method types.** This last section of the TTypeData structure is the one you'll find least useful at run time. The method type data exists only to allow the design-time module manager to generate the appropriate method declaration and parameter list for an event handler method when you double-click on the event property editor in the Object Inspector. This is the only part of the TTypeData structure for which TypInfo does not provide helper routines — there's nothing a running program can do with the names of the parameters expected by a particular method type. If you're getting excited at the possibility of using this method type data to have your program dynamically figure out how to call an arbitrary event, forget it. The method type data doesn't tell you anything about the size of the parameter data or how it is passed on the stack or in registers. All the method type data stores is the names of the parameters and the names of their types, which can be any valid identifier.

RTTI Routines

RTTI's variable-length fields and nested structures are compact and fairly easy for the compiler to generate at full throttle. However, these structures do make traversing the RTTI tree more difficult, so TypInfo defines several access routines that slice and dice the packed type information for you. At the same time, these access routines insulate you from the actual implementation of the tree structure, giving Borland room to reorganize the structures as needed in future versions of Delphi.

TypeInfo

TypeInfo is a compiler intrinsic function (like SizeOf) that returns a pointer to a nonclass type's TTypeInfo RTTI record, if any. If you have declared an enumeration TChessPiece in a $M+ block, you can get its type info by calling TypeInfo(TChessPiece). If the specified type does not have any RTTI, TypeInfo returns `nil`. (An intrinsic function is something the compiler can evaluate at compile time without generating machine code for a run-time function call.)

TObject.ClassInfo

```
class function TObject.ClassInfo: Pointer;
```

When you want access to the RTTI of a class type, call the class's ClassInfo function. If the class type doesn't have any RTTI, ClassInfo returns `nil`. ClassInfo is a class method, so you can call it with or without an object instance. Pass the value returned by your class's ClassInfo function to the TypInfo unit routines that require a PTypeInfo parameter.

GetPropInfo

```
function GetPropInfo(TypeInfo: PTypeInfo;
  const PropName: String): PPropInfo;
```

GetPropInfo gives you access to the TPropInfo structure associated with a particular published property.

When you're poking around in RTTI for anything more than just getting and setting property values, you'll almost always start with a call to this function. If the specified property name does not exist in the specified class's type info (or the class doesn't have any type info), GetPropInfo returns `nil`.

GetPropInfos and GetPropList

```
procedure GetPropInfos(TypeInfo: PTypeInfo; PropList: PPropList);
function GetPropList(TypeInfo: PTypeInfo; TypeKinds: TTypeKinds;
   PropList: PPropList): Integer;
```

The GetPropInfos and GetPropList routines are high-volume versions of GetPropInfo. GetPropList fills an array of pointers with all the PropInfo pointers associated with the specified class type. You must allocate the array of pointers and ensure that it is large enough to hold all the PropInfos of the class type. Calculate the PropInfo count like this:

```
GetTypeData(MyClass.ClassInfo)^.PropCount.
```

GetPropInfos is a filter function that will return only the PropInfos of properties whose type is in the TypeKinds parameter search criteria. The PropInfo pointers are returned in an array of pointers you allocate and pass to the function, and the function result is the number of items in the result set. TTypeKinds is a set of TTypeKind, the enumeration that lists all the RTTI-supported types. You must allocate the array of pointers. You can overestimate the required array size by just using the count of all published properties in the class, just as for GetPropList. To allocate exactly enough memory needed by the PropInfos array for your particular query, call GetPropInfos with a `nil` PropList to get the count of properties in the result set, allocate the PropInfo array using that count (Count * SizeOf(Pointer)), and then call GetPropInfos again, this time passing in the pointer array.

Property Get Routines

```
function GetOrdProp(Instance: TObject;
   PropInfo: PPropInfo): Longint;
function GetStrProp(Instance: TObject;
   PropInfo: PPropInfo): string;
function GetFloatProp(Instance: TObject;
   PropInfo: PPropInfo): Extended;
function GetVariantProp(Instance: TObject;
   PropInfo: PPropInfo): Variant;
function GetMethodProp(Instance: TObject;
   PropInfo: PPropInfo): TMethod;
```

The five property get routines in TypInfo allow you to fetch the data from any published property, using program code that knows nothing (at compile time) about the specific class types it operates on. These TypInfo routines take care of all the work of fetching the property value regardless of what kind of property access technique is required—direct field reference, static method call, `virtual` method call, indexed static method call, or indexed `virtual` method call.

The operation of each should be pretty obvious from their function declarations. You pass in a PropInfo pointer for the property whose value you want and a pointer to the object instance from which the value should be taken. Only GetOrdProp does anything beyond the obvious. You use GetOrdProp to fetch values of just about any property whose data fits in 32 bits—all the integer types, char, enumerated types, sets, and class types. Remember that instance variables are always pointers to the instance data on the heap, so a class type property is just a 32-bit pointer, easily typecast to and from a 32-bit integer. Sets work here because you can only publish set types with less than 32 elements. Sets are implemented as 1 bit per element, so published sets can be typecast as 32-bit integers for the purposes of moving data back and forth.

Property Set Routines

```
procedure SetOrdProp(Instance: TObject; PropInfo: PPropInfo;
  Value: Longint);
procedure SetStrProp(Instance: TObject; PropInfo: PPropInfo;
  const Value: string);
procedure SetFloatProp(Instance: TObject; PropInfo: PPropInfo;
  Value: Extended);
procedure SetVariantProp(Instance: TObject; PropInfo: PPropInfo;
  const Value: Variant);
procedure SetMethodProp(Instance: TObject; PropInfo: PPropInfo;
  const Value: TMethod);
```

The five property set routines in TypInfo allow you to write data into any published property without specific compile-time knowledge of the class type. Like the TypInfo property get routines, these set routines figure out from the PropInfo's TypeData what needs to be done to write the value to the property, be it by direct field access, static method call, or `virtual` method call. Like the get routines, the set routines are pretty obvious, except perhaps for SetOrdProp's broader purpose to write set and class instance properties as well as ordinals. Again, typecasting is the trick.

GetEnumName and GetEnumValue

```
function GetEnumName(TypeInfo: PTypeInfo; Value: Integer):
  string;
```

```
function GetEnumValue(TypeInfo: PTypeInfo;
  const Name: string): Integer;
```

GetEnumName is handy for converting the ordinal value of an enumerated type to its more readable string identifier. GetEnumValue goes in the other direction, returning the ordinal value of an identifier in an enumerated type, if any. If the identifier is not part of the enumerated type indicated by the TypeInfo parameter, GetEnumValue returns –1. If the value you pass to GetEnumName is out of range for the enumerated type indicated by TypeInfo, the function result is undefined. In other words, you'll get a garbage string back.

IsStoredProp

```
function IsStoredProp(Instance: TObject;
  PropInfo: PPropInfo): Boolean;
```

The VCL streaming class TWriter uses IsStoredProp to determine whether a property needs to be written to the stream. Like the property get and set routines, IsStoredProp takes care of the details of calling the static or `virtual` method referenced by the property's `stored` directive, if any.

GetTypeData

```
function GetTypeData(TypeInfo: PTypeInfo): PTypeData;
```

GetTypeData is a utility routine to get a pointer to the TypeData structure packed up tight against the end of the TypeInfo's Name string.

RTTI Example Project: Persistent User Data

With all the carrying-on earlier in this chapter about the disadvantages of using RTTI, you may well have doubts that RTTI is as useful as you were first led to believe. Don't lose hope just yet. Most of the hazards of RTTI cited earlier were related to exposing internal names to the end user, and thus causing documentation and translation problems. There are plenty of other areas of Delphi programming that don't involve strings displayed in the user interface. RTTI can greatly simplify and automate internal operations. Let's now take a look at one example of how you can put RTTI to work for you.

The Task

Most software of any complexity has user-configurable options to control the operation of the software. These user-configurable options are often presented in dialogs using shoals of checkboxes, radio buttons, and edit controls. When you modify these options at run time, you usually expect the modifications to "stick" so that the program will use your modified settings the next time you run it. You need some kind of persistent storage for the program's configuration settings, you need to load those settings into the program's configuration dialog controls before displaying it, and you need to store modifications to those settings when the user closes the dialog. As the number of options needing controls, dialogs, and persistent storage increases, so does the volume of grunt work required to maintain the source code.

Since VCL's streaming system stores a complete description of a form, including the data in its controls, you might be tempted to implement persistent user settings by just streaming the form to a file. Form streaming would certainly do the job, but it's major overkill—you don't need to store everything in the form; all you need is to record the data corresponding to the user's input. The stream image for a simple form (a DFM file) with several controls is typically around 2K in size and can be much larger if the form contains bitmaps or high-density multi-page controls. However, the controls on that form manage only a handful of on/off states or text strings—hardly 500 bytes of actual user data. Thus, the first problem with this approach is that it wastes disk space.

The second problem with using form streaming to record user data is that a binary form file is not easily modified by the end user. For better or for worse, people need to be able to configure software without running the software. If the only way to configure your program is to run your program, you'll quickly find yourself in a chicken-and-egg conundrum if the program's start-up configuration settings are somehow damaged or invalidated. For example: User moves program files to a different directory. So, binary files are out. You could convert the DFM into text using the ObjectBinaryToText routine in the Classes unit, but this would make the file size two to three times larger and expose an enormous amount of program detail to the end user. Most users would be unable to recognize the configuration data they can change (such as the on/off state of a checkbox) from the program data they should not (such as the x,y screen location of the checkbox control) and would have the ability to *really* mess up your program.

The third and fourth problems with using form streaming to store user data are the maintenance hazards and the general difficulty of reading stream data into an already existing form instance. When you ship version 2 of your program with a slightly different configuration dialog (some new options added, some old ones removed), you'll have a difficult time extracting just the user's configuration data from the old form files. You can't just load the old form into the new program because the new program might not even have the code for some of the controls used in the first version of the program. On a more fundamental level, when you load a form from a stream, the VCL streaming system assumes that it needs to create new instances of every TComponent it finds in the stream. Loading a form twice would result in two copies of every control in the form, if you could get past the problem of duplicate control names in the form. You could solve that by deleting all the components in the form before reading it from the stream, but it's really beside the point. This is all patchwork and hacks to make the wrong solution work.

The Solution

What we need is a system that will store just the user data contained in a control and will store it in a manner easily editable by end users using external tools. The traditional user-editable configuration storage place for 16-bit Windows programs is Windows INI files. For 32-bit Windows programs, the system registry is the preferred medium for storing program options. Both systems allow you to associate a key name with a data value and to group key names together in sections or directories.

Most program options can be adequately represented by a group of radio buttons (mutually exclusive list of choices), a group of checkboxes (nonexclusive choices), or an edit control (text input). The user data for each of these controls is contained in a single published property: TRadiobutton.Checked, TCheckbox.State, and TEdit.Text. Since these properties are published and these controls descend from TPersistent, these properties have RTTI and are accessible through TypInfo routines.

The Implementation

We can use the name of each component on the form as the key name and the value of the user data property as the key value and can place all these keys in a group having the form's class name. Using RTTI, we can create a small set of utility routines that can store the user data of just about any form to an INI file or branch of the system registry. Listing 5.5 shows the interface section of the USERDATA unit, which implements such a set of utility routines.

Listing 5.5 The USERDATA unit lets you load and store just the user data in your forms.

```
unit userdata;
interface
uses SysUtils, Classes, INIFiles, Registry;

procedure SaveDataToINIFile(Instance: TComponent;
  const Filename: String);
procedure SaveDataToINI(Instance: TComponent; INI: TINIFile);
procedure SaveDataToStrings(Instance: TComponent; Items:
TStrings);
procedure SaveDataToRegistry(Instance: TComponent;
  const Path: String);

procedure LoadDataFromINIFile(Instance: TComponent;
  const Filename: String);
procedure LoadDataFromINI(Instance: TComponent; INI: TINIFile);
procedure LoadDataFromStrings(Instance: TComponent;
  Items: TStrings);
procedure LoadDataFromRegistry(Instance: TComponent;
  const Path: String);

procedure RegisterDataProp(const ClassName, PropName: String);
```

Using the USERDATA unit, you can capture the user data of an options dialog and store it in an INI text file, an in-memory string list, or a branch of the HKEY_CURRENT_USER section of the system registry. Normally, you will pass a form instance variable into the Instance parameter of these routines, and all its components will be handled automatically.

The RegisterDataProp procedure allows you to specify the user data property for additional control classes. Only one property name can be associated with each class name. Registering a class name twice will raise an exception. Classes are registered by class name to avoid touching the class type. Registering a control using a class reference would force the smart linker to pull in a lot of the control's code, even if the control wasn't used anywhere in the program. Registering by class name means you can register everything you *might* need and then forget about it, with no significant memory or EXE size costs.

Listing 5.6 shows the core of the USERDATA unit's implementation. An internal TDataFiler class implements the LoadData and StoreData logic and RTTI handling while leaving the actual persistent storage mechanism undefined. Three descendant classes override TDataFiler's abstract virtual methods WriteStr and ReadStr to implement storage in INI files, TStringLists, or a registry path.

Listing 5.6 The core of the USERDATA unit is its internal TDataFiler class and its LoadData and StoreData methods.

```
implementation
uses TypInfo
type
  TDataFiler = class
    function ReadStr(const Key, Default: string):string;
      virtual; abstract;
    procedure WriteStr(const Key, Value: string); virtual; abstract;
    function ReadInt(const Key: string; Default: Longint): Longint;
    procedure WriteInt(const Key: string; Value: Longint);
    procedure LoadData(Instance: TComponent);
    procedure SaveData(Instance: TComponent);
  end;

  TDataINIFiler = class(TDataFiler)
    FINIFile: TINIFile;
    FSection: string;
    constructor Create(INIFile: TINIFile; const Section: string);
    function ReadStr(const Key, Default: string):string; override;
    procedure WriteStr(const Key, Value: string); override;
  end;

  TDataStringFiler = class(TDataFiler)
    FStrings: TStrings;
    constructor Create(SList: TStrings);
    function ReadStr(const Key, Default: string):string; override;
    procedure WriteStr(const Key, Value: string); override;
  end;

  TDataRegistryFiler = class(TDataFiler)
    FRegINI: TRegINIFile;
    FSection: string;
    constructor Create(RegINI: TRegINIFile; const Section: string);
    function ReadStr(const Key, Default: string): string; override;
    procedure WriteStr(const Key, Value: string); override;
  end;

procedure TDataFiler.LoadData(Instance: TComponent);
var
```

```
    P : TComponent;
    X: Integer;
    PropInfo: PPropInfo;
begin
  for X := 0 to Instance.ComponentCount - 1 do
  begin
    P := Instance.Components[X];
    if (Length(P.Name) > 0) and FindDataProp(P, PropInfo) then
      case PropInfo^.PropType^.Kind of
        tkString,
        tkLString: SetStrProp(P, PropInfo,
          ReadStr(P.Name, GetStrProp(P,PropInfo)));
        tkInteger: SetOrdProp(P, PropInfo,
          ReadInt(P.Name, GetOrdProp(P,PropInfo)));
        tkEnumeration: SetOrdProp(P, PropInfo,
          GetEnumValue(PropInfo^.PropType,
            ReadStr(P.Name,
              GetEnumName(PropInfo^.PropType,
                GetOrdProp(P,PropInfo)))));
      end;
  end;
end;

procedure TDataFiler.SaveData(Instance: TComponent);
var
  X: Integer;
  P: TComponent;
  PropInfo: PPropInfo;
begin
  for X := 0 to Instance.ComponentCount-1 do
  begin
    P := Instance.Components[x];
    if (Length(P.Name) > 0) and FindDataProp(P, PropInfo) then
      case PropInfo^.PropType^.Kind of
        tkString,
        tkLString: WriteStr(P.Name, GetStrProp(P,PropInfo));
        tkInteger: WriteInt(P.Name, GetOrdProp(P,PropInfo));
        tkEnumeration: WriteStr(P.Name,
          GetEnumName(PropInfo^.PropType,
            GetOrdProp(P,PropInfo)));
      end;
  end;
end;
```

> **Note**
> Incidentally, this USERDATA unit was originally developed in Delphi 1.0. In upgrading it to 32-bit Delphi 2.0, it made sense to add registry support since that's where 32-bit Windows applications are supposed to store user preferences and program options (for small amounts of data, less than a few kilobytes). All that was needed to add registry support was to add the LoadDataFromRegistry and SaveDataToRegistry procedures, declare a new TDataRegistryFiler descendant of TDataFiler, and implement its WriteStr and ReadStr methods to write the data to the registry using the standard TRegINIFile class—well, that and the normal code grooming that seems obligatory when dusting off code you haven't looked at in 18 months. (If the Surgeon General were a programmer, code grooming would be listed as obsessive-compulsive behavior. Know your neurosis!)

For each component owned by the passed-in component, the TDataFiler.LoadData and SaveData methods check to see that the component has a name and that its class name is in the list of registered class/property names. They fetch the property's PropInfo and handle the property data using TypInfo's RTTI utility routines. Notice that for enumerated type properties, the enum identifier is stored instead of its ordinal value to make the stored (editable) data more readable. Note that only string, integer, and enumerated types are supported in this code. Support for other data types can be added when the need arises. (In other words, it's left as an exercise for the reader.)

The Application

RTTI2 is a sample application that uses this new USERDATA unit to store the contents of a nontrivial Sandwich Preferences dialog (see Figure 5.1). The main form of the application is just a button that calls an Execute method of the preferences dialog (see Listing 5.7).

Listing 5.7 This Execute method stores the form's user data in the system registry.

```
const
  AppRegPath = '\Software\Delphi Component Design\RTTI2';

procedure TSandwichPrefs.Execute;
begin
  LoadDataFromRegistry(Self, AppRegPath);
  if ShowModal = mrOk then
    SaveDataToRegistry(Self, AppRegPath);
end;
```

RUN-TIME TYPE INFORMATION

Figure 5.1 The RTTI2 sample application's Sandwich Preferences dialog. (Must be lunchtime.)

The Execute method loads the stored user data (if any) from the HKEY_CURRENT_USER section of the registry, under the path \Software\Delphi Component Design\RTTI2. It then displays the form as a modal dialog and, if the user closes it by clicking the OK button, stores the form's user data back to the registry. The registry entries written by the app are shown in Figure 5.2.

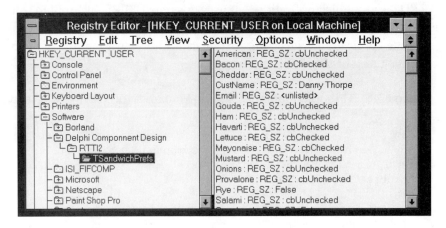

Figure 5.2 The registry entries created by the RTTI2 sample app.

The complete source code for the RTTI2 project, its Sandwich Preferences form, and the USERDATA unit can be found on the CD-ROM that accompanies this book.

Summary

Here are the RTTI rules of thumb covered in this chapter:

- Remember that published property names, class names, and other identifiers (elements of enumerations and sets) will be readable in your EXE file by snoopers with hex-dump utilities.

- Don't use RTTI for strings displayed in the user interface. User interface display strings should be tailored to the user's frame of reference and native language, which RTTI can't do.

- When using TypInfo routines, plan for change. Isolate the code that uses TypInfo so that it will be easier to update if/when TypInfo changes in future versions of Delphi.

- Use the TypInfo routines to navigate the RTTI structures instead of crawling the RTTI structures directly. The RTTI structures sketched by TypInfo are more likely to change in the future than the access routines defined in TypInfo.

- Be careful of defeating the smart linker. Accessing the RTTI of a property or class using a class reference (like TMyClass.ClassInfo) touches the class type and VMT. As explained in Chapter 3, touching the class type forces the linker to link in all the associated code even if that class is never directly used or instantiated in the program.

Chapter 6

Streaming

S*treaming* is a generic term for the process of writing an object's state to a stream, or restoring an object's state from a stream. A stream is an abstraction of primarily sequential data storage, such as a file on disk, a resizable chunk of memory, or a blob in a database. Historically, streaming an object's internal data has been a tedious, manual, and error-prone process in virtually all development tools. A programmer had to write code to write the object's data to the stream and write code to read the object's data from the stream (in the same order and format as they were written), plus write code to register the object type with the streaming system so that the object could be created when its signature was encountered in a stream. As much as a third to one-half of the entire implementation of many objects was devoted solely to storing and loading the object's state.

Delphi's property-based streaming system automatically handles almost all component data storage needs with no programmer intervention. Delphi's streaming system is the result of a unique synergy between the compiler and core VCL classes that makes Delphi's visual design-time environment and Object Inspector possible. This chapter explains how the Delphi streaming system handles 95% of your component's data needs automatically, and it explores the programming opportunities available to you should you ever need to venture into that last 5% in your own components.

Property-Based Streaming

In Delphi's Object Pascal language, properties are a language representation of data owned or managed by a class. Almost all the data exposed by a class is exposed with properties. Storing the current state of an object instance is primarily a matter of capturing the data it contains. Property-based streaming is the union of these two concepts: If all the data of an object is in its properties, you can capture the state of the object by capturing the data of its properties.

STREAMING

The property declarations in your class types provide a great deal of information to the compiler about how the data the property represents can be manipulated—how to read it, how to write it, and so on. If a property's data can be taken at face value, you can declare the property to read directly from an internal data field. If the property's data is synthesized or depends upon other internal state information, you can declare the property to fetch its data through a call to an internal function. Whenever any code reads from that property, it will wind up calling your internal function to obtain the actual data. So, if you know about the properties of a class, you can manipulate the class's simple data and its not-so-simple data.

For published properties, the Delphi compiler reduces all this information down to Run-Time Type Information (RTTI) structures in the compiled program. As we saw in Chapter 5, RTTI allows generic routines in the running program to find out what published properties exist in any class, their data types, and how to access that data. With RTTI, you have the information you need to capture the data of an object, and with that data you have persistent object storage. VCL's streaming classes are the generic routines that make Delphi's persistent object storage automatic for almost all classes and data needs.

Self-Descriptive Data

Property values written to a stream are not just dumped to disk willy-nilly. If all that were written for each property was its data, a generic routine would have a hard time figuring out where one property's data ends and another's begins and validating the data as it is read in. Instead, Delphi's streaming system tags each property data value in the stream with a data type indicator and the name of the property identifier. With this information embedded in the data stream, generic routines can traverse the stream recognizing the data type, data size, and property name of each property data value in the stream, without knowing anything about the class type those data values are for.

Writing the name of every property does use more disk space than writing a pure binary stream of non-delimited data values, but the benefits of automatic data validation, people-readable descriptive error messages, and stream internal consistency checks far outweigh the cost of a little more disk space.

Storing Property Deltas

Delphi's streaming system does not write all the published properties of an object to the stream. Delphi objects are assumed to have a consistent initial state when constructed. The streaming system constructs object instances before setting their property values from stream data. Since the object (and its data) starts out in a known default state, all you really need from the stream is the property data that is *different* from the object's default state. Delphi's streaming system only writes property values that are different from their default value, as indicated by the `default` directive in the property declaration. This greatly reduces the size of a typical object's stream image and more than makes up for the stream space added by the self-descriptive data tags.

Thus, an object's stream image is not a binary snapshot of the object's internal state. Delphi streams are a set of property assignment instructions to change an object from its default state to its state at the time it was written to the stream. Delphi streams store property deltas, not binary snapshots.

Property Deltas and Visual Form Inheritance

Storing only properties whose values are different from their defaults was a nifty way to reduce the stream size and improve streaming performance in Delphi 1.0. In Delphi 2.0, property deltas are critical to the operation of visual form inheritance—building a form that inherits compile-time code and design-time configuration data from an ancestor form. When writing such a form and its components to a stream, property values are compared, not to the form's own declared default property values, but to the property values of its ancestor form. The ancestor form determines the descendant form's initial state, so all that needs to be written to the stream is how the descendant form's properties differ from the ancestor's properties.

When a form is written to a stream, its ancestor form's data is written first, followed by any data in the form itself that differs from its ancestor. When reading, the ancestor form is created and its properties loaded first, the descendant form is created, the ancestor property values are copied to the descendant, and, finally, the properties of the descendant form that differ from the ancestor are read from the stream. This property difference analysis applies to the properties of the ancestor and descendant forms as well as to all components in the ancestor and descendant forms.

This means that efficient streaming is no longer just a nifty option, as it was in Delphi 1.0. If you write your own custom data to the stream, you are responsible for comparing your component's data with that of the form inheritance ancestor and writing only the parts that are different. If you do not, your component cannot fully participate in the interactive powers of visual form inheritance. If your component is dropped into an ancestor form, it will be replicated in descendants of that form, just like any other component. However, if your component doesn't do its part to reduce its stream image to the absolute minimum, the replicated descendant component instances will disconnect from the ancestor instance and will not reflect changes made to the ancestor instance's properties. This is not an issue for normal published properties, only for custom properties for which you implement your own streaming support.

Component Ownership and Parentage

Components created by the streaming system will have their Owner and Parent properties set to the stream's current Owner and Parent property values. The nested scopes of the stream file format reflect the visual containment relationships between controls: The inner component's Parent property will be set to point to the component its property data is nested inside of in the stream. The owner of components created from a stream is assumed to be the root component, which is usually the form. This ownership assumption can be altered, but only with code. Ownership of controls cannot be expressed in the stream data. For a button in a panel in a form, the button's parent is the panel and its owner is the form.

A component that owns internal aggregate components will probably need to enlist some special streaming support to temporarily change the stream's notion of component owner to itself while loading its internal aggregates from the stream. TNotebook is an example: The pages of the notebook are components owned by the notebook control, but the components in the pages should be owned by the form. We'll see exactly how TNotebook does this later in this chapter.

Sibling Pointers and Other Cross-Links

Component-type properties that refer to other components owned by the same form are called *sibling pointers*. For example, TDataSource components are usually connected to TTable or TQuery components. Properties that refer to components in other forms are called *cross-links*. If you establish a cross-link using IDE design-time tools, for example, by connecting a TDataSource in Form1 to a TTable in Form2, then you're using visual form linking (and marketing buzzwords). The streaming system stores such properties by writing the referenced component's name to the stream. The referenced component is not written to the stream just by the act of reference.

When the streaming system reads a component reference property, the referenced component may not yet exist if it was written after the component that referenced it. The referenced component may not exist at all if it was not written in the same streaming operation as the referencing component. The streaming system creates a fixup record to note which property contains a reference to which component name and then proceeds with reading the rest of the current component's properties.

After all the components described by the stream have been created and their properties loaded, the streaming system tries to resolve all the fixup records that were created along the way. If a referenced component is not found in the set of components loaded in this stream operation, the referring property is set to `nil`. Otherwise, the referring property is set to point to the component whose name matches the fixup reference. The property's value is undefined (`nil`, usually) until after the streaming system performs this fixup pass. The first point at which the property's value is usable is in the component's Loaded method. References to other components are preserved across streaming only if both ends of the reference are streamed at the same time.

The Tools of Streaming

Writing a component to a stream requires the cooperation of three objects: a stream, a filer, and, of course, a component. Thanks to utility routines like the Classes unit's global WriteComponentResFile procedure, you don't have to get directly involved with all three objects, but all three are present in all component streaming operations whether you create the parts or a utility routine creates them for you.

TStream is an abstract class that represents file I/O in a very generic sense—Read, Write, and Seek. Descendants of TStream implement this generic I/O interface for specific storage systems: TFileStream handles disk files; THandleStream manages Win32 generic file handles (which may be handles to nondisk files such as named pipes); TMemoryStream and TResourceStream read and write blocks of system memory; and TBlobStream reads and writes data in database blobs. Streams handle the movement of data, but they do not have any knowledge of the data they move.

TFiler is an abstract class that is the root of the VCL streaming system. TFiler defines an abstract interface that components can use to define their own custom property data. TFiler does not define any data read or write capabilities. The real muscle of VCL's streaming system is split between TFiler's descendants, TReader and TWriter. VCL uses two classes for streaming to keep each part of the system as clean and focused as possible and to reduce the size of the compiled code. Almost all Delphi applications will need to read components from streams, but relatively few Delphi apps ever need to write components to streams. Writing component property data also requires more work (and more code) than reading property data, so spinning off the writing logic into a separate TWriter class shaves more than 15K of machine code off most Delphi apps.

TWriter contains all the intelligence required to write the published properties of any component to a stream and support routines for components to use to write custom property data if necessary. TWriter performs differential data analysis on published properties against their declared default values or against the corresponding property values in an ancestor instance, if one is present.

TReader is responsible for decoding the stream data to locate class types named in the stream, create component instances, read stream data into component properties, and deal with loading inherited forms and their descendants.

So much for the overview. Let's get down to the brass tacks.

Writing to the Stream with TWriter

The process by which VCL writes properties and components to a stream has many steps, but they are fairly easy to follow once you understand the roles of the participants. In this section, we'll examine the steps in the process of writing components to the stream.

Initiating Output

There are a number of ways to fire up the streaming system to write out a component, depending on where you want the output to go and how lazy you are.

WriteComponentResFile

WriteComponentResFile is the simplest way to write a component. You give it a file name and a component instance, and it takes care of creating a stream, creating a writer, writing the component, and arranging the stream data in a Windows resource (RES) file format, just like a DFM file.

TStream.WriteComponent and WriteComponentRes

If you want more control over the creation of the file or you want to write the component into memory or into a database blob, you can create an instance of a stream yourself and use it to write the component. The TStream class offers two ways to write a component: TStream.WriteComponentRes and TStream.WriteComponent.

TStream.WriteDescendent and WriteDescendentRes

TStream.WriteDescendent [sic] and TStream.WriteDescendentRes are lower-level routines that take a component instance and an ancestor instance as parameters. WriteComponent and WriteComponentRes pass their component instance parameter and a `nil` ancestor pointer to their respective WriteDescendent routines to do the actual work of streaming. When an ancestor instance is available, the streaming system compares the component's property values against the corresponding ancestor instance's property values to decide whether to write the component's property values to the stream. The Delphi IDE uses these WriteDescendent routines to write visually inherited forms to disk. It's unlikely you will ever call these routines directly.

TStream.WriteDescendentRes writes a Windows RES file header to the stream and then calls WriteDescendent. The resource header makes the file a valid resource file that can then be linked into a project's EXE or DLL module. TStream.WriteDescendent creates an instance of TWriter and calls TWriter.WriteDescendent.

Even though the TWriter class contains WriteComponent and WriteDescendent methods, you should never call these to initiate streaming of a component. These routines should only be used within the context of a streaming operation already in progress. It's unlikely that you'll ever create an instance of TWriter in your own Delphi applications or components.

TWriter.WriteDescendent

TWriter.WriteDescendent makes note of the passed-in ancestor (if any) and component. The writer assigns the component to its Root property and assigns the ancestor to its RootAncestor property. We'll see what these properties are used for in a minute.

TWriter writes a Delphi stream signature value to the stream and then calls TWriter.WriteComponent. At this point, the VCL streaming system is set up and on a roll.

TWriter.WriteComponent

TWriter.WriteComponent is the first routine in the streaming sequence so far that is called recursively for each child component that exists inside the root component. Everything before this has been stream setup and once-only headers.

TWriter.WriteComponent sets the csWriting flag in the current component instance's ComponentState property. If the current component is a child component, TWriter.WriteComponent locates the corresponding child in the root ancestor (if any) and assigns that child to the writer's Ancestor property. The writer's Ancestor property refers to the component instance in the ancestor form (in visual form inheritance) that corresponds to the component instance currently being streamed. For example, if Form1 contains a Button1 component, and Form2 visually inherits from Form1 (inheriting its own instance of Button1), then while the writer is writing the properties of Form2's Button1 instance to the stream, the writer's Ancestor property will point to Form1's Button1 instance. TWriter.Ancestor is `nil` for components that are added to a descendant form. TWriter.WriteComponent then calls the component's WriteState method.

TComponent.WriteState

TComponent.WriteState is a virtual method that the streaming system calls to allow the component an opportunity to prepare itself for streaming, such as to consolidate memory structures for more efficient streaming. When your component has made its preparations, it should call its inherited WriteState method, which will trickle up to TComponent.WriteState, which sends execution back into the writer with a call to Writer.WriteData(Self).

TComponent.WriteState is your component's first opportunity to actively participate in the streaming process. However, it's unlikely that you will ever override TComponent.WriteState. Only one component (TDBGrid) overrides WriteState out of the 100+ standard Delphi components and 100,000 lines of VCL and Delphi IDE source code.

Skipping Inherited Calls

If you find it necessary to call Writer.WriteData yourself to avoid some behavior in your inherited WriteState, you should review your choice of ancestor. While it is certainly valid to override a virtual method and not call the inherited routine, that is usually done only when the virtual method is a "leaf node" of the call tree and responsible for providing a single service that is intended (by the author of the ancestor class) to be completely replaced by descendants. TComponent.WriteState is not a leaf node; it is the middle step in a chain of operations. Short-circuiting the chain by not calling the inherited method and then duplicating parts of the inherited implementation (by calling Writer.WriteData yourself) undermine your code's long-term viability. If future implementations of the inherited method change to support new features, your component cannot share in those new features if you skip the inherited method. If the ancestor's new features are required for proper operation in the updated streaming system, your shortcutting components won't work at all.

TWriter.WriteData

TWriter.WriteData is where the real work begins. WriteData starts out by writing a tag indicating whether the component uses inherited data or just streams normally, followed by the component's class name (ClassName) and instance name (Name property).

WriteData then writes the component's properties to the stream using TypInfo routines to access the RTTI for the component's published properties. If the TWriter.Ancestor property is not `nil`, each component property is compared to the corresponding ancestor instance's property and written to the stream only if the values differ. If the component has no corresponding ancestor—because it is new in the descendant form or because the root component (form) is not the product of visual form inheritance—TWriter.WriteData writes the component's property values to the stream if they differ from the default property values declared in the component's class declaration.

Property data in a stream exists as a pair of values: the string name of the property and the type-tagged data value of the property. A type-tagged data value is a byte that describes the type and size of the following data and the data itself. (See the TValueType enumeration in classes.pas in your VCL source code directory.) Note that the process of writing properties requires calling the read methods of the component's published properties. If your read methods do strange and perilous things, like incrementing an internal counter or pointer each time the property is accessed, you may have to add code to the read method to test for csWriting in the component's ComponentState. Of course, getting rid of the strange and perilous behavior would resolve this streaming issue, too.

Writing Class-Type Properties

When TWriter encounters a published property whose type is a class, how it handles that property depends upon the class type of the object instance the property refers to, not the type of the property declaration itself. If the referenced instance's class type is not a descendant of TPersistent, nothing is written to the stream. Only TPersistent classes can be streamed in published class-type properties.

If the referenced instance is a TComponent, TWriter writes the component's name as the property value. This is the sibling or cross-reference pointer mentioned earlier in this chapter. If the referenced component is owned by a different form than the component currently being streamed, the name reference written to the stream includes the name of the other form, followed by a period, followed by the name of the component.

If the referenced instance is a TCollection, TWriter writes the contents of the collection as a list of item blocks. Each item in the collection is written like a TPersistent class, described next. The main difference is that collection items are not individually named; they are streamed as a delimited list of property groups, one group per collection item.

If the referenced instance is a TPersistent descendant but is not a TComponent or TCollection, the writer writes the instance's published properties to the stream. The names of the properties are prepended with the current property name, so nested properties of a component's TitleFont property would be identified in the stream as TitleFont.Size, TitleFont.Style, and so on.

TPersistent.DefineProperties

After all the published properties of an object instance have been written to the stream, the writer calls the instance's DefineProperties method. DefineProperties is a virtual method introduced in TPersistent. TPersistent classes can override DefineProperties to register stream read and write routines for "hidden" properties—properties that appear in the stream but that do not appear in the Object Inspector at design time. DefineProperties applies to TComponents as well as lightweight TPersistent utility classes.

In the sequence of streaming operations, the DefineProperties method is a component's second opportunity to actively participate in the streaming process.

> **Define Properties Example 1: Nonvisual Components' Top and Left**
>
> Nonvisual components, such as TTable or TOpenFileDialog, have hidden Top and Left properties inherited from TComponent. Since nonvisual components have no visual representation, it would be strange to publish Top and Left properties that could be edited in the Object Inspector or modified at run time. However, you do want to record the screen position of the design-time icon of the component so that nonvisual components will stay where you put them when you open and close forms at design time. The solution has two parts: TComponent overrides DefineProperties to read and write hidden Top and Left properties in the stream, and a component designer built to manage nonvisual components at design time pokes the location of the design-time component icon into the component's DesignInterface property. DesignInterface is a public (not published) property of TComponent that is used only by the nonvisual component designer at design time.

TFiler.DefineProperty

Inside your component's DefineProperties method, you can define a hidden property by calling Filer.DefineProperty. As the plural implies, your DefineProperties method can define multiple hidden properties by calling Filer.DefineProperty multiple times, once for each property. Both the component reading and component writing processes call DefineProperties, so the type of DefineProperties' Filer parameter is TFiler, the common ancestor of TReader and TWriter. The declaration of TFiler.DefineProperty is as follows:

```
procedure DefineProperty(const Name: string;
     ReadData: TReaderProc; WriteData: TWriterProc;
     HasData: Boolean);
```

To call TFiler.DefineProperty, your component passes a pointer to a read method, a pointer to a write method, and an indication of whether the property data needs to be written. If the filer is actually a TReader, it will call the ReadData method pointer you provide to read the property's data. If the filer is actually a TWriter, it will call the WriteData method pointer you provide, if HasData is True. The ReadData or WriteData method pointer can be `nil`. If you want your hidden property to be write-only, for example, you can leave ReadData `nil`. A read-only hidden property isn't particularly useful because the only way the hidden data could get into the stream to begin with is if your component wrote it with a WriteData method. If you don't write it, you have nothing to read.

In the methods you pass to TFiler.DefineProperty, you can call filer methods to retrieve the actual data from the stream. The TWriterProc method type receives a TWriter as a parameter, so you can call writer methods such as WriteInteger or WriteString in your hidden property's WriteData method. If the data you need to write does not fit well into the simple types supported by the writer's type-tagged data, you should use TFiler.DefineBinaryProperty instead of TFiler.DefineProperty to register your hidden property so that you can dump your hidden data as a single binary blob. TFiler.DefineBinaryProperty is discussed in the next section.

DefineProperties Example 2: TStrings. TStrings needs to store its internal list of strings in the stream. TStrings overrides DefineProperties to specify read and write methods for its string list, as shown in Listing 6.1.

Listing 6.1 TStrings overrides DefineProperties to store its list of strings on the stream.

```
procedure TStrings.ReadData(Reader: TReader);
begin
  Reader.ReadListBegin;
  Clear;
  while not Reader.EndOfList do Add(Reader.ReadString);
  Reader.ReadListEnd;
end;

procedure TStrings.WriteData(Writer: TWriter);
var
  I: Integer;
begin
  Writer.WriteListBegin;
  for I := 0 to Count - 1 do Writer.WriteString(Get(I));
  Writer.WriteListEnd;
end;

procedure TStrings.DefineProperties(Filer: TFiler);

  function DoWrite: Boolean;
  begin
    if Filer.Ancestor <> nil then
    begin
      Result := True;
      if Filer.Ancestor is TStrings then
        Result := not Equals(TStrings(Filer.Ancestor))
    end
    else Result := Count > 0;
  end;

begin
  Filer.DefineProperty('Strings', ReadData, WriteData, DoWrite);
end;
```

Notice first the DoWrite local function in Listing 6.1. If an ancestor instance is present, the TStrings object compares its string list contents to that of the ancestor. If there are any differences, DoWrite returns True, and the hidden Strings property needs to write its data. If there is no ancestor, DoWrite returns True if there are any strings in the list at all.

Comparing Property Data to Ancestor

This example illustrates a major difference between streaming in Delphi 1.0 and Delphi 2.0. As mentioned earlier, visual form inheritance and propagation of changes made in ancestor properties to descendants depend upon properties writing the absolute minimum amount of data by comparing their values to their ancestor values. For normal published properties, VCL takes care of these new chores for you. For defined hidden properties, though, it is entirely up to you to perform the ancestor value comparisons and to write as little data as possible. If you fail to do this, your component will not fully participate in visual form inheritance's dynamic updates—changes made to your property in a component in a visual form inheritance ancestor form will not propagate to the corresponding component(s) in descendant form(s). When you pass False to the HasData parameter of TFiler.DefineProperty, the streaming system knows that the descendant property data is identical to the ancestor, so changes to the ancestor property should be applied to that descendant.

Any 16-bit Delphi 1.0 component you port to 32-bit Delphi 2.0 that defines hidden properties by overriding DefineProperties will need to add ancestor checking to its HasData checks.

TStrings.WriteData is the method TStrings.DefineProperties passes as the WriteData parameter in the call to Filer.DefineProperty. TStrings.WriteData writes a begin-list token (Writer.WriteListBegin), then writes each of the strings in its list (Writer.WriteString), and concludes by writing an end-of-list token (Writer.WriteListEnd). The begin and end markers help the streaming system recognize groups of related data and treat them as a single entity. Writing the data using the type-tagging methods of TWriter enables the VCL stream-to-text converter, ObjectBinaryToText, to recognize the data values and display them in an appropriate text representation.

Accommodating Manual Editing of Stream Data

Since streams can be converted to text and edited by application programmers, you should avoid writing interdependent data to the stream. For example, you might be tempted to write the count of items in a list before writing the list, perhaps to make it easier to read the list later. Notice that the string list never writes the number of items in the string list; it only writes the items themselves. The reason is simple: The stream data can be edited by the application writer, and it's very likely that items would be added or deleted from the list without also updating the count. The solution is to avoid writing the count at all and simply read string values until an end-of-list marker is encountered. What little you lose by this in read optimizations you gain in flexibility.

TFiler.DefineBinaryProperty

When your property data is not easily broken down into discrete fields, you can dump the property data to the stream as an amorphous binary blob. You set this up by calling Filer.DefineBinaryProperty in your component's DefineProperties method. The rules of use are the same as for Filer.DefineProperty. The only difference is that the read and write methods receive a stream object as a parameter instead of a reader or writer. In a write method, your component dumps its binary data into this stream object, and VCL will then copy that stream data to the actual component stream. In a read method, VCL passes you a stream that contains all of your blob data.

Avoid using binary properties except when absolutely necessary. The text representation of binary data is a hexadecimal data stream, which is extremely difficult to browse or edit. Bitmap images are an example of binary properties.

TComponent.GetChildren

Once the writer writes all the published properties and hidden defined properties of the current component, execution returns to TWriter.WriteData. WriteData's next step is to locate all the children of the current component and write each of them to the stream. WriteData does this by calling the TComponent.GetChildren virtual method. GetChildren's only parameter is a callback method that GetChildren is supposed to call for each child component that should be streamed. Your component can override GetChildren to filter out child components you don't want to appear in the stream, for example.

The notion of hierarchical containment supported by the VCL streaming system corresponds to the visual containment indicated by the Parent property of VCL controls. Across the board, VCL controls have only two notions of containment: Owner and Parent. Since the VCL streaming system assumes all components recorded in a stream are owned by the stream's root component (unless you specify otherwise—we'll get to that in the TReader section), all the streaming system has to keep track of is the visual containment of controls in the stream. This also makes the text representation of the component stream more intuitive: For a button inside a panel inside a form, the text representation of that form's stream image will show a button nested inside a panel nested inside a form.

Note that we're talking about Parent properties of *controls* through all this. TComponent doesn't know about visual things like Parent relationships. The Parent property is introduced by the TControl class, the first class in the VCL hierarchy to support on-screen representations. When writing a TComponent (not derived from

TControl), the writer calls TComponent.GetChildren, but TComponent.GetChildren doesn't do anything. A nonvisual TComponent that owns child components will not write those owned components when it is written to the stream. TWinControl overrides GetChildren to return all the controls in its Controls list. GetChildren was defined in TComponent primarily to avoid having to make the streaming system aware of TWinControl. You could use this GetChildren virtual method to define your own containership scheme (not based on visual controls and Parent relationships) for your own nonvisual component.

In cases of visual form inheritance, GetChildren serves a dual purpose. TWriter calls GetChildren of the ancestor instance first, passing it a pointer to an internal TWriter method that notes (but does not write to the stream) the child objects returned by the ancestor instance. TWriter then calls GetChildren on the current component instance, passing TWriter.WriteComponent as the method pointer parameter. TWriter.WriteData calls your component's GetChildren method, which calls the method pointer parameter for each child, which actually calls TWriter.WriteComponent for each child. The writer calls GetChildren on the current and ancestor components so that the writer can figure out which children in the current component are new and which are inherited.

In visual form inheritance, after TWriter.WriteData has gone through all the current component's properties and all the current component's child components (and their children, recursively), it checks to see whether anything was actually written to the stream. If no property data or child component data was written, WriteData backs out the flags, class name, and component name it wrote to the stream for the current component instance. If a component instance is identical to its ancestor instance properties and children, nothing is written to the stream at all.

> **Porting 16-Bit Code That Uses Write-Components**
>
> In Delphi 1.0, TWriter.WriteData called a TComponent.WriteComponents virtual method of the current component. You could override WriteComponents to pick which child components you wanted to have streamed and could call Writer.WriteComponent for each child directly. TComponent.WriteComponents was removed in Delphi 2.0 and replaced with the more versatile TComponent.GetChildren, primarily to support visual form inheritance and associated ancestor instance property deltas. To port a Delphi 1.0 component that overrides WriteComponents to Delphi 2.0, rename your component's WriteComponents override method to GetChildren, change the parameter lists accordingly, and in the body of the method call the Proc method pointer parameter for each child component instead of calling Writer.WriteComponent.

TWriter Shutdown

TWriter.WriteData returns to your component's WriteState method, which returns to TWriter.WriteComponent. WriteComponent clears the csWriting flag from the current instance's ComponentState property and then returns to whatever called WriteComponent (TWriter.WriteDescendent or the parent component's GetChildren). This marks the end of writing a component and its children to a stream.

Reading from the Stream with TReader

The process of reading components from a stream is largely a mirror image of the writing process. Reading has a few extra steps to allow components to reconstruct their complete state from the minimal information stored on the stream.

Starting the Read Process

You can load a component from a stream by calling the stand-alone functions ReadComponentResFile or ReadComponentRes or by calling the TStream functions ReadComponent or ReadComponentRes. Use ReadComponentResFile to load a component from a named file on disk. Use ReadComponentRes to load a component from a resource linked into the EXE or DLL module. Use the TStream methods to read a component from an arbitrary stream you opened yourself. TStream.ReadComponentRes expects a Windows RES file header at the start of the stream; TStream.ReadComponent does not.

Note that all the read routines take an Instance parameter and their function result is also an instance. If you pass `nil` to the Instance parameter, the stream reader will create an instance of whatever class it finds in the stream data and then will set the instance's properties according to the data in the stream. If you pass an object instance to the Instance parameter, the stream reader sets the instance's properties according to the data in the stream. You will almost always pass `nil` in the Instance parameter to let the streaming system create the appropriate object instance from scratch.

TStream.ReadComponent

After taking care of busywork such as opening streams, skipping over resource headers, and so forth, each of those ReadComponentxyz routines winds up calling TStream.ReadComponent. TStream.ReadComponent creates an instance of TReader and calls TReader.ReadRootComponent. As with TWriter, you should never need to create an instance of TReader yourself.

TReader.ReadRootComponent

TReader.ReadRootComponent is responsible for setting up the entire component-loading process. ReadRootComponent reads a VCL stream signature (4 bytes), a set of flags indicating form inheritance options, and a component class name.

If the Instance parameter is `nil`, the reader looks up the class name in an internal list of self-registered root classes (forms, usually) and creates an instance of that class using a class reference variable stored with the class name in the internal list of classes. The reader then reads the component's name from the stream.

Note that the component doesn't know it is being created as part of a streaming process. The component's constructor initializes its instance data in a void, oblivious to whether it is being created by the stream reader or by your button click code. After the component is constructed, the streaming system assigns stream data to the component's properties. This is quite different from previous object streaming systems, where objects had special constructors devoted solely to constructing the instance and initializing the instance data from the stream at the same time. Delphi uses only one constructor to create instances for any purpose. The downside to this is that properties may be assigned twice (once in the constructor and again by the stream reader), but the upside is that component writers don't have to worry about it.

If the Instance parameter is not `nil`, the reader ignores the class name it read from the stream. The reader reads the component name from the stream and checks it for uniqueness among the global components (forms, usually) of the application. If necessary, the reader alters the name (by appending an underscore and a number) to make it unique.

ReadRootComponent assigns the component instance to the reader's Root property and sets the csLoading and csReading flags in the component's ComponentState property. The reader then calls the component's ReadState method.

TComponent.ReadState

ReadState is a virtual method defined in TComponent that exists for the same reason as TComponent.WriteState: It allows the component an opportunity to participate in the streaming process. The reader calls a component's ReadState method before assigning any stream data to the component's properties (other than Name). ReadState is the first point at which your component knows its properties are about to be replaced with data from a stream. TComponent.ReadState simply calls Reader.ReadData.

TReader.ReadData

TReader.ReadData creates a temporary fixup list, where references to sibling objects are noted while the components are in the process of loading. Once all the components are loaded, the reader replaces the fixups with pointers to the actual sibling objects or `nil` if the referenced object doesn't exist. The fixup list eliminates problems associated with order of component creation and circular references by resolving cross-references after all the child components have been loaded.

Reading Properties

Next, the reader reads the property values for the current component from the stream. The reader reverses the data conversions performed by the writer, converting identifiers of enumerated or set types into ordinal values, reading integers, strings, floats, and so forth, and reading data into the properties of TPersistent class properties, such as Font properties. Data for defined properties can be mixed in with published properties. Just because TWriter writes defined properties after published properties doesn't prevent the application writer from moving things around while editing a form as text.

For properties that refer to TComponent types, the reader reads the name of the referenced component from the stream and adds a fixup record to the reader's fixup list. For collection properties, the reader repeatedly adds a new collection item and reads its properties from the stream until it finds an end-of-list marker. Remember, the TCollection class already knows what type of collection item it can create, so the reader has only to call Collection.Add to make a new item.

For event properties, the reader reads a method name from the stream and looks up that name in the root component's RTTI to get a code address to store in the property's method pointer. The root instance is also stored in the property's method pointer (method pointers always have two parts: a code pointer and an instance pointer). Event properties always refer to methods of the reader's root component.

> **Note**
>
> Since you can change the reader's root property in midstream, it is technically possible to make streamable event properties refer to published methods of something other than the form. This practice is not recommended unless the class whose event properties you are setting is a helper class completely hidden inside your component implementation. Components should not manipulate event properties that application writers have access to.

Reading Components

After reading the property values for the current component, TReader.ReadData prepares to create and read the child components (if any) of the current component. First, the reader saves the current values of its Parent and Owner properties and calls the current component's GetChildParent and GetChildOwner virtual methods to get new values for these properties, respectively. These methods allow the current component to control the ownership and visual container of its child components. TComponent.GetChildParent returns Self, and TComponent.GetChildOwner returns `nil`. If the current component's GetChildOwner method returns `nil`, the reader assigns Root to Owner.

This arrangement covers the child-containment needs of more than 98% of Delphi components. The other 2% are components like TNotebook that contain internal helper objects owned by the component instead of the form. TNotebook overrides its GetChildOwner method to return Self so that the notebook page controls will have the notebook as their owner. Notebook pages retain the default TComponent.GetChildOwner implementation, so when reading a notebook page, the reader's Owner property reverts to the root component (the form), making all the components on the notebook page owned by the form and parented (visually contained) by the notebook page. VCL's stream reader gravitates toward having the form own all components created from the stream—you have to work to make the reader create components with a different owner, but you don't have to do anything to return to the norm.

TReader.ReadData calls TReader.ReadComponent to create each child object indicated by the stream data. ReadComponent performs the same steps as ReadRootComponent, but the reader calls ReadComponent recursively for each nested level of child objects. ReadRootComponent is called only once.

Winding Down the Read Process

Once the reader has streamed in all the children of the current component instance and all their property values, the reader resolves any outstanding fixup references, restores the original values of its Owner and Parent properties and returns to TComponent.ReadState. After all the children of the root component have been read in, the reader calls each component's Loaded method. Loaded is a virtual method defined in TComponent, and it is the first opportunity your component has to collect itself after its properties have been streamed in. Loaded is also the first point at which a component can safely use properties that reference sibling components.

Converting Between Binary and Text

A lot of people like the Delphi IDE's ability to convert form files into editable text in an edit window. Most folks, though, don't realize how simple it is to convert a form file (binary component stream) back and forth between binary and text representations. This text conversion isn't new with Delphi 2.0, either. You can open form files as text in the Delphi 1.0 code editor simply by opening a form's DFM file instead of its PAS file (File: Open: foo.dfm). All Delphi 2.0 added to the mix was an Edit as Text menu item on the form designer's pop-up menu, which made the conversion feature more obvious and easier to access.

To convert a binary form into text in your own applications, you will need to prepare two streams: one that contains the binary stream input and one to receive the text stream output. Any kind of stream will do—files on disk, memory streams, or database blob streams. Just be sure to open the input stream for reading and to open the output stream for writing. If the binary stream has a RES file header (like a DFM file or a component you stored by calling TStream.WriteComponentRes), use ObjectResourceToText to convert the stream to text. If the binary stream is something you cooked up just moments ago with a call to TStream.WriteComponent, use ObjectBinaryToText to convert it to text.

The text stream output of these routines is neatly formatted with line breaks and two-space indents to indicate nested scopes. All you have to do to dump that text into a memo control, for example, is reset the stream position to zero and call Memo1.LoadFromStream.

To reverse the flow, use ObjectTextToBinary to produce a raw binary component stream or ObjectTextToResource to produce a binary component stream with a RES file header. Syntax errors or other user editing goofs will raise an exception.

> **When to Save in Resource File Format**
>
> If there is ever the possibility that the component stream you're writing will need to be linked into a project, you must write it as a resource file—TStream.WriteComponentRes. If you're only writing components to temporary internal memory streams, there's no need for the RES file header information, so just use TStream.WriteComponent. In general, if you're saving the component stream to a permanent file on disk, it's best to save it in resource file format.

Streaming Opportunities for Component Writers

Published Properties

Published properties are by far the easiest way to get persistent data storage and design-time editing support for data in your component. Always give published properties first priority in your component design. Record structures can usually be replaced with lightweight TPersistent helper classes to provide record-like access and still retain automatic streaming support. Array property data must be streamed using DefineProperties and cannot be edited with the Object Inspector at design time. You can use a component editor to build design-time editing tools for data held in defined properties, as we'll see in Chapter 13.

Default Value

The `default` directive in a published property declaration tells the streaming system what value the property has immediately after the component is constructed. The default value declaration does not affect the initialization of that property in the component's constructor—it's your responsibility to initialize the property to its correct initial value. When writing property values to a stream, TWriter compares a property's value to the property's declared default value. If the two are equal, TWriter does not write that property value to the stream.

In the absence of explicit assignments of initial values to properties in a component's constructor, all properties have an initial value of zero—an empty set for set properties, zero for integer, float, and enumerated type properties, `nil` for event properties, and empty string for string properties. Empty string is the only default value possible for string properties since you cannot declare a default value for string properties.

Stored Option

The `stored` directive in a published property declaration can take the value True (property is always written to stream) or False (property is never written to stream) or can refer to a Boolean function that will be called while streaming to determine whether the property's value should be written. If a property declaration contains a `stored` directive, the streaming system ignores any default value declared for the property. You can think of a property with no `stored` directive as having an implicit stored function associated with it that compares the property's current value to the property's declared default value.

The stored function is useful for sorting out interproperty dependencies within a component. For example, many components have a Font property and a ParentFont property. If ParentFont is True, the Font property reflects the Font property settings of the component's parent. If you modify the Font property, ParentFont changes to False. Assigning True to ParentFont discards your font settings and restores the Font property to match the parent's Font property.

In streaming this pair of properties, you can imagine a host of catch-22 situations. There's no problem writing both the Font and ParentFont properties to the stream, but when you read them back in, one will defeat the other. If you read in the Font property first, that will modify the Font and set ParentFont to False. If you then read a value of True into ParentFont, it will discard changes made to the Font property.

The solution here is to make storage of the Font property conditional to the state of the ParentFont property by declaring a stored function on the Font property. If ParentFont is True, there is no need to store Font at all. If ParentFont is False, the Font property is independent and needs to be stored.

You can also use the `stored` directive to implement a published string property with a nonempty default value. Declare the property to use a stored function and have that function compare the actual property value to the initial value your constructor assigns to the string property.

Order of Streaming

Properties are streamed in the order they appear in the class declaration, starting with ancestor properties first. It's usually a point of source code style to alphabetize properties in a class declaration, and most of the time this has no effect on streaming. Interdependent component properties, though, can sometimes require a special order of assignment or output. Such order of assignment requirements are a hazard, though, since the application writer can easily move things around when editing a form as text.

DefineProperties

DefineProperties is your second largest opportunity to perform specialized data storage, after published properties. DefineProperties is most often used to store array property data or data that cannot be expressed in a simple type, such as bitmap pixel data. A less common use of DefineProperties is to store component data that you do not want to appear in the Object Inspector at design time. Note that this is not a security feature. Defined properties are completely visible and editable when viewing a form as text.

ReadState and WriteState

Your last and lowest-level opportunity to control how your component stores its data is to override the ReadState and/or WriteState methods inherited from TComponent. Overriding these methods is very rare—only two or three of the 100+ standard VCL components override ReadState (like TNotebook), and only one overrides WriteState (TDBGrid). In all cases, the overrides perform housekeeping chores in addition to calling the inherited method to perform the actual streaming. The page component used by TNotebook, for example, overrides ReadState to insert itself into TNotebook's internal list of pages after calling the inherited method. Do not abuse ReadState and WriteState to make your component store itself in a manner completely alien to VCL. Work with the system and use the supplied channels for customization—namely, published properties and defined properties.

Summary

The Delphi streaming system is the very heart of the entire Delphi programming model. The streaming system is the thread that connects the design-time environment, compiled program code, and extensible component architecture into a tightly integrated and powerful system.

Chapter 7

Messaging

Why should we care about message processing? Simple. Messages are your components' only connection to the outside world. Sure, you can call out to a bunch of Windows API functions, but when does your code get a chance to execute? In a Windows application, 99% of the code executes only in direct or indirect response to a message. Messages are your eyes and ears, your means to find out what's going on. The functions of the Windows API are simply your fingers, your means to make things happen. You can do a lot of component building without giving too much thought to how messages interact with your component, but understanding the flow of message information in your Delphi app will help you take maximum advantage of the built-in systems and help you avoid cutting off message circulation to vital parts of your application.

Message processing in Delphi can be rather conveniently divided into two domains: things that happen inside a window's window procedure and things that happen outside and leading up to the call to the window procedure. This chapter studies the path a message takes through a Delphi application, starting outside the application, moving into the application message loop (the outer domain), and working all the way through the Delphi message dispatch mechanisms (the inner domain). Along the way, we'll pick up tidbits on when to use messages instead of virtual methods, discover the three points at which you can intercept component messages, see how messages simplify interprocess and interthread communication and synchronization, and find out just exactly what a message really is.

Win32 Messaging

Microsoft Windows is an event-driven programming environment. *Event-driven* means that most of an application's behavior comes from responding to external events—notifications of user input with the keyboard or mouse or notifications from the system to redraw a portion of the application's screen area, for example. These notifications circulate in the form of messages. A message is a small data packet containing a message id number and up to 8 bytes of data whose format and meaning depend upon the message id.

Each Windows application has a message queue, a temporary holding area for messages posted to windows of the application. (Actually, each thread in an application can have its own message queue, but this is usually considered far too much trouble to bother with.) The operating system posts messages to the message queue to inform the application of user input events or system events that affect the application's windows. The application can retrieve the posted messages at its convenience some time later. The message queue is generally treated as a first-in, first-out (FIFO) queue, but messages can be retrieved out of queue order, and some messages (WM_PAINT) gravitate toward the tail of the queue so that they are always the last message fetched from the queue.

Windows requires applications to regularly poll the operating system to see whether there are any new messages waiting in the application's message queue. The code that performs this polling is called the *message loop* of the application. The message loop's job is to fetch messages from the message queue, examine them for potential application-wide processing, and route the messages to the appropriate window procedure for final processing. Since a Windows application's entire lifetime is spent waiting for and processing messages, the message loop is the engine that drives the execution of the rest of the app.

You can send messages to an application using PostMessage or SendMessage. PostMessage places the message in the recipient's message queue for later processing and returns control to the caller immediately. The recipient will receive the message at some later time when the recipient calls GetMessage or PeekMessage. SendMessage shortcuts the message queue, sending the message directly to the recipient window's window procedure. SendMessage does not return to the caller until the receiver has finished processing the message. PostMessage is asynchronous; SendMessage is synchronous. PostMessage is fast (for the caller), but it doesn't allow the sender to receive any feedback from the recipient within the context of the PostMessage call. SendMessage takes longer (from the caller's perspective) because the operating system must force a task switch to call the recipient's window procedure, but the sender can receive feedback from the recipient through the SendMessage function result. (A value assigned to the recipient's Message.Result field shows up in the caller as the SendMessage function result.)

Every window is identified and manipulated through a unique window handle. With the window handle you can access a host of attributes associated with the window—its width, height, and origin, the window's style, and a pointer to

> **Win32 Abolishes Message Processing?**
>
> One of the big selling points of the Win32 operating systems over Windows 3.1 is that Win32 is preemptively multitasked, whereas Windows 3.1 is cooperatively multitasked. Preemptive multitasking means that execution of your application can be suspended to give CPU time to another process (a task switch) at any time, anywhere in the execution of your code. With cooperative multitasking, task switches occur only when you call certain operating system functions, such as PeekMessage or GetMessage. In a cooperatively multitasked environment like Win3.1, if any application stops checking its message queue even temporarily, the entire system grinds to a halt. Win3.1 applications must "cooperate" to coexist.
>
> So, Win32 apps don't have to process messages, right? Wrong! A Win32 app that doesn't check its message queue won't cripple the operating system or affect other running programs, but it also won't be able to receive user input, redraw its windows, or even participate in most forms of interprocess communication. Timely message processing is still important to your Win32 app's well-being, but it is no longer critical to the well-being of the rest of the system.
>
> Incidentally, Win32 console applications aren't an exception to this message processing rule. Console applications don't require any application code to process messages because the Win32 console subsystem does it for you. A console app has a window handle, and window handles require message processing.

its window procedure. A window procedure is a function responsible for processing every message sent to a particular kind of window. Just as one method of a class is used by all instances of that class (and its descendants), one window procedure may be tied to many window instances.

> **What Shall We Call It Today?**
>
> In response to a Microsoft spin-du-jour remark that Windows really is an object-oriented operating system, a Borlander quipped, "Sure, windows are objects—objects with only one virtual method (the window procedure) and only one level of inheritance (the window class)!"

The Message Loop

In the body of code in a Delphi project source file, you'll find one or more calls to Application.CreateForm, followed by a call to Application.Run. CreateForm initializes the main form and whatever secondary forms you told Delphi to create automatically at start-up. Application.Run contains the application's main message loop. The call to Application.Run doesn't return until the application receives a WM_QUIT message, when the user or the system closes the application.

TApplication.Run takes care of a few chores (like making sure a main form exists) and then drops into a loop:

```
repeat
  HandleMessage;
until Terminated;
```

TApplication.HandleMessage is equally simplistic:

```
if not ProcessMessages then Idle;
```

If there are no more messages waiting in the message queue, HandleMessage lets the application drop into an idle state. TApplication.ProcessMessages (plural) spins in a loop calling ProcessMessage (singular) until the message queue is empty.

TApplication.ProcessMessage (singular), shown in Listing 7.1, is the true message pump of a Delphi application. ProcessMessage runs each message it pulls from the application's message queue through several message filter routines. These filters provide application-wide message preprocessing services, such as menu shortcut key processing. If the message makes it past these filters, it goes on to the TranslateMessage and DispatchMessage API functions. TranslateMessage is primarily responsible for generating WM_CHAR messages in response to WM_KEYDOWN messages. DispatchMessage calls the window procedure of the window the message is addressed to, passing along the message structure. DispatchMessage is where the message jumps from the outer domain of the application message queue and application-wide message handling to the inner domain of a particular window and component.

Listing 7.1 TApplication.ProcessMessage is the central message pump of a Delphi application.

```
function TApplication.ProcessMessage: Boolean;
var
  Handled: Boolean;
  Msg: TMsg;
begin
  Result := False;
  if PeekMessage(Msg, 0, 0, 0, PM_REMOVE) then
  begin
    Result := True;
```

```
      if Msg.Message <> WM_QUIT then
      begin
        Handled := False;
        if Assigned(FOnMessage) then FOnMessage(Msg, Handled);
        if not IsHintMsg(Msg) and not Handled and not IsMDIMsg(Msg)
          and not IsKeyMsg(Msg) and not IsDlgMsg(Msg) then
        begin
          TranslateMessage(Msg);
          DispatchMessage(Msg);
        end;
      end
      else
        FTerminate := True;
    end;
end;
```

TApplication.ProcessMessage (singular) is a protected member of TApplication mostly because application writers and component writers have little need to process *exactly* one message at a time. (If you need that level of detail, you're probably also interested in only a particular kind of message, and for that you should use the PeekMessage API function directly.) TApplication.ProcessMessages (plural and public) is the method you should use when you want to let your application "come up for air" during long loops or calculations. In 16-bit applications, where failing to process messages periodically would turn the whole system an asphyxiated shade of blue, message pump routines were often given colorful names like

```
procedure Gasp;
```

Running the Gauntlet of Filters

Let's take a closer look at what each of those filters in ProcessMessage do.

Application.OnMessage

First, there's the Application.OnMessage event. An application writer can assign a method of a form to this event (in the form's constructor or OnCreate event, usually) in order to get first crack at all the messages that pass through the application's message queue for all windows in the application. An OnMessage event handler can prevent further processing of a particular message by setting the Handled Boolean parameter to True.

Application.OnMessage is handy for implementing a particular message response that applies to all controls in all forms of the application, but that also makes it a rather dangerous freeway to play in. Application.OnMessage is by far the most time-critical routine an application writer will ever plug into simply because of the sheer volume of messages that race through even the simplest Windows application. Bursts of several thousand messages per second are not uncommon. Sloppy coding techniques that are harmless in a button click event handler can degrade the performance of your application noticeably when placed in an OnMessage event handler. To minimize performance costs, an OnMessage event handler should immediately check the message id for the particular message(s) you're interested in and let the rest pass without further delay. Avoid time-consuming operations in an OnMessage event handler, such as file I/O, memory allocation, and graphics drawing. And as discussed in Chapter 2, component writers should never modify event properties that the application writer has access to, including TApplication events.

IsHintMsg and IsMDIMsg

The call to IsHintMsg in Listing 7.1 lets the currently displayed pop-up hint window (if any) hide itself when the user moves the mouse. The IsMDIMsg function calls the TranslateMDISysAccel API function to process MDI accelerator keys (such as Ctrl+F6 for Next MDI Window) in MDI forms.

IsKeyMsg

IsKeyMsg lets the message's recipient window preview keystroke messages under the guise of a CN_BASE notification message (WM_KEYDOWN is previewed under CN_KEYDOWN, for example, and WM_CHAR is previewed under CN_CHAR). TWinControl uses these keystroke notifications to check for matching shortcut keys in the pop-up menu of itself and its parent components and in its parent form's main menu. TWinControl fires off a number of messages to process the keystroke, including CM_CHILDKEY, CM_WANTSPECIALKEY, WM_GETDLGCODE, CM_DIALOGKEY, and CM_DIALOGCHAR. CM_DIALOGKEY is the message Delphi controls use to participate in form focus navigation behavior, such as tab or arrow keys to move between controls on a form or the Enter key to click the default button of the form. Controls use CM_DIALOGCHAR to act upon shortcut keys embedded in their captions. TLabel responds to CM_DIALOGCHAR to compare the character in the message to the accelerator character in its caption (preceded by a single ampersand, &). If it finds a match, the label focuses its associated FocusControl (if any).

IsDlgMsg

The last filter function in ProcessMessage, IsDlgMsg, is a wrapper around the IsDialogMessage API function. IsDialogMessage implements the Windows default dialog manager. A dialog manager is the thing that moves focus between controls when you press the tab key, among other things. Because the behavior of the Windows default dialog manager is very difficult to alter or extend, Delphi implements its own dialog manager with the IsKeyMsg filter function and TWinControl message handlers just mentioned. This IsDialogMessage call allows non-VCL windows that require the services of the Windows default dialog manager to live comfortably in a Delphi application. Windows created by non-Delphi DLLs, such as the Windows common dialogs, are an example of non-VCL windows living in a Delphi application.

Why Preview Keystroke Messages?

Why does VCL use all these keystroke preview messages to implement its dialog management instead of listening for the normal keystroke messages? First, VCL has to support windows that require the Windows default dialog manager (IsDialogMessage), and Windows requires that IsDialogMessage must be called before TranslateMessage and DispatchMessage. Since IsDialogMessage "eats" the messages it handles and VCL's own dialog management needs to see those same messages, VCL must look at the messages before IsDialogMessage. Thus, IsKeyMsg appears ahead of IsDlgMsg in the ProcessMessage list of filter functions.

Second, if a particular WM_KEYDOWN message is used for dialog management purposes, you don't want TranslateMessage to synthesize and post a corresponding WM_CHAR message. The best way to prevent that is to not call TranslateMessage. Thus, dialog management keystroke processing must occur before the normal processing of keystroke messages.

IsKeyMsg promotes the keystroke messages to CN_BASE notifications so that components can distinguish between dialog key processing and normal keystroke/data-entry processing. Most keystroke messages pass through the focused component twice: once as a CN_BASE preview and again as a normal WM_KEYDOWN/WM_CHAR/WM_KEYUP message sequence if nothing reacts to the CN_BASE preview.

TApplication.Idle—The Pause That Refreshes

When the message queue is empty, TApplication.HandleMessage calls TApplication.Idle. Idle eventually puts the application into a very CPU-efficient idle state by calling the WaitMessage Windows function. On its way to dreamland, Idle catches up on a few VCL housekeeping chores, sending CM_MOUSELEAVE and CM_MOUSEENTER messages to the control that was and is (respectively) under the mouse cursor, hiding the pop-up hint window, updating the Application.Hint property from the control under the mouse cursor, calling the Application.OnIdle event, dragging the kids in, and putting the cat out. (Locking the doors isn't a high priority because we live in a private address space of a secure environment.) With all this going on, it's a wonder that an application has any idle time to itself.

The truth is, most apps wind up calling Idle several times per second, even during flurries of message activity such as when the user pointlessly waves the mouse around. However, once the app goes idle, it will remain idle for an unpredictable length of time—until some external event posts a message to the application's message queue. The idle period may be only a few milliseconds, as in the case of mindless mouse waving, or as long as minutes or hours or longer, as in the case of a minimized application sitting in a quiet corner of the desktop. While an application's message loop is idle, it consumes essentially zero CPU cycles, which leaves more CPU time available for other processes in the system and even other threads in your own app.

TApplication.OnIdle Event: Just-in-Time Updates

The TApplication.OnIdle event is handy for implementing noncritical, low-priority behaviors in an application without the complications of threads. (OnIdle is for application writers, not component writers.) You should think of OnIdle as executing every now and then when the application *transitions* from an active period to a quiet period, rather than viewing OnIdle as executing continuously when nothing else is going on. For example, the TApplication.Idle method, which calls the OnIdle event, updates the application's Hint property from the control currently under the mouse cursor. This update could have been done in response to every mousemove message, but that would have been overkill: How quickly can the user read a status line hint? It doesn't matter how many times the hint might change during a flurry of mouse activity. All that matters to the user is that the hint text is accurate when the dust settles a few milliseconds later.

Just-in-time "catch-up" techniques such as this are far more efficient of CPU resources than brute-force continuous updates and are more efficient than using timer messages to perform delayed updates. A fast timer update (100 milliseconds or less) is as wasteful of CPU time as continuous updates. A slow timer update (500 milliseconds or more) conserves CPU time as effectively as OnIdle, but it usually introduces an annoyingly noticeable lag time between a user action and the program's response to that action. Catch-up updates in OnIdle are inherently self-adjusting dynamic systems that minimize both CPU load and response times.

OnIdle State Machines: Inside-Out Calculation Loops

The Application.OnIdle event has a Done Boolean parameter that you can set to False to indicate that you don't want the app to go idle just yet. You might use this if your OnIdle code is broken into multiple steps and advances through these steps with each subsequent call to OnIdle—a state machine. For example, you might use OnIdle to read files as a background "task" without the hassles of setting up an actual background thread of execution. Reading all the files in one OnIdle call would block the message loop for too long and cause a noticeable pause in the application's operation. You could instead read one file per OnIdle invocation. However, you still want to read all the files as quickly as possible, so while you still have files left to read, you can set the Done parameter to False to prevent the app from going idle and to force another lap through the message loop. If there are still no messages waiting in the message loop, execution will return to your OnIdle event handler very quickly, where you can start working on the next file. When you have no more files to process, set Done to True to allow the app to go idle.

Typically, when you need to execute a lengthy calculation loop but still want the application to be responsive to user input, you insert a call to Application.ProcessMessages in your calculation loop. The OnIdle file-handling scenario just described is an example of turning the calculation loop inside out: Instead of moving message handling into your calculation loop, move your calculations into the message loop. This OnIdle state machine technique was about the only way to perform background processing in 16-bit Windows applications, but threads have stolen its thunder in 32-bit Windows. Simple OnIdle state machines in Win32 apps are still easier to write, easier to manage, easier to debug, and faster to execute than background threads, but state machine implementations of complex processes can become unmanageable faster than thread implementations of the same.

Local Message Loops = Modal Dialog Windows

When you display a modal dialog, the application shifts into a mode (hence, the name) where the user's attention is completely focused on that dialog. The rest of the application is disabled until you close that dialog. If you were to put a fly on the wall of Application.Run, you would discover that while the modal dialog is active, no messages go through Application.Run's repeat loop. Yet the modal dialog responds to user input messages just fine. How can this be?

To simplify the process of disabling the application windows, waiting for the user to close the modal dialog, and then reenabling the disabled windows, a modal dialog uses a local message loop. A *local message loop* is just like the repeat loop in Application.Run, except that it's somewhere else in the application. Say you have a button click event that calls AForm.ShowModal. When the user clicks on the button, a mouse message is posted to the application's message queue. The main message loop (in Application.Run) picks up that mouse message and dispatches it to the button control, where it winds up in the button's OnClick event handler (we'll study just how that happens in the next section). That OnClick handler calls AForm.ShowModal. ShowModal disables the application's windows and enters its own loop that calls Application.HandleMessage repeatedly until the form's ModalResult property is set to something nonzero by a user action (clicking a button or pressing Esc). While ShowModal is spinning its wheels waiting for the user to do something, the main message loop (in Application.Run) is still waiting for the call to DispatchMessage (which called the original button OnClick, which called ShowModal) to return. If a button on AForm brings up yet another modal dialog, AForm's ShowModal message loop will be suspended until the new modal form's message loop exits and returns.

Since these local message loops call Application.HandleMessages to do the actual message processing, all the normal Delphi message processing takes place. If you took it upon yourself to call PeekMessage, TranslateMessage, and DispatchMessage in your own homegrown message pump, your Delphi application would not be happy. Pop-up hints, menu hot keys, control shortcut keys, and form navigation keys would all cease to exist while the homegrown message pump was operating.

TApplication.HandleMessage is a public method for situations where you need to implement a custom local message loop (like ShowModal) and want to retain the standard Delphi message filter behavior *and* the application idle behavior. Because HandleMessage can put the application into an idle state for an indefinite period of time, you shouldn't use HandleMessage just to let your app take a gasp every now and then during a long calculation or loop. Use ProcessMessages when you have work to do but need to process messages occasionally to allow the app to update its display or perform other message-based work. Use HandleMessage when you have nothing else to do but wait for a message-based exit condition. When all you're doing is processing messages, you don't care if the app goes idle—you can't do anything until you see the next message anyway.

When the message queue is empty, HandleMessage will let the app go idle, which reduces CPU use to zero. A loop that does nothing but call ProcessMessages will continue to consume a lot of CPU time even when there are no messages to be processed.

Application Start-up and Shutdown—Message Limbo

Everything that executes before Application.Run is part of the application's start-up code; everything after Application.Run is the application's shutdown code. Since the initialization sections of all the units in the application execute prior to the project file's main `begin...end` block, and since the finalization sections of those units are executed after the project file's main `begin...end` block, there can be a lot more going on in the start-up and shutdown phases of the application than the project file alone indicates. The Forms unit's finalization section, for example, destroys the Application object, which, in turn, destroys all the forms it contains and all the components they contain, which is just about everything in the application.

The important point to note here is that the application has no active message loop during its start-up and shutdown phases. The application's message queue exists at all times, but messages posted to your app won't be processed until the message loop starts up. For messages posted during start-up, that could be quite a while—whole seconds in a large application that opens lots of database connections at start-up, for example. Messages posted to an application that is shutting down will never be processed.

Since almost all screen redrawing of controls happens only in response to WM_PAINT messages, changes made to controls during application start-up won't be displayed on-screen until the message loop starts up. Applications that do a lot of time-consuming work in their start-up phase typically display a status dialog during start-up to indicate the application's progress through its start-up sequence. You can do this quite easily in Delphi (just create and show your status form *after* the main form has been created, and destroy the status form just before the call to Application.Run), but many programmers are surprised to discover that changing the caption of a label on the status form doesn't appear to do anything. The reason is that for the changed caption to show on-screen, the status form must receive a WM_PAINT message, which won't happen until the message loop starts retrieving messages. The solution is simple: Don't wait for the WM_PAINT message. After modifying the label caption, force the form to catch up on any pending WM_PAINT messages by calling the form's Update method.

Receiving Messages

Now that we've covered the outer domain of a Delphi application's message handling, let's take a look at what goes on in the inner domain—the window procedure and points beyond. While the outer domain is primarily the realm of the application, the inner domain is the realm of the component. Component-level message processing is certainly one aspect of application writing (forms are components, after all), but for component writers, message processing is the only game in town. A component's streaming support is important, but only for initialization. A component's programming interface is important, but only when the application writer calls it. A component's message support is critical because messages are driven by the system, not the whims of the application writer. With messages, you can make your components more autonomous, requiring less configuration and nursing by the application writer.

Recall that the message loop's last task in processing a message is to call DispatchMessage if the message isn't handled by a filter first. DispatchMessage is a Windows function that looks up the window procedure address of the window handle the message is addressed to and calls that window procedure, passing along the message information.

Component-Window Bonding

Every TWinControl instance has its own window handle. For each TWinControl instance, VCL synthesizes (at run time) machine code for a unique window procedure and inserts the address of that code into the component's window handle. The synthesized window procedure loads the instance pointer of the component associated with the window handle into a register and jumps to StdWndProc, a utility routine deep inside the Forms unit that packages up the message parameters and calls the component's window procedure method (TWinControl.MainWndProc, usually).

This arrangement gives components a two-way bond to their associated window handles: The component has a window handle to talk to its associated window, and the window has a window procedure address unique to its associated component. The Windows operating system knows nothing about VCL objects, but when a message is sent to a particular VCL-owned window handle, execution jumps immediately "into" the corresponding VCL component.

While we're on the subject, there is a third bond between a component and its window. Windows supports attaching data to a window handle using integer indexes and API functions SetProp and GetProp. Windows refers to this data as "window properties," a term that has nothing to do with Delphi component properties. When VCL creates a window handle, it assigns the component instance pointer to the window handle as a window property. To help ensure that the integer window property index used to assign the property doesn't conflict with other uses of window properties, VCL calls GlobalAddAtom to convert a unique string into an integer guaranteed to be unique on a particular machine. That integer atom is the window property index under which the component's instance pointer is stored in the window handle. The unique string is the concatenation of "Delphi" with the application's GetCurrentProcessID value represented as 8 hexadecimal digits.

So, if you have a window handle and you want to get the component instance pointer associated with that window handle, you can construct a string the same way VCL does. Call GlobalAddAtom to get the same integer index VCL uses, and fetch the component instance pointer from the window handle with a call to GetProp. Or, you could just call VCL's FindControl function, which does the work for you.

Note that since global atoms, window handles, and window handle properties can be accessed by any application, it's possible for one application to obtain the instance pointer of a VCL component located in another application. Since pointers aren't valid between Win32 apps, this isn't particularly useful in Win32 unless you're writing a debugger or program analysis tools that can reach into other applications' address spaces. Nevertheless, it's still pretty neat.

If your application (or a DLL your application uses) attaches information to window handles using window properties (SetProp/GetProp), you should use GlobalAddAtom to obtain integer property indexes that are guaranteed to be unique so that you don't accidentally stomp on the window property indexes used by VCL, Windows, or anybody else.

With these techniques, VCL establishes a triple bond between a window handle and a component. The window talks directly to the component (window procedure), you can obtain the window handle from the component instance, and you can obtain the component instance from the window handle. This kind of symmetry is common in Delphi; after all, symmetry and triple bonds are what make diamonds last forever.

The Three Message-Handling Opportunities

When creating a TControl descendant class, you have three opportunities to intercept and process messages sent to the control: WndProc, a message method, and DefaultHandler. These three intercept points allow you to process messages before, during, and after (respectively) the normal VCL message processing process. Let's look at how the message gets to these three intercept points and then discuss how you can use them.

As mentioned earlier, messages for a component's window handle are sent to the component's unique window procedure address, which calls the StdWndProc utility routine to package up the message data and call the component's message-handling entry point. For TWinControl descendants, this is TWinControl.MainWndProc. Note that while the window procedure address is unique to each component *instance*, StdWndProc is shared by all window-owning components, and the code in MainWndProc and all points beyond are shared by all instances of the component *class*.

MainWndProc calls TWinControl.WndProc inside a layer of exception handlers, as shown in Listing 7.2. The `try...finally` exception handler releases temporary resources (device contexts) that may be allocated during the processing of each message, and the `try...except` handler traps all exceptions that may occur while processing a message.

Listing 7.2 TWinControl.MainWndProc implements VCL's default exception handler.

```
procedure TWinControl.MainWndProc(var Message: TMessage);
begin
  try
    try
      WndProc(Message);
    finally
      FreeDeviceContexts;
      FreeMemoryContexts;
    end;
  except
    Application.HandleException(Self);
  end;
end;
```

This is VCL's default exception handler, and it is the reason Delphi applications can continue operating after an exception has occurred. Exceptions raised while processing a message will find their way into this exception handler, where they will be processed by Application.HandleException. The default behavior of HandleException is to display the exception message information in a message box, but application writers can override this behavior by plugging into the Application.OnException event. An exception raised while processing a message aborts the processing of that message but does not terminate the program.

Opportunity 1: WndProc

TWinControl.MainWndProc calls WndProc, passing along the message information. Since WndProc is a virtual method (introduced in TControl), this call will jump to the most recent WndProc method override in the component's class. Overriding WndProc in your component class gives you first cut at handling messages, before your ancestor classes, as well as the last chance to handle messages after all other message processing (by your other component methods and by your ancestor classes) has been completed. WndProc code before the call to the inherited WndProc sees messages before the rest of the component; WndProc code after the call to the inherited sees WndProc messages after the rest of the component. If your WndProc doesn't pass a particular message on to its inherited WndProc, the rest of the component will never see the message. Of course, if you forget to call the inherited WndProc at all in your WndProc override, your component will be dead in the water.

TWinControl.WndProc does some processing for several kinds of messages and calls its inherited TControl.WndProc. TControl.WndProc also looks for a few messages before calling TObject.Dispatch. The specific details of the messages these routines handle are far too numerous to cover here. Instead of covering which messages a component processes, we'll stick to how messages circulate through a component. When you know where to look, a few minutes' perusal of the VCL source code is usually all it takes to find out which messages the VCL base classes or a particular component handles and what action is taken upon receiving a particular message. *Use the source, Luke!*

Notice that WndProc first appears in TControl, a component that, by definition, does not have a window handle. Though it has no window handle, TControl receives messages forwarded by its parent control. TControl is thus an active participant in the messaging system, responding primarily to mouse messages and messages that affect the control's appearance (WM_PAINT, font change, and color change messages). This allows the TGraphicControl branch of the VCL component hierarchy to participate in message handling without the overhead of owning a window handle. TGraphic controls like TLabel and TSpeedButton are lightweight components that consume very few Windows system resources and often repaint faster than their fully laden brethren.

TObject.Dispatch

TObject.Dispatch is responsible for dispatching a message to the appropriate message method of the component. How it accomplishes this is a story unto itself.

Recall from Chapter 3, Virtual Methods and Polymorphism, that dynamic methods are called by searching for a compiler-generated method id in a compiler-generated Dynamic Method Table (DMT) that is part of the component's class information. Message methods declared in a class, for example,

```
procedure Foo(var Msg); message 1234;
```

are also stored in the DMT, substituting the declared message id for the compiler-generated method id. Compiler-generated method ids for dynamic methods are always negative; message numbers are always positive.

Dispatch takes a single untyped `var` parameter. Dispatch treats the first 4 bytes of data referred to by the `var` parameter as a message id number, looks up that message id in the component's DMT, and calls the method address it finds in the DMT. Note that Dispatch doesn't require any particular data structure type; it simply treats the first 4 bytes of whatever data you pass in as the message number.

For a call to a dynamic method, the compiler generates machine code to pass the compiler-generated method id to an internal System unit subroutine that searches the DMT and calls the corresponding method address. TObject.Dispatch passes the message id it extracts from its untyped `var` parameter to the same System unit subroutine to find and call message methods.

Opportunity 2: Message Methods

Your second opportunity to intercept messages passing through your component is in a message method. Message methods are always specific to a particular message number, which makes the code in message methods more focused and easier to read than the huge multimessage `case` statements commonly found in WndProc methods.

Though message methods are dispatched through the same mechanism as dynamic methods, calls to message methods are not polymorphic. A call to MyObject.MyDynamic is polymorphic because the compiler generates code to search for and call the most recently defined override, as determined by the type of the instance, not the type of the variable. A call to MyObject.MyMessage is always compiled as a static call to the method in the class type identified by the variable, not the type of the instance in the variable. If you want to invoke a message method polymorphically, call Dispatch with a message structure containing the appropriate message number.

Since the name of a message method is not significant to how it is dispatched, it's possible to have different method names in ancestor and descendant classes that process the same message number. For this reason, you don't need to specify a method name (nor a message data parameter) when you call `inherited` from within your message method body.

Like dynamic methods, a call to an inherited message method is resolved to a static call to the corresponding method in the ancestor. Unlike dynamic methods, though, when there is no corresponding message method in any ancestor class, the compiler replaces the inherited call with a call to the DefaultHandler virtual method, introduced in TObject. If you don't call `inherited` in your message method, neither ancestor message methods nor DefaultHandler will see the message.

The size of the data that accompanies Windows messages is the same for every message (8 bytes), but how those 8 bytes are chopped up into data fields varies with each family of messages. In a multimessage-handling routine like WndProc, you have to treat the message structure generically and typecast the message structure to access specific data fields in message-specific portions of the routine. Since a message method handles only one kind of message, you only need to view the message structure in the data format associated with the particular message.

Delphi message methods must have a single `var` parameter to receive the message data, but the type of the `var` parameter is arbitrary, determined by the message number and your needs. If your message method doesn't refer to the message data at all, you can just declare the message method with a typeless `var` parameter:

```
procedure Foo(var Msg); message 1234;
```

If your message method does need to use the message data, you can declare the message method with a `var` parameter with a type appropriate to the message number:

```
procedure WMCommand(var Msg: TWMCommand); message WM_COMMAND;
```

Delphi doesn't care what the type is, as long as the message method has a `var` parameter. (See the messages.pas unit in the Delphi RTL source code for the complete list of Windows message-specific record types.)

Implicit Message Cracking

This flexibility in using message-specific data structures makes Delphi's message-handling system fully portable between 16-bit and 32-bit Windows environments. Because some data types change size in the move to 32-bit Windows, the placement of data fields in the message structure is different between 16- and 32-bit Windows for some messages, such as WM_COMMAND. The 16-bit code that treats message data as a generic TMessage structure and manually extracts message data from the LParam and WParam fields of the TMessage structure will not work in 32-bit Windows, for certain Windows messages. Delphi solves this problem by encouraging the use of message-specific data structures to access message data. When your code accesses data using a field name of a message-specific data structure, your code is oblivious to any relocation of that field within the data structure that may occur in the move to 32-bit Windows.

C and C++ development tools solve this data relocation problem with a host of macros, or "message crackers," that are conditionally defined to fetch data from particular locations in the message structure depending upon which version of Windows you're targeting. Delphi solves the data relocation problem using types: The same message record types are defined in 16-bit and 32-bit versions of Delphi (in messages.pas), but the placement and size of the data fields in the message structures are redefined in each version to match the changes in Windows. All you have to do to take advantage of this is use message-specific record types for the var parameter in your message method declarations; Delphi takes care of the rest.

Opportunity 3: DefaultHandler

Your third opportunity to intercept messages passing through your component is to override the TObject.DefaultHandler virtual method. In DefaultHandler, you can define default behavior for any messages sent to a component through Dispatch. TObject.Dispatch calls DefaultHandler when Dispatch can't find any message methods in a component for a particular message number. TWinControl overrides DefaultHandler to pass Windows messages on to the window procedure that was associated with the window handle before VCL bound its own component-instance window procedure to the window handle. In a sense, this is like calling an inherited method. You can access that prior window procedure address through DefWndProc, a protected property of TWinControl.

DefaultHandler is the best place to put default message-handling code that applies to multiple messages. You can achieve the same results in WndProc, but you run a greater risk of cutting off messages to your component in WndProc than in DefaultHandler. WndProc is best for preempting normal message handling; DefaultHandler is best for augmenting normal message handling.

Doubling Your Fun

Keep in mind that a message goes out through the same path it came in by. Execution goes through your WndProc, one or more inherited WndProcs, Dispatch, one or more message methods, and the DefaultHandler; it then turns around and returns through the message methods, the inherited WndProcs, and your WndProc and finally exits to whatever sent you the message to begin with (DispatchMessage in the message loop, for example). In this light, you actually have six distinct opportunities to handle messages: inbound (prior to the call to inherited) and outbound (after the call to `inherited`) in each of the three message intercept opportunities.

Marking a Message as Handled

When writing code to process a particular message in your component, it's good practice to set the message result field to 1 to indicate that you have completely handled that message (assuming you have, of course). This will notify any code that sees the message after you that no further action should be taken on that message. Setting the message result is required for some Windows messages (WM_ERASEBKGND and WM_SETCURSOR leap to mind) to prevent Windows from taking further action.

Similarly, any code you put in a WndProc, message method, or DefaultHandler should first check the message result field for 0 before acting upon the message. This is particularly important for code in the outbound half of the method, after the message has made the rounds.

Sending Messages

Now that we've seen how a component receives messages, let's take a look at the many ways you can send messages to components. Messaging techniques can be categorized by synchronization (asynchronous or synchronous messages) and locality (external or internal targets).

External Messages

External messages are messages that you send to windows in other applications. External messages usually cross process boundaries, which places strict constraints on what kind of data you can attach to the message. Since the advent of DDE and OLE, application-to-application custom messages have become quite rare.

When sending messages to other applications, you can't send any data that contains pointers to items in your application's address space. For example, you can send a pointer to a string in the LParam of a message to another application, but the receiving application can't use that pointer to access the string data because the receiving application doesn't have access to your process address space. If you want to send more than 8 bytes of actual data, you'll have to work out some sort of shared memory scheme with the other application.

Sending data pointers in a message is perfectly valid when the receiver is inside your application address space. Custom controls implemented in a DLL, for example, live inside your process address space, so they can use your pointers and you can use theirs.

Using RegisterWindowMessage

When sending messages to other applications, you have to be careful about what message numbers you use. You need to select a message number that is not only unique within your application but also different from any other custom interapplication message numbers used by other applications. The best way to avoid message number collisions is to use RegisterWindowMessage to register a unique message description string to obtain an integer message number that uniquely identifies that message system-wide on that particular machine (much like GlobalAddAtom). Any other application that calls RegisterWindowMessage with the same string will get the same integer message number you got, and thus sender and receiver will be using the same message number.

Handling Registered Window Messages

If you're planning to receive an interapplication message in your Delphi app, you may have already figured out that you can't declare a message method in your form class to handle the custom message. Message method ids must be constant expressions that can be resolved at compile time, but RegisterWindowMessage produces the needed message number only at run time. To handle custom registered window messages, override DefaultHandler to check the received message number against a variable containing the message number obtained from RegisterWindowMessage.

Internal Messages

Internal messages are messages sent to controls inside your application. Internal messages have none of the restrictions on pointer data that external messages are strapped with, and there is no need to go through any registration system to define custom messages for your application's internal use. As we'll see at the end of this chapter, there are also certain programming advantages to sending messages between controls instead of calling methods.

Asynchronous Messaging Using PostMessage

When you use PostMessage to send a message to a window handle, the message data is placed in the receiving application's message queue and the PostMessage call returns immediately. PostMessage is called *asynchronous* because the sender doesn't wait for the receiver to process the message. PostMessage is the only readily available means to perform an asynchronous message notification. All other messaging routines are synchronous, meaning they don't return until the receiver has completely processed the message.

PostMessage is good for sending notifications and data to another window (inside your app or in another app) when no response is required and the message can be processed "out of band" (processed outside the sender's context). Care must be taken to ensure that data bundled with the message will still be valid when the message is processed later. Passing a pointer to a local variable in a posted message will most likely fail because by the time the message is retrieved from the message queue, the sending routine will have already exited and destroyed its local variables. You can pass pointers to allocated memory or object instances in the data of the posted message if you remember *not* to free the allocated resources in the sender and *do* remember to free the allocated resources at the receiving end.

Case Study: Using Asynchronous Updates to Improve Performance PostMessage is also good for deferring an action to some later time—to move the action "out of band." A control can post a message to itself to perform some noncritical chore when the message is retrieved from the message queue some time later. For example, in the TConsole component source code that accompanies this book, the component has an option called *lazy scrolling*. When lazy scrolling is turned off and enough text is written to the control that requires the control to scroll its display up, the control will perform the scroll-and-redraw operation immediately, before returning to the code that wrote the text into the control. Almost any operation that requires updating the screen image takes hundreds of times longer than normal data processing. Scrolling the control's display in the middle of processing new text made it difficult for the control to keep up with a high rate of text input, as is the case when using the TConsole to display text coming from a high-speed modem connection.

The lazy scrolling option removes this performance bottleneck by taking the screen update out of the text input processing cycle. With lazy scrolling enabled, the control posts a message to itself to remind it to scroll the display some time later. This alone provides some performance improvement, allowing the control to update its display after the current flurry of text input settles down. This is another form of the just-in-time updates introduced in the TApplication.OnIdle section earlier.

With the small addition of making the lazy scroll message accumulate multiple scroll requests (if the lazy scroll custom message is already in the message queue, remove it, add the new scroll request to the scroll data in the existing message, and post the message back into the message queue), the lazy scrolling technique improves data throughput by an order of magnitude over the in-band scrolling technique. When several lines of text arrive in a burst, the lazy scrolling technique scrolls and redraws the screen once, where the in-line scrolling requires multiple scroll-and-redraw operations—one for each line of text received.

Synchronous Messaging Using SendMessage

SendMessage skips over the message queue and calls the window procedure of the receiving window handle directly, just as DispatchMessage does in the message loop. SendMessage is called *synchronous* because it doesn't return until the message has been processed by the receiver. If the receiving window handle is in another application, SendMessage must also perform a context switch, a costly extra step that PostMessage doesn't have to contend with. Since SendMessage is the function of choice for communicating with the Windows standard controls (TEdit, TButton, and so forth) and most custom controls implemented in DLLs, messages sent with SendMessage vastly outnumber messages sent with PostMessage. However, since SendMessage messages don't pass through the application's main message loop, they don't pass through the gauntlet of message loop filter functions or through the Application.OnMessage event. The only way to eavesdrop on SendMessage messages is to install a Windows message hook, an ugly proposition at best.

Since SendMessage doesn't return until the receiver has processed the message, it's easy to manage resources allocated and passed to the receiver in the message data. You just allocate the resource (say, memory), use it, pass it to the receiver with a call to SendMessage, and then free the resource. Similarly, you can safely pass pointers to local variables through SendMessage since the local variables will be valid throughout the lifetime of the call to the receiver. The same rules of pointers and process address spaces discussed for PostMessage between applications apply to SendMessage between applications, of course.

SendMessage Pitfalls SendMessage's greatest strength—that it calls directly into the window procedure of the receiving message—is also its greatest liability. SendMessage can't actually call directly into another application since the application could well be executing its own business somewhere else. When calling into another application, SendMessage must wait for the other application to reach a point at which SendMessage can safely jump in. That safe point is none other than the other application's message loop! SendMessage can't jump in until the other application calls a message retrieval function (PeekMessage, GetMessage, or WaitMessage). If the other application is busily grinding away in a compute loop and not checking its message loop regularly, your so-called fast and direct SendMessage call will suspend your application until it can get through to the other app.

Even worse, it's not hard to fall into a SendMessage deadlock. If application A performs a SendMessage to application B and, in the processing of that message, application B tries to perform a SendMessage to application A, the applications will be deadlocked. Application A is blocked waiting for SendMessage to return from application B, and application B is blocked waiting for application A to check its messages so that B can proceed with its SendMessage call. Neither application is processing any messages, so there is no way to escape the deadlock once it has been entered, except by forcibly terminating both applications.

You can avoid such deadlocks by being more careful in the design of your interapplication message protocols and by calling InSendMessage to find out whether the message your application is currently processing was sent to you by SendMessage.

OLE, RPC, and SendMessage Blocking OLE interface methods call between applications using the same internal mechanism SendMessage uses. OLE method calls have to wait for the target application to return to its message loop before the call can go through. Remote Procedure Calls (RPC), another way to call between processes, also use this technique. If application A makes a SendMessage call into application B, application A can't receive any OLE calls from any application until the SendMessage call returns and application A returns to its message loop. This is definitely a case where PostMessage can cure a thousand synchronization headaches.

Perform

TControl.Perform is the VCL internal lightweight equivalent of SendMessage. Perform takes message parameters, bundles them up in a message data structure, and then calls the control's WndProc method. Perform has a few advantages over SendMessage: Perform doesn't require a call to the operating system, it doesn't require a window handle, and it's immune to the SendMessage deadlock problem. However, Perform only works for VCL components, not arbitrary window handles, and Perform can't send messages to other applications (thus, the deadlock immunity). Also, anything that replaces the window's window procedure after your control has established its triple bond won't see messages sent with Perform because it doesn't go through the window handle. This is something to be aware of but usually is not important enough to worry about. When you need to send a message to another component, use Perform instead of SendMessage.

Broadcast

TWinControl.Broadcast sends the same message to all the child controls (members of the Controls[] array property) of the TWinControl. If one of the child controls marks the message as handled (by setting Msg.Result to a nonzero value), Broadcast bails out immediately. For example, TWinControl uses Broadcast to notify all its immediate children when the system colors change (CM_SYSCOLORCHANGE).

Dispatch

As we saw earlier, WndProc uses Dispatch to send window messages to the appropriate message methods in the component. Messaging isn't limited to components with window handles or even to components. You can use Dispatch to send any sort of message to message methods of any Delphi class. Every Delphi class inherits Dispatch (and DefaultHandler) from TObject, any Delphi class can have message methods, and any data structure can be passed to Dispatch as message data as long as the first 4 bytes contain the message number.

The only thing to watch out for is using Dispatch on TWinControl classes. Calling Dispatch instead of, say, Perform, leaves the TWinControl's WndProc out in the cold. If the message you're sending with Dispatch is your own, this omission is harmless. If the message is a Windows or VCL message, though, you should use Perform so that the WndProc will have its opportunity to see the message.

Miscellanea

Windowless Window Handles—AllocateHWnd

Some components don't need a window to display themselves, but they do need a window handle to perform special message processing. For example, the TTimer control owns a hidden window handle so that it can receive timer messages. Nonvisible components can create hidden utility window handles for themselves by calling AllocateHWnd in the Forms unit. AllocateHWnd takes a method pointer parameter to use as the window's window procedure. Declare a method in your component with the same parameter list as TWinControl.WndProc and pass that method to the AllocateHWnd call. Your window procedure method will then receive all the messages sent to the hidden utility window. Destroy the utility window handle by calling DeallocateHWnd, usually in your component's destructor.

Application.HookMainWindow

All the forms in a Delphi application are owned by a central, hidden application window. Application.Handle gives you the window handle of the hidden application window. Since Windows and other applications can send messages to the application window (such as drag-n-drop on the application icon when the app is minimized), you may have a need to eavesdrop on messages received by the application window. You can do this by inserting a method of your component into the Application.HookMainWindow chain of eavesdroppers. Your component's hook method must be a function that returns a Boolean and takes a `var` message parameter. When your hook method is called, you can do what you like with the application message and can set the function result to True to indicate that the message has been handled and that neither further hooks nor the application message handler should receive the message. Use Application.UnHookMainWindow to remove your component from the chain of eavesdroppers.

For example, the Windows common dialogs DLL requires a window handle to use as the parent of the dialog it will create. The VCL common dialog components have no window handles of their own, so they pass the Application object's window handle as the parent of the common dialog. Unfortunately, the common dialogs DLL sends feedback and notification messages to that parent window. The VCL dialog components use Application.HookMainWindow to listen for common dialog notification messages for such events as the user clicking on the Help button on the common dialog.

Summary

Messaging has the following advantages:

- **Messages transcend class types.** Messages allow your component to communicate with other components without knowing anything about the type of the other components. This reduces your component's direct exposure to and dependency on other component types and units.

- **Messages are polymorphic.** Each component class can handle a message differently. Messages are more flexible than virtual methods because messages have none of the method name or method parameter requirements of virtual methods.

- **Messages have a low risk of failure.** If the receiver doesn't know how to respond to a custom message, it does nothing.

- **Messages can cross process and thread boundaries.** The easiest way to communicate with another process or thread is to post or send a message.

Here are the drawbacks of messaging:

- **Message handling is slower than direct calls.** As should now be clear from this chapter, a message passes through a lot of code on its way through a component.

- **Messaging code can be difficult to read.** Messages are an indirection, so it can be difficult sometimes to see which components will receive a message and how they will respond to it. Similarly, it can be difficult to figure out the contexts in which a message method can be called.

- **SendMessage can lead to deadlocks.** Use PostMessage or check InSendMessage to avoid SendMessage deadlock. Also keep in mind that most forms of synchronous interprocess communication (DDE, OLE, and RPC) are susceptible to SendMessage deadlocks.

- **Message methods defeat smart linking.** Message methods are, by definition, always needed at run time, so all message method code is linked into an application when the class type is touched.

Chapter 8

More VCL Subsystems

In addition to the major systems covered in earlier chapters, Delphi's VCL architecture contains a number of smaller subsystems that component writers need to be aware of. Some of these systems provide little-known services you can take advantage of, while others are conventions that your components should support. This chapter focuses on several of these smaller VCL systems, including component free notifications, component assignment semantics, color palettes, and graphics operations.

FreeNotification

By definition, components never work alone. You can implement a component as a combination of internal classes and you can implement a component to share some of its work with other classes, outside its domain. An aggregate component usually keeps all its internal implementation classes completely hidden, so it can maintain strict ownership of its innards. When nothing outside the component can access the internal instances, there is no ambiguity about who is supposed to free the internal instances or in what order.

When a component relies upon object instances that live outside its domain of control, the component has to contend with the possibility that those object instances may be altered or destroyed by something outside the component's domain. Because so much of Delphi is built up from cooperative, dynamic relationships between components, TComponent implements a notification system where one component can establish a link to another component that will last as long as both components exist. Regardless of which component initiated the link, when either component is destroyed, it automatically notifies the other of its eminent demise. Typically, the surviving component's response to this notification is to remove all references to the expiring component from its internal lists and fields so that the surviving component no longer has any reference to the expiring component.

Establishing the Link

TComponent.FreeNotification initiates a link between two components. When component A calls component B.FreeNotification(A), B adds A to its internal free notifications list, and then reciprocates by calling A.FreeNotification(B). FreeNotifications are always bidirectional. If A and B have a common owner (A is directly or indirectly owned by B's owner), FreeNotification does not need to create a link between them. Components with a common owner will receive notification of each other's destruction through the common owner.

FreeNotification primarily exists to support references between components in different forms. However, you can use FreeNotification in just about any situation where your component needs to be informed when another component is destroyed, regardless of where the other component lives. If FreeNotification figures out that your link request is redundant (that the two components will receive free notifications anyway because they share a common owner), FreeNotification does nothing.

For example, the TDBGrid contains column objects that can contain references to database field components. The lifetimes of the field components displayed by a TDBGrid are determined by their owning dataset or form and could be different from the lifetime of the TDBGrid itself. Thus, the TDBGrid and its column objects need to know when the fields they reference are destroyed so that the columns can clear those references and redraw themselves.

Receiving Notifications

When a component is inserted into its owner, it calls its owner's Notification method. When a component is removed from its owner, it calls the Notification method of its owner and of each of the components on its internal free notifications list. TComponent.Notification is a protected virtual method that you can override in your component to listen for these notifications.

The Notification method takes two parameters: the component that is the subject of the notification and the kind of notification. Notification is called whenever a component is inserted into its owner (opInsert) and whenever a component is removed from its owner (opRemove). Since components remove themselves from their owner when they are destroyed, opRemove is the notification to listen for to find out when companion components are destroyed.

TComponent.Notification responds to opRemove notifications by removing the expiring component from the current component's internal free notifications list, and by calling Notification on all the components owned by the current component.

Notifications cascade down the ownership tree, which is why components with a common immediate owner don't need an explicit FreeNotification link.

Since Notification is called as one of the last steps in the component's destruction, the expiring component's instance pointer is still valid, but the component itself probably isn't. You should only use the component instance parameter for its memory address to locate and clear matching references to that memory address from your component's internal data. Do not call methods or access properties of the expiring component in the Notification method of the surviving component.

Note that both participants in these notifications must be TComponents or TComponent descendants. In the TDBGrid column example mentioned earlier, you may find it interesting that the column objects are not TComponents. The column objects are lightweight TCollectionItem descendants, indirect descendants of TPersistent. To find out when database field components are destroyed, the column objects use their owning TDBGrid as their surrogate endpoint in the free notifications link. TDBGrid overrides Notification to listen for opRemove notifications and updates its column objects when it finds that a field object is being destroyed.

Assign and AssignTo

Assignment of data to component properties is one of the most fundamental operations in Delphi. Since component properties can refer to object instances and object instances with properties can be treated like record structures with data fields, you need a way to allow the Delphi programmer to assign one class-type component property the "value" of another class-type property. However, just making the simple instance variable assignment A := B won't do: You'll lose the object instance that variable A was referring to, and you'll wind up with two variables referring to the same object instance. This is a problem if both A and B assume they own the object instance they refer to—if A destroys the object instance, B will point to garbage.

To make A := B perform as expected, all you need to do is make A take on the attributes of B. If you can do this without destroying either object instance, you avoid problems of object ownership and ownership transfer. VCL implements an object attribute transfer convention using the TPersistent.Assign method and its less common reciprocal, TPersistent.AssignTo. Where C++ has copy constructors, implicitly created temporary instances, and assignment operators, Delphi has Assign methods and property write methods.

Making the Assignment

First, let's talk about how to set up a class-type property to support direct assignment. Let's say we're implementing a string list property of type TStrings. In the property declaration, specify a method in the property's write clause, as shown in Listing 8.1. For this discussion of assignment, it doesn't matter whether the property read clause is a method or a field.

Listing 8.1 The SetList method lets the MyStrings property support direct assignment.

```
type
  TMyComponent = class(TComponent)
  private
    FList: TStringList;
    procedure SetList(NewList: TStrings);
  public
    constructor Create(Owner: TComponent); override;
    destructor Destroy; override;
    property MyStrings: TStrings read FList write SetList;
  end;

constructor TMyComponent.Create(Owner: TComponent);
begin
  inherited Create(Owner);
  FList := TStringList.Create;
end;
destructor TMyComponent.Destroy;
begin
  FList.Free;
  inherited Destroy;
end;
procedure TMyComponent.SetList(NewList: TStrings);
begin
  FList.Assign(NewList);
end;
```

Implement the SetList method to call the Assign method of the internal string list instance, passing in the NewList parameter. The TStrings implementation of Assign takes care of the details of copying the list contents from the NewList instance into the current string list instance, essentially cloning the list.

Implementing Assign

When building your own component class, you need to think about whether you should support assignment between instances of your class and what it means to make such assignments. The destination instance should usually release all resources it has allocated and copy or acquire a shared reference to the resources owned by the source instance. In the simplest case, you just copy property values from the source instance (the parameter to Assign) to the destination instance (Self in Assign). In extreme cases, it may be simpler to dump the source instance into a temporary memory stream and load the destination instance from that memory stream.

Most VCL components don't implement any support for assignment between instances. Most VCL helper classes—TPersistent descendants intended for use as properties in components, such as TFont, TPen, and TBrush—do support assignment. A few special classes, such as TClipboard, contain extensive assignment support.

You should consider what class types your component will recognize as compatible sources. You could support assignment of instances of other component types to your component if it makes sense and is convenient for the Delphi application writer. Most classes recognize only their own class type in their Assign implementations.

Your Assign implementation should be prepared for `nil` as a source parameter. If it makes sense for your component, assignment of a `nil` source parameter should revert your component to its default initialized state. If your component cannot support `nil` assignments, treat `nil` like any other source parameter you don't support: Pass it on to the inherited Assign method.

To implement Assign, you override TPersistent.Assign in your TPersistent-derived class declaration and write code to test the source parameter for `nil` or compatible class type(s). Source instance class types you don't recognize or handle completely should be passed on to the inherited Assign method. Listing 8.2 shows the implementation of TStrings.Assign, which clears the destination string list and copies each of the strings from the source list to the destination list.

Listing 8.2 A simple implementation of Assign.

```
procedure TStrings.Assign(Source: TPersistent);
begin
  if Source is TStrings then
  begin
    BeginUpdate;
```

```
      try
        Clear;
        AddStrings(TStrings(Source));
      finally
        EndUpdate;
      end;
  end else inherited Assign(Source);
end;
```

Since TStrings is an abstract base class used by many components for string data properties, this Assign implementation makes it easy to assign Listbox1.Lines := Memo1.Lines or Header1.Sections := StringGrid.Rows[10]. In each case, the property type is a class descended from TStrings, and the property write methods use Assign to transfer the data between the string lists.

The AssignTo Turnabout

When your Assign method calls its inherited method, your ancestor class has an opportunity to examine the source instance's class type and either handle the assignment or pass the source instance on to its inherited method. If none of the Assign implementations in your class's ancestry know what to do with the source instance, execution will eventually find its way to TPersistent.Assign. If the source parameter is `nil`, TPersistent raises an exception; otherwise, TPersistent.Assign turns around and calls the AssignTo method of the source instance, passing the destination instance as a parameter. The process of implementing AssignTo is identical to Assign, except that the roles are reversed (the parameter is the destination, and Self is the source).

The AssignTo turnabout says, "If A doesn't know how to extract data from B, perhaps B knows how to transfer data into A." This allows new classes to participate in assignment to and from old classes without modifying the code of the old classes. In broader terms, the combination of Assign and AssignTo allows a class to implement assignment semantics for assignments *to* instances of that class from known class types, as well as assignments *from* instances of that class to other known class types.

Non-Self Class Tests and Smart Linking

Be careful of what class types you touch when implementing your Assign and AssignTo methods. Remember that an IS test touches the class information of the named class type, which links in all the virtual methods of the class and all the code they refer to. Testing an instance against your own class type or an inherited class type incurs no code size penalties (you're already using your class), but testing an instance against some other class type usually forces the linker to link in that other class, even if it's never used or constructed anywhere in the application. Since Assign and AssignTo are virtual methods, sloppy coding can lead to a multilevel cascade effect where use of class A in a program touches class B (because A.Assign contains an IS B test) and class B touches classes C and D (because B.Assign contains IS C and IS D tests), and so on, which is a classic cause of code bloat.

The best strategy to combat this code bloat is to eliminate codependencies in Assign and AssignTo. One way to avoid touching specific types is to use base class types instead of multiple specific descendant class types. If you can get the info you need using C and D's common ancestor type instead of the C and D actual types, you reduce the code bloat costs to just the implementation of the common ancestor class instead of the implementations of both C and D.

You can sacrifice one class to carry the burden of cross-class assignment for several classes. If one class already requires the presence of the other classes, put all the Assign/AssignTo logic in that class. In the preceding example, if there is no way to avoid B's use of C and D, you can at least lighten A by flipping A.Assign's code into B.AssignTo. Instead of A.Assign containing an IS B test, B.AssignTo can have an IS A test. B gets a little heavier, but A gets a lot lighter. A real-world example of this is the TPicture class. TPicture can contain a bitmap, a metafile, an icon, or a custom graphic image, so using a TPicture class in a project will most likely pull those other graphics classes into the EXE as well. You want to be able to assign image data from a TPicture into a graphics class, like Bitmap.Assign(Picture), for example. Problem: You don't want the graphics class's Assign methods to reference TPicture because TPicture touches so many other things. Solution: Make TPicture.AssignTo do the work of transferring its image into an arbitrary graphics class.

Frequency of use plays into this as well. The cost of a frequently used class touching a seldom used class is very high; the seldom used class is dragged in even though it is not used. The cost of a seldom-used class touching a frequently-used class is quite low; the frequently used class is probably already in the project for other reasons. For example, the clipboard unit provides special support for handling various clipboard data formats. This support is handy but is not needed by most Delphi applications. Instead of having the graphics classes support assignment to the clipboard component (and thus drag infrequently used clipboard code into all Delphi apps), the clipboard component supports assignment from the graphics classes in its AssignTo method. The clipboard component is the seldom used class, while the graphics classes are frequently used classes.

Transferring Data via Properties or Direct Field Access

When implementing Assign or AssignTo, it may be necessary to circumvent the normal property assignment practices of your component to avoid triggering multiple change notifications in your component or to prevent the data transfer operation from changing the state of the source instance. Since most Assign implementations deal only with source instances compatible with their own class type, Assign usually has complete access to the private fields at the heart of both the destination and source instances.

For example, one simple way to implement TBitmap.Assign would be to just assign the source's bitmap handle and palette handle into the destination's bitmap and palette properties. However, referring to the source's Handle property will force it to create a bitmap handle if it doesn't already have one (VCL's handle creation deferral strategies are covered in Chapter 10). Creating a handle is a time-consuming task, and grabbing the handle marks the bitmap as modified (since VCL can't know what you're going to do with the raw handle, it must assume you're going to draw onto it). Instead of referring to the source's Handle property, TBitmap.Assign reaches into the private fields of the source TBitmap so that the destination instance can share the bitmap data owned by the source instance without changing the source instance's state. Like all the VCL graphics classes, TBitmap implements copy-on-write resource caching. Modifications to one bitmap instance whose image data is shared with other bitmap instances will force it to make its own complete copy of the image data before applying the modifications.

Clipboard Support

The best example of Assign and AssignTo in action is the TClipboard class and its interaction with components. TClipboard includes built-in support for transferring clipboard data to and from the standard graphics classes—for example, TBitmap and TPicture. Through TPicture, TClipboard also supports any custom graphics classes that have been registered through TPicture.RegisterClipboardFormat. To copy data to the clipboard, you call Clipboard.Assign(MyObject). To paste data from the clipboard into your object, you call MyObject.Assign(Clipboard).

If you create a new component that has special clipboard data requirements, you may be tempted to create a new clipboard class type derived from TClipboard, override the Assign method, and add your special support code directly to the clipboard. Don't do this! If you replace the stock clipboard object with your own custom clipboard instance, you'll have to destroy the stock clipboard and create your replacement in the unit initialization code (since the clipboard object must always be available). Now, what happens if somebody else does the same thing to implement his or her own custom clipboard support? If these two custom clipboards wind up in the same project (they will, trust me), one of the custom clipboard implementations will end up destroying the other, and the code that relies on the existence of the losing custom clipboard will most likely cause an access violation. Again, don't do this! The clipboard is a global resource; there can be only one, so leave it alone.

To get the custom clipboard support you need, just implement your special clipboard support code in your component's Assign (paste from clipboard) and AssignTo (copy to clipboard) methods, and remind your customers (the application writers) to use Assign to perform clipboard operations on your component.

GetPalette and PaletteChanged

Components that need to display more colors than the standard 20 Windows system colors either will have to require 24-bit true color video modes or will have to implement color palette support. As you dig into your first project requiring color palette coordination, the first option will seem less and less absurd. Unless you're fortunate enough to be able to require 24-bit color video support of your end users, though, you'll just have to read up on the Windows palette system and slog through it like the rest of us.

Well, actually, perhaps not. All you really need to do to add palette support to a VCL component is override the protected TControl.GetPalette virtual method in your component to return the handle of the palette of colors your component wants to display itself with. VCL will call your GetPalette method when appropriate and do all the work of merging your preferred palette of colors with the palette of system colors actually available. If your component has focus, its color palette has first priority in the system palette and your component will look great. If your component doesn't have focus, its palette colors are mixed in with whatever is left after the focused window or application has asserted its own palette, and your component may not look so great. However, displaying muted and muddy colors when your component doesn't have focus (which is most of the time) is better than the solarized, postapocalyptic, alien-landscape color effects that result from not performing any palette operations at all.

Windows sends the WM_QUERYNEWPALETTE message to top-level windows (such as Delphi forms) in search of an initial foreground color palette, which is provided by the focused window or one of its child controls. VCL responds to WM_QUERYNEWPALETTE by calling the PaletteChanged virtual method introduced in TControl with a Foreground parameter of True. PaletteChanged calls GetPalette to fetch your control's palette handle. If your control provides a palette handle (result <> 0), PaletteChanged realizes your palette (merges it with the system palette), sets its function result to True, and exits. If your control doesn't provide a palette handle, your control's PaletteChanged calls PaletteChanged of each of the controls parented by your control until one of them returns True, indicating it realized a palette.

VCL calls PaletteChanged with Foreground = False in response to the WM_PALETTECHANGED message. Windows sends this message to all top-level windows after an application asserts a foreground palette. When the Foreground parameter is False, the PaletteChanged cascade runs through all the controls in a form, allowing them the opportunity to do the best they can with the new colors in the system palette.

> **Infinitely Colorful Recursion**
>
> Since WM_PALETTECHANGED follows every WM_QUERYNEWPALETTE, and WM_QUERYNEWPALETTE is sent in response to somebody realizing a palette as a foreground palette, all you need to do to bring Windows to its knees is realize a foreground palette in response to WM_PALETTECHANGED. Grab some popcorn, sit back, and watch the pretty colors switch back and forth indefinitely.
>
> Unless, of course, you're running in a high-color video mode (more than 8 bits per pixel). All palette operations are no-ops in high-color modes, and your app will never receive a WM_QUERYNEWPALETTE or WM_PALETTECHANGED message when running on high-color systems. This also means your component's GetPalette and PaletteChanged methods will never be called when running on high-color systems, so don't do anything but palette support in these methods.

If you are writing a component wrapper around a third-party DLL custom control that needs palette support, the custom control may require that you forward WM_QUERYNEWPALETTE messages to it so that it can realize its palette—that is, merge the colors it wants with the colors it can get. The easiest way to do this is to override PaletteChanged in your component wrapper to send a fake WM_QUERYNEWPALETTE message to the custom control implementation when the PaletteChanged Foreground parameter is True. If the custom control implementation realizes a palette, set your PaletteChanged function result to True and exit. Otherwise, call your inherited PaletteChanged method to let the normal palette processing continue.

Graphics

Every component that has a visible presence on the screen uses graphics drawing routines to some degree. The VCL graphics classes eliminate a lot of the grunt work normally associated with Windows graphics operations. VCL takes care of allocating resources as needed, freeing resources when they are no longer in use, and managing the intricacies of the great state machine known as Windows GDI.

While graphics in general is far too large a topic to tackle here, there are several features of the VCL graphics architecture that are often overlooked or misunderstood. In this section, we'll review resource minimization techniques in VCL, how to "decorate" your components with graphics properties, how to use graphics classes to improve performance or display quality, and how to extend VCL to support additional graphics file formats.

Sharing Resources with a Vengeance

All the VCL graphics classes implement a resource-sharing scheme that allows multiple graphics objects to share the same Windows bitmap, font, and other handles. Creating handles for just about any kind of Windows resource is expensive both in terms of memory and in terms of performance. Sharing handles between graphics objects minimizes an application's consumption of system resource handles and system memory and minimizes the number of times the application has to wait for Windows to create a new handle. Though 32-bit Windows apps aren't constantly bumping into system resource limits the way 16-bit Windows 3.1 apps do, there are still limits. Windows NT's system resource pool is limited only by system memory (which is "virtually" endless with a large enough swap file), but burning up resource handles like there's no tomorrow will eventually exhaust the system's physical memory and put the machine into a disk-thrashing frenzy. Windows 95's system resource pool still has some 16-bit pockets with limits on the number of handles that it can, um, handle.

The extra effort VCL makes to implement resource sharing is still very important to Delphi application performance. Originally, resource sharing was simply a matter of survival for 16-bit Delphi apps. In today's 32-bit Windows environments, resource sharing has become a key performance advantage for 32-bit Delphi apps.

How does VCL determine when a graphics object can share the handle of another graphics object? In simple graphics objects like fonts, pens, and brushes, the data that uniquely identifies the characteristics of the resource is quite small. A font name and font size are just about all you need to uniquely define a font, for example. For these simple classes, VCL just compares the characteristic data to find a matching resource that can be shared. A font object, for example, requests a font resource structure having a particular set of attributes from a global font cache inside the graphics unit. If the font cache already contains a font resource structure with those attributes, the cache lets the font object use that existing font resource structure, incrementing the structure's reference count in the process. If the cache doesn't have a match, it creates a new font resource structure with those attributes. When a font object no longer needs a font resource structure, it tells the cache to decrement the font resource structure's reference count. When the reference count drops to zero, the cache destroys the font resource structure and the font handle contained within it. VCL uses separate global resource caches for font, pen, and brush handles.

So, a font object can share its font handle with other font objects just by having the same font name, font size, and other properties as the other font objects. Calling the Assign method of font, pen, and brush objects is another way to share handles: The destination object releases its cached resource structure and acquires a reference to the source object's cached resource structure.

Images can't be uniquely characterized by a few bytes of data—you would have to compare every pixel between two bitmaps to determine that they are identical. The only way to make two bitmap objects share the same handle is to use the Assign method. This is the big difference between TGraphicsObject classes (like TFont) and TGraphic classes (like TBitmap): TGraphicsObject classes are always using shared resources maintained by a central cache object; TGraphic classes share resources only if you call Assign in your code.

Consider the following scenarios:

1. If you call LoadBitmap 10 times to load the same bitmap into 10 speed buttons, you'll wind up with 10 different bitmap handles, and your memory use will be 10 times the size of the bitmap.

2. If you call LoadBitmap once and assign that bitmap handle to the Glyph.Handle property of 10 speed buttons, you have a logic bug: Assigning to the Handle property transfers ownership of that handle to the object you're giving it to. You'll have one happy speed button and nine jealous mutineers waiting for an excuse to raise an exception.

3. If you call Speedbutton1.Glyph.LoadFromFile('foo.bmp') and then use Assign to copy that bitmap to the other speed button's glyphs, like Speedbutton2.Glyph.Assign(Speedbutton1.Glyph), for example, you'll have 10 happy speed buttons sharing one busy bitmap.

4. By dropping 10 speed buttons on a form at design time and loading the same bitmap into each, you'll have a scenario identical to scenario #1. That is, 10 copies of the bitmap exist in memory at design time, 10 copies are written to the DFM file, and 10 copies are loaded at run time.

5. If you set the bitmap of only one speed button at design time and then assign the glyphs around using code in the form's OnCreate event, you're back to using only one bitmap handle at run time, landing you a 10-times reduction in memory use and form load time.

Decorating Your Components with Fonts, Pens, and Brushes

Adding Font, Pen and Brush graphics object properties to your component classes requires these boilerplate steps:

1. Declare the published graphics object property to use a method in its property write clause. The read clause is up to you.

2. Declare a private instance variable to hold the graphics object.

3. Declare a private change notification method for the graphics object. This can be used by multiple graphics objects in your component.

4. Instantiate the graphics object in your component's constructor. Assign the change notification method to the graphics object's OnChange event property.

5. Free the graphics object in your component's destructor.

6. Implement the property's write method to call your graphics object's Assign method.

7. Implement the change notification method to call Invalidate to redraw your component.

8. Use the graphics object in your component's drawing code. Assign the graphics object to the drawing canvas's corresponding property (Canvas.Font := MyFont). (This is the step you'll forget to do.)

These steps can be used to implement almost any helper object as a property, including bitmap objects, canvases, or your own helper classes.

Using Bitmaps

TBitmap encapsulates a surprising number of Windows graphics concepts. TBitmap loads and stores BMP file image data in a variety of color depths and manages its own color palette when drawing its image. TBitmap has its own canvas that you can use to draw on the bitmap image, encapsulating the notion of a memory device context and offscreen memory bitmap.

Performance Tradeoffs with DIB versus DDB

When you call TBitmap.LoadFromFile to load a BMP file into a bitmap object, the bitmap object keeps a copy of the original file data in a memory stream. The bitmap does not create a bitmap handle unless you refer to the bitmap's Handle property in your own code. The bitmap can draw its image directly from the pixel data in the memory stream using the StretchDIBits Windows API call. Stretch-DIBits takes about twice as long as StretchBlt to draw pixels on the screen, but StretchDIBits doesn't require a bitmap handle to draw the image. Since creating the bitmap handle from the device-independent bitmap (DIB) file information is a very time-consuming task, using StretchDIBits and the DIB memory stream actually results in faster file-to-screen image load performance than using StretchBlt and a device-dependent bitmap handle (DDB). Since most applications redraw images infrequently, using the slower StretchDIBits is a reasonable trade-off for faster image loading. Remember, bitmaps selected at design time are stored in the DFM file, so bitmap loading performance directly impacts form loading performance and application start-up time.

If your component will be redrawing the same bitmap image frequently, you can get faster drawing performance by forcing the bitmap object to create the DDB bitmap handle. Just read the bitmap's Handle property to force it to create a native DDB bitmap handle.

File Format Preservation

A bitmap's internal DIB memory stream stays around as long as the bitmap object can be sure that the bitmap image still matches the contents of the DIB memory stream. When the bitmap image is altered or is potentially altered, the bitmap object frees its DIB memory stream, and the bitmap lives solely on the image in the bitmap handle. When you instruct the bitmap to save its image to a file, it writes the DIB memory stream to the file. If the DIB memory stream has been destroyed because of image modifications, a new DIB memory stream is created and filled with DIB pixel data extracted from the bitmap handle before writing the DIB memory stream to the file.

If you load a BMP file into a bitmap, display the image, and then write the image out to another BMP file, the pixel format and color information in the new file will be identical to the original BMP file. However, if you load, display, modify, and then write the image out to a file, the new file's pixel color depth (bits per pixel, bpp) will reflect the color depth of the current video mode. This can lead to 16-color, 4-bpp images that suddenly turn into 8-bpp or 24-bpp files. Like toothpaste out of its tube, it's hard to pack an image back into its original pixel format once it has been promoted to a larger number of colors. A TBitmap's original file information is destroyed by accessing its Handle property, calling its ReleaseHandle or ReleasePalette methods, drawing on the bitmap's canvas, or accessing the canvas's Handle property.

Graphics File Format Extensions

Delphi's standard TGraphic classes (TMetafile, TBitmap, and TIcon) cover the image file handling needs of your typical Windows program. However, these are only the tip of the iceberg. You can create your own graphics classes to handle other graphics file formats, such as GIF and JPEG files, and register them with the TPicture class. TPicture is a generic image handling class that provides polymorphism of image data. With a TBitmap instance, you can only read and display BMP files. With a TPicture instance, you can read and display any file format that has been registered and any clipboard format that has been registered.

To create your own graphics file handler, create a class that derives from TGraphic and override and implement all the abstract virtual methods declared in TGraphic. The most important methods for you to concentrate on are LoadFromStream, GetWidth, GetHeight, Draw, and SaveToStream, in that order. If your file format is fairly simple, you might get away with inheriting your class from TBitmap. Graphics file formats that involve image compression will probably do better to inherit directly from TGraphic and implement a public property of type TBitmap that provides the decompressed image data. LoadFromStream can decompress the image data into the TBitmap property image. Draw can just forward the draw operation to the class's bitmap property, like this:

```
procedure TMyGIFImage.Draw(ACanvas: TCanvas; const Rect: TRect);
begin
  ACanvas.StretchDraw(Rect, FBitmap);
end;
```

In this way, the graphic can be treated as a displayable image source (it implements Draw), but it doesn't have to support all the operations of a TBitmap. For example, with lossy compression file formats like JPEG, you don't want to recompress the image data every time SaveToStream is called because as more image information is discarded on each load/save cycle, the image would quickly decay to a lifeless blur. Image compression should occur only when requested, perhaps by a call to a Compress method that takes a source bitmap as an input parameter.

Fractal Image File Graphics Class

I've long been a fan of nonlinear dynamics and fractal mathematics, even before pretty picture books of fractal artwork captured the eye of the general public several years ago. One of the first wave of researchers to focus on fractal mathematics, Michael Barnsley, was also one of the first to move to capitalize on this new science. Barnsley founded Iterated Systems with the vision of applying fractal transformations and image decomposition to the task of image compression. Iterated Systems' Fractal Image File (FIF) format is the result of that vision and quite a lot of work.

Most image compression techniques use statistical analysis to characterize an image by the frequency of incidence of individual pixel color values. In contrast, the data in a FIF file describes the composition of an image more than its individual pixels. Fractal compression seeks to find transformations that will make the image fold in upon itself, reducing the volume of data required to reproduce the significant detail of the image. The resulting FIF data is often 100 times smaller than the original raw image pixels, on par with other lossy image compression systems such as JPEG, but retains considerably more image detail and color accuracy and introduces fewer artifacts than JPEG. While FIF compression requires considerably more computation time than other systems, decompression is uncharacteristically fast. Perhaps the most unusual aspect of FIF decompression is that it is resolution independent. You can compress a 1000-by-500, 24-bpp image into a 20K FIF file and then decompress the FIF file to 3000-by-1500 pixels without the image decaying into unrecognizable blobs of color. Certainly, artifacts of lossy compression are more apparent when you've expanded the FIF image to four or five times the original dimensions, but try doing that with a BMP or JPEG file and see what happens. Where JPEG's compression artifacts are often described as "fuzzballs" or "dog hair," FIF compression artifacts more resemble brush strokes in a painting.

But don't take my word for it—see for yourself. In the files that accompany this book are Iterated Systems' FIF decompression library (and royalty-free distribution license), source code implementing a new TFIFImage class for Delphi, and a Delphi application, ImgView.dpr, to show it off. You can create new FIF files from your own images with the included Fractal Imager shareware application.

Why FIF and not GIF, JPEG, or TIFF?

Why on earth have I taken off after a file format you've probably never heard of instead of writing a graphics class for a more common image file format like GIF, JPEG, or TIFF? Simple. GIF and TIFF use the LZW compression algorithm, for which LZW patent-holder Unisys now requires licensing and per-copy royalty payments. JPEG source is free, but it requires more support code (that I would have to write) than FIF and produces inferior results. So now you know: I'm cheap and I'm lazy.

On one hand, FIF is an interesting technology in its own right. On the other hand, that's really beside the point. Let's get back to talking about writing Delphi components, like TFIFImage.

As shown in Listing 8.3, the FIF unit contains two classes: TFIFData and TFIFImage. TFIFData is a private internal class that owns the actual compressed data of a FIF image. TFIFImage manages the attributes and display of one view of that compressed data. TFIFData is reference counted so that it can be shared among multiple TFIFImage instances. Each TFIFImage instance has its own copy of the decompressed image stored in its Bitmap property. The image is not decompressed until it is needed—either when TFIFImage.Draw is called or when something accesses the Bitmap property.

Listing 8.3 The TFIFImage graphics class adds support for the FIF graphics format to Delphi's built-in graphics systems.

```
type
  TFIFData = class
  private
    FRefCount: Longint;
    FData: TCustomMemoryStream;
    FOriginal: TFIFOriginalImageInfo;
    FAttributesLoaded: Boolean;
  protected
    procedure AttributesNeeded;
    procedure Reference;
    procedure Release;
    property RefCount: Longint read FRefCount;
  end;
```

```
    TColorFormat = (RGB8, RGB15, RGB24);
    TProgressAction = (paStart, paRunning, paEnd);
    TProgressEvent = procedure (Sender: TObject;
      Action: TProgressAction;
      PercentComplete: Longint) of object;

    TFIFImage = class(TGraphic)
    private
      FImage: TFIFData;   // original compressed image data
      FBitmap: TBitmap;   // decompressed image
      FWidth: Integer;    // desired pixel width of decompressed image
      FHeight: Integer;   // desired pixel height of decompressed image
      FOnLoading: TProgressEvent;
      FSession: TFIFDecodeSession;
      FFastestSize: Boolean; // rounds size down for best speed
      FColorFormat: TColorFormat;
      procedure BitmapChanged(Sender: TObject);
      function GetBitmap: TBitmap;
      function GetOriginalHeight: Longint;
      function GetOriginalWidth: Longint;
      procedure SetFastestSize(Value: Boolean);
      procedure SetColorFormat(Value: TColorFormat);
    protected
      procedure Changed(Sender: TObject);
      procedure Draw(ACanvas: TCanvas; const Rect: TRect); override;
      procedure  FIFCallback(Session: TFIFDecodeSession;
         Action: TProgressAction; PercentComplete: Longint); virtual;
      function GetEmpty: Boolean; override;
      function GetHeight: Integer; override;
      function GetWidth: Integer; override;
      procedure NewImage;
      procedure ReadData(Stream: TStream); override;
      procedure ReadStream(Size: Longint; Stream: TStream);
      procedure SetHeight(Value: Integer); override;
      procedure SetWidth(Value: Integer); override;
      procedure WriteData(Stream: TStream); override;
    public
      constructor Create; override;
      destructor Destroy; override;
      procedure Assign(Source: TPersistent); override;
      procedure LoadFromStream(Stream: TStream); override;
      procedure SaveToStream(Stream: TStream); override;
      procedure LoadFromClipboardFormat(AFormat: Word; AData: THandle;
         APalette: HPALETTE); override;
      procedure SaveToClipboardFormat(var AFormat: Word;
         var AData: THandle; var APalette: HPALETTE); override;
      property Bitmap: TBitmap read GetBitmap;
      property ColorFormat: TColorFormat read FColorFormat
```

```
      write SetColorFormat;
    property FastestSize: Boolean read FFastestSize
      write SetFastestSize;
    property OriginalWidth: Longint read GetOriginalWidth;
    property OriginalHeight: Longint read GetOriginalHeight;
    property OnLoading: TProgressEvent read FOnLoading
      write FOnLoading;
  end;
```

ColorFormat, FastestSize, Width, and Height determine the parameters that GetBitmap uses to request the FIF decompression DLL to prepare an image with a particular pixel color depth and output resolution. FastestSize allows the decompressor to round the output resolution down to the nearest internal natural boundary in the FIF data to speed up decompression. OriginalHeight and OriginalWidth provide the pixel height and width of the original source image used to create the FIF file. These are the default values for the Height and Width properties as well. To scale the image, modify its height or width property.

All the properties use write methods so that when the property changes, the current bitmap image will be destroyed. The bitmap will be recreated from the original FIF data the next time the Bitmap property is accessed. This allows you to modify multiple properties without incurring the decompression cost on each modification.

Assign and the streaming routines all have standard implementations. The streaming routines use only the FIF compressed data, not the expanded bitmap image. LoadFromClipboardFormat is stubbed out (it does nothing). SaveToClipboardFormat forwards the request to the Bitmap object.

The FIF unit registers the TFIFImage class with the graphics unit's list of file formats in the unit initialization section, shown in Listing 8.4. The first parameter is the file extension to associate the graphics class with, followed by the full text description of the file format. TPicture.LoadFromFile scans the list of registered file extensions for a match with the given file and creates an instance of the first graphics class it finds a match with. Thus, TPicture.LoadFromFile will automatically create instances of the graphics classes you design (if you remember to register them).

Listing 8.4 In FIF.PAS, this call to a TPicture class method makes the new TFIFImage class a native part of the Delphi graphics architecture.

```
initialization
  TPicture.RegisterFileFormat('FIF',
    'Fractal Image File', TFIFImage);
end;
```

The file extension and description strings are used by the GraphicFilter function in graphics.pas to build a string of filter expressions suitable for assigning to an open file dialog's Filter property. The main form of the ImgView application makes this assignment in its FormCreate event, as shown in Listing 8.5.

Listing 8.5 GraphicFilter builds a file filter string describing all registered graphics classes, including the newly registered TFIFImage class, for use in the open file dialog's List Files of Type combobox.

```
procedure TImgViewForm.FormCreate(Sender: TObject);
begin
  OpenDialog1.Filter := GraphicFilter(TGraphic);
  Colors1.Enabled := Image1.Picture.Graphic is TFIFImage;
  Caption := Application.Title;
end;
```

TFIFImage contains an OnLoading event to allow a form to display a progress indicator while a large image is decompressing. This event is called by the FIFCallback procedure, which is called (indirectly) by the decompressor DLL periodically while decompressing the image. OnLoading is of type TProgressEvent, which takes three parameters: a Sender, an Action, and a PercentComplete. Sender is the TFIFImage instance. Action can be paStart, paRunning, or paEnd, indicating the state of the decompression. Once OnLoading has been called with paStart, you are guaranteed that OnLoading will later be called with paEnd, so you can use these notifications to allocate and free resources used by your event handler during the decompression cycle.

For example, Listing 8.6 shows the ImgView main form's Open1Click and UpdateProgressBar procedures. Open1Click shows an open file common dialog to let the user select a file to load and loads the file into the image control. If the TGraphic instance created by Image1.Picture is a TFIFImage, the form hooks its OnLoading event to point to its own UpdateProgressBar method. UpdateProgressBar sets the application's mouse cursor to an hourglass (or whatever cursor you've configured your Windows environment to use for the "wait" symbol—mine is the "drumming fingers" animated cursor) when it receives a paStart notification. In the paRunning notification, it displays the progress in a text message on the status bar.

Listing 8.6 The ImgView main form hooks the FIFImage instance's OnLoading event to display progress messages on the status line.

```
procedure TImgViewForm.Open1Click(Sender: TObject);
begin
  if OpenDialog1.Execute then
  begin
    Image1.Autosize := True;
    Image1.Picture.LoadFromFile(OpenDialog1.Filename);
    Colors1.Enabled := Image1.Picture.Graphic is TFIFImage;
    if Image1.Picture.Graphic is TFIFImage then
      TFIFImage(Image1.Picture.Graphic).OnLoading :=
        UpdateProgressBar;
    Filename := OpenDialog1.Filename;
    FitToWindow;
    UpdateCaption;
  end;
end;
procedure TImgViewForm.UpdateProgressBar(Sender: TObject;
  Action: TProgressAction; PercentComplete: Longint);
begin
  case Action of
    paStart: Screen.Cursor := crHourGlass;
    paRunning:
      begin
        StatusBar1.SimpleText := Format(
          'Decompressing: %d%% complete.', [PercentComplete]);
        StatusBar1.Update;
      end;
    paEnd:
      begin
        Screen.Cursor := crDefault;
        StatusBar1.SimpleText := '';
      end;
  end;
end;
```

Notice the call to StatusBar1.Update. No message processing takes place while the decompressor is churning away. If we simply invalidate the status bar (which happens automatically when you modify its SimpleText property), it will put a WM_PAINT message in our message queue, but that message won't be retrieved until execution returns to the application message loop after the decompression step has finished.

Calling StatusBar1.Update forces the status bar control to redraw itself immediately if it has been invalidated. Calling Application.ProcessMessages would also work, but that opens up the possibility of reentrancy (recursion) and allows a lot more stuff to go on during the callback, which slows down the decompression cycle. This application doesn't have anything else to do but wait for the decompression to finish, so it keeps the callback operations to a minimum by not calling Application.ProcessMessages.

Finally, UpdateProgressBar responds to the paEnd notification by clearing the status line string and restoring the application's cursor. The OnLoading event will be fired with paEnd after paStart even if an exception occurs during decompression.

To abort the decompression of an image, call Abort in the OnLoading event. Abort is a SysUtils routine that raises a silent exception—an exception class derived directly from TObject instead of the normal TException. Abort is called a *silent* exception because the default VCL exception handler (Application.HandleException) will not report Abort exceptions to the end user.

Play around with the ImgView application a bit. You can load WMF, EMF, BMP, ICO, and now FIF files with it. Be sure to try left- and right-mouse clicks on the image to zoom in and out. Not bad for 200 lines of application code, eh?

Summary

VCL contains large, hard-to-miss system services as well as smaller, more subtle conventions and utility services. Using TComponent.FreeNotification, you can link components with different lifetimes so that when one goes away, the other can clear its pointers and link states. By implementing Assign and/or AssignTo, you can provide an easy way to transfer data and state information between complex components and implement class-type properties with value semantics. Controls that need to display more than the handful of VGA system colors can plug into VCL's color palette management system simply by overriding and implementing GetPalette. Graphics components are among my personal favorites. Since pixels will always outnumber available CPU cycles, efficiency always counts in graphics work. Sharing resources and avoiding costly references to handle properties are essential to building a small, fast component. Finally, through the extensible graphics architecture, you can add support for additional image file formats to your Delphi applications without having to write separate image viewer components for each file format. If it's a TGraphic and it's registered with TPicture, plain old TImage (and TDBImage) will display whatever it is.

Chapter 9

OLE and COM Interfaces

OLE is often perceived as a huge impenetrable mass of code and interfaces mostly because Microsoft's flagship OLE applications are typically huge impenetrable masses of code and features. The bad news is that most of the OLE documentation focuses on Microsoft-supplied support libraries and code emitters that are very good at making mountains out of molehills. The good news is that OLE is supported by the operating system, segmented into a variety of services that you can use in your Delphi applications without adding significant overhead to your programs. The trick is to tackle OLE one interface at a time and to learn to distinguish between what OLE offers and what you really need. This chapter reviews what OLE and COM are, examines what happens when you use an OLE object in a Delphi application, and shows you how to implement OLE interfaces by building a simple OLE automation server in Delphi from scratch. Since we want to explore how OLE works at a low level, this chapter avoids the high-level TAutoObject OLE Automation server built into Delphi 2.0 that hides all the ugly OLE details.

OLE—Interprocess Communication

OLE is actually a network of subsystems, many of which can be used independently of the others. All of the myriad OLE features, complexities, subsystems, and protocols boil down to one thing: communication—specifically, communication between different bodies of code. Once you have communication, you can build all sorts of elaborate systems to share data between different bodies of code, to notify each other of changes, to provide services, and to query services that are available, and so on. Everything that is OLE is in some way related to communicating information between bodies of code.

OLE implements an interprocess communication mechanism upon which all other OLE services are built. This mechanism comes in several flavors optimized for varying degrees of remoteness, but the communication layer is invisible to the client application using OLE objects, as well as to the server application that implements OLE objects. As far as applications are concerned, OLE objects look just like the application's native objects, except that OLE objects are obtained from or given to an external party.

OLE Automation is one small facet of OLE that is intimately tied to OLE's core purpose of communication. In a nutshell, OLE Automation provides a standard interface that one application can use to prod another application into performing an action or to set or query state information within the other application. Automation is a good place to start your OLE experience because it's a relatively small set of APIs and interfaces, the mechanisms conceptually map directly onto OOP concepts you should already be familiar with, and it can serve as a metaphor for the communication mechanism that lies at the heart of nearly everything in OLE.

In the interest of clarity, we will ignore many aspects of *how* OLE does its magic. OLE is flexible to a fault: Nearly everything can be customized, including the lowest-level communication mechanisms. Many of the thousands of pages of OLE documentation deal with how to customize everything, which can get in the way of finding simple answers to simple questions. As with any technology, just keep in mind that there is always a deeper level of detail than what you are currently aware of. Lest you forget, OLE will remind you of this regularly.

COM = Abstract Interfaces

Recall from Chapter 3 that an abstract interface class is a class that contains only abstract virtual method declarations. An abstract interface contains no static methods or data fields and does not have any implementation. It's just a syntactic facade that makes the compiler think that class actually exists in your application.

OLE is a specification for interprocess communication using abstract virtual interfaces. COM (for Common Object Model) is the Microsoft specification for how those abstract virtual interfaces are arranged. Basically, a COM object must contain a pointer to a table of function addresses that are the callable methods of the COM object. Delphi's VMTs (virtual method tables) are precisely the list of function addresses that COM requires.

OLE defines a number of standard interfaces that OLE servers can implement and that OLE clients can use to communicate with an OLE server. (You can also define your own custom interfaces, but that's just icing on the cake.) Notice who implements the interface—the OLE server application, not OLE. OLE just defines what the abstract virtual interface should look like and the semantics of each method in the interface but OLE doesn't actually implement the behavior of most of the interfaces you'll encounter.

An OLE server provides an implementation of an OLE interface, and registers that implementation with OLE so that other apps can find and use it. An OLE client typically calls an OLE API function to locate and obtain an instance of a particular interface type, which the OLE client then interacts with by calling methods defined in the abstract virtual interface. The OLE client calls a method of the interface, and that winds up executing code in the OLE server implementation of that interface.

Fabricating Proxies to Bridge the Gap

OLE is doing a lot of behind-the-scenes work to make such interprocess communication succeed. For example, it would appear that the client is merely calling code in the OLE server. That would be the case if the client were just using an object instance obtained directly from a DLL (as discussed in Chapter 3), but that's not the case in OLE when the object is implemented in a separate application or on a remote machine. When a client calls OLE to request an instance of a particular interface, OLE does obtain such an instance from the server app, but OLE does not give that instance pointer to the client. OLE internally fabricates a proxy instance for the client so that when the client calls a method of the interface, it actually calls a helper routine set up by OLE. The helper routine will take care of performing the necessary context switches before calling the corresponding method in the OLE server. The OLE server returns from the call back to the helper, which switches context back to the client before returning to the client. The setup and teardown code surrounding the context-switching process is called *marshaling*. The actual interprocess calls are made through a service called Remote Procedure Calls (RPC) or locally optimized derivatives.

True to form, OLE has a variety of degrees to which it participates in this call cycle. Between 16-bit applications, the context switch is about the same as what SendMessage does—change the DS and SS registers, copy parameters, then leap. Between 32-bit applications, the wall separating processes is at least 6 feet thick, so the context switch performed by OLE can be much more complicated. (OLE calls also work between 16- and 32-bit apps.) When communicating between applications, remember that you are never calling directly into the target app. There will always be some marshaling and task switch overhead in interprocess communication.

Marshaling usually requires copying parameter data from the client's to the server's process address space. You'll notice as we build our OLE Automation server that data for string parameters is always allocated using SysAllocString, an OLE API function that puts the string data in a shared global memory area accessible to both the client and the server. This relieves the marshaling routines from having to copy large volumes of data or deal with string length semantics.

Loading In-Process Servers

If the OLE object is implemented in a DLL instead of an application, OLE can load it as an *in-process server*. An in-process OLE server eliminates virtually all the proxies, marshaling, and other interprocess overhead by setting up shop inside the client's process address space. The OLE object can directly access parameters passed to it by the client application, so there is no need for marshaling to copy parameter data back and forth. OLE in-process servers are the domain of OLE Controls, originally referred to as OCX controls but more recently relabeled "ActiveX" by the Microsoft marketing circus. With the interprocess communication overhead out of the way, OCX controls have the potential to execute as fast as native controls in an application. Unfortunately, OCX is inextricably OLE, so while a method call may be direct, getting there is not (just take a look at OLE2.pas!). Implementing an OCX control requires implementing about a dozen OLE-defined interfaces, plus whatever custom interfaces your control requires. For the moment, creating OCX controls from scratch in Delphi is beyond the scope of this chapter.

Delphi OLE Automation Server: Design Strategy

To illustrate what's involved in implementing an OLE interface, let's build a simple OLE Automation server in Delphi that allows other applications to read the properties of components in the Delphi application. Note that the purpose of this exercise is to explore the bare-metal OLE interfaces and issues, not to find the easiest way to add OLE Automation to your applications. The easiest way, by far, to add OLE Automation capabilities to your application is to use the Automation Expert in Delphi 2.0. The exercise we're about to embark upon will give you some insight into how the Delphi Automation Expert and Automation Server component are implemented.

To make a native object participate in OLE Automation processes, you can either build your application using OLE objects as your native architecture or can make OLE enabler objects that bind to your native objects and act as a bridge between OLE-speak and your native architecture. Since OLE is designed to solve interprocess communication issues, it's a poor choice to implement objects used only within an application (it's like using a Boeing 747 to pick up bread and milk at the corner market).

Building OLE enabler classes is the approach we'll use for our Delphi OLE Automation server. The enabler classes will implement OLE's IDispatch interface, which is the center of the OLE Automation universe. IDispatch defines methods that allow the client to get and set property values of an object in the server and to call methods of server objects with parameters and return values. Our implementation of IDispatch will keep a pointer to a real VCL object that the IDispatch instance represents. When an OLE client asks our IDispatch to get a property value, our IDispatch will get the value from the real VCL object and package the result in an OLE-friendly format.

OLE interfaces can allow the client to obtain access to other objects in an application. Once a client has obtained an OLE interface, it can often navigate all over the server application's object space, hopping from one interface instance to another.

In Delphi applications, the Application object is the root container of all the objects in the application. From the Application object, you can get a list of all the currently open forms. From a given form, you can get a list of all the components in that form. From each component, you can get a variety of data and state information through its published properties.

Therefore, we will use the Application object as our OLE Automation gateway. If a client can obtain an OLE interface to your program's Application object, it can reach just about everything in your Delphi application. Security paranoia aside, allowing an OLE client the greatest breadth of access to your OLE Automation server app with a minimal amount of effort is the principal goal of this exercise.

IUnknown (UJane?)

IUnknown is a standard OLE interface that is as pervasive in OLE as TObject is in Delphi. All OLE interfaces descend from or include IUnknown. IUnknown defines reference-counting methods (AddRef and Release) and a method to obtain other interfaces (QueryInterface).

Implementing IDispatch

The IDispatch interface has four critical methods: AddRef and Release (inherited from IUnknown), plus GetIDsOfNames and Invoke. In Listing 9.1, we declare our IObjectDispatch as a descendant of the IDispatch abstract virtual interface class and override *all* the inherited methods. Don't forget to include the abstract methods that IDispatch inherits from IUnknown. For an OLE interface to work reliably, *all* the OLE-defined methods must be overridden and given method bodies in the server, even if that implementation does nothing more than return a result code of E_NOTIMPL. Note that there is a big difference between implementing a method body that returns E_NOTIMPL and leaving an abstract virtual method without a method body. The first case provides code that can be called, and that politely tells the caller not to do that. The second case does not provide any code, so calls to it will jump to an error routine that will terminate the server application and quite possibly crash the client app as well. (OLE is very unforgiving of server-side flake-outs.)

Listing 9.1 Our IDispatch implementation descends from IDispatch and overrides all its abstract methods (continued in Listing 9.2).

```
type
  IObjectDispatch = class(IDispatch)
  private
    RefCount: Integer;
    FObject: TObject;
  public
    constructor Create(AObject: TObject);
    function QueryInterface(const iid: TIID; var Obj): HResult;
      override;
    function AddRef: Longint; override;
    function Release: Longint; override;
    function GetTypeInfoCount(var pctinfo: Integer): HResult;
      override;
    function GetTypeInfo(itinfo: Integer; lcid: TLCID;
      var tinfo: ITypeInfo): HResult; override;
    function GetIDsOfNames(const iid: TIID; rgszNames: POleStrList;
      cNames: Integer; lcid: TLCID; rgdispid: PDispIDList): HResult;
      override;
    function Invoke(dispIDMember: TDispID; const iid: TIID;
      lcid: TLCID; flags: Word; var dispParams: TDispParams;
      varResult: PVariant; excepInfo: PExcepInfo;
      argErr: PInteger): HResult; override;
  end;

constructor IObjectDispatch.Create(AObject: TObject);
begin
  inherited Create;
  FObject := AObject;
```

```
    RefCount := 1;
end;

function IObjectDispatch.QueryInterface(const iid: TIID;
                                       var Obj): HResult;
begin
  if IsEqualGUID(iid, IID_IUNKNOWN)
      or IsEqualGUID(iid, IID_IDispatch) then
  begin
    TObject(Obj) := Self;
    AddRef;
    Result := NOERROR;
  end
  else
    Result := E_NOINTERFACE;
end;

function IObjectDispatch.AddRef: Longint;
begin
  Inc(RefCount);
  Result := RefCount;
end;

function IObjectDispatch.Release: Longint;
begin
  Dec(RefCount);
  Result := RefCount;
  if RefCount = 0 then Free;
end;

function IObjectDispatch.GetTypeInfoCount(
                   var pctinfo: Integer): HResult;
begin
  pctinfo := 0;
  Result := E_NOTIMPL;
end;

function IObjectDispatch.GetTypeInfo(itinfo: Integer;
             lcid: TLCID; var tinfo: ITypeInfo): HResult;
begin
  Result := E_NOTIMPL;
end;
```

OLE objects are reference counted so that multiple clients (or multiple subroutines within the same client) can connect and disconnect from an interface without worrying about who should finally delete the interface object. Everyone calls AddRef when connecting to an OLE interface, and everyone calls Release when disconnecting from it. When the interface object's internal reference count reaches zero, it will delete itself.

Obtaining an interface object through OLE almost always performs an implicit AddRef on that interface. All the client really has to do is call Release when that interface is no longer needed.

Our IObjectDispatch implementation contains an integer field RefCount that is incremented by AddRef and decremented by Release. If RefCount drops to zero, Release frees the instance.

Mapping Names to Unique Dispatch IDs

When a client wants to get or set the value of a property of our server object, it will call our Invoke method. To identify which property it wants, the client must pass an integer id to Invoke. The client first calls the interface's GetIDsOfNames method to obtain the integer id of a property name and then calls Invoke using that id.

So, we need to implement our IObjectDispatch.GetIDsOfNames to map a string name to an integer id. Since that id will come back to us in the Invoke method, it would behoove us to pick an id mapping that is convenient for Invoke.

We could create a list of property names and use the index of a name in that list as its Invoke id. However, we would need such a list for every object type in our applications that we want to make OLE automatable. Since many properties are inherited from one class to the next, there would be a lot of duplication of string data between those lists—enough to justify some sort of tiered multilist system that mirrors the inheritance hierarchy. This could get complicated!

It *is* complicated, but not for you and me. Delphi components already have such a table of names, generated by the compiler for every published property— the Run-Time Type Information. Recall from Chapter 5 that using the utility functions in the VCL TypInfo unit, we can use RTTI to extract valuable name and type information about any published property of any Delphi component—VCL core or third-party add-ons. Of course, published properties are only part of a Delphi component. However, they are certainly a very large part of the picture—and ample for the purposes of this exercise.

Mapping Property Names to Unique IDs

The TypInfo unit contains routines to locate a property info record for a property by name and routines to set and get property values of any component. The function GetPropInfo returns a pointer to a compiler-generated property info record. This pointer is a 4-byte value that is unique to the property within the given class for the current execution of the server program. Since the RTTI property info records are stored in the executable code of your app, the pointer value will probably never change from one run of the application to the next. However, if this code is going into a DLL, it is possible that the DLL may be loaded at a different address in memory when loaded by different applications, if the DLL's address range overlaps with another DLL that has already been loaded. Regardless, pointers to the code area will not change while the program is running, so we can get by with using the address of a property's PropInfo structure as the property's unique integer id.

The id needed by Invoke and provided by GetIDsOfNames is a 4-byte integer. We can have GetIDsOfNames typecast and return the property info pointer as a longint id. Invoke can then typecast such an id back into a property info pointer and gain direct access to the info it needs most—the type of the property and its get and set routines.

OLE has no requirements that ids be consecutive, so this mapping of pointer to id is perfectly valid. The main disadvantage is that the ids are not guaranteed to be identical between runs of the server if the server is implemented in a DLL. It is legal for OLE Automation client applications to use "early binding" to capture the IDispatch id values of methods and property names and hard-code them into the client app to eliminate the overhead of calling GetIDsOfNames before each Invoke. However, early binding requires that the dispatch id remain constant across multiple runs of the application. It's extremely unlikely that an application will be loaded to an address different from its default base address, so this simple pointer typecast trick is adequate for an OLE Automation server in an EXE.

Mapping Child Component Names to Unique IDs

Another cheap source of useful names is TComponent.Name. A component can own other components, so it would be nice to gain access to the children of a component through the OLE interface. A simple way to do that is to expose the names of child components as properties of the owning component. This would allow an OLE client possessing an interface to a form in your server app to obtain IDispatch interfaces for any of the named components on the form just by asking for the component by name.

Because of the way Windows 95 and Windows NT define the process address space of an application, the machine code of the application will always be loaded at a logical address greater than 1MB. Since RTTI tables are stored in the machine code of the application, this means property info pointers will always have an integer value larger than 1 million. Since it is extremely unlikely that a single form or other component will ever contain a million child components, we have plenty of room to map child component names to ids in the 0..1M range. OLE defines a standard property with an id of 0 ('Value'), so we'll start our component name id range at 16 instead of 0.

In Listing 9.2, the IObjectDispatch.GetIDsOfNames method checks that the iid parameter is a null GUID (discussed shortly), as specified by the OLE documentation, and checks that the cNames parameter is exactly 1. GetIDsOfNames is only good for fetching a single method or property name; any other names provided in the same call are parameter names. We aren't interested in passing parameters by name, so we simply require that the name count be 1.

Listing 9.2 TObjectDispatch.GetIDsOfNames maps property and child component names into unique integer IDs.

```
function IObjectDispatch.GetIDsOfNames(const iid: TIID;
  rgszNames: POleStrList; cNames: Integer; lcid: TLCID;
  rgdispid: PDispIDList): HResult;
var
  Child: TComponent;
  PropName: String;
begin
  Result := E_NOINTERFACE;
  if not IsEqualGUID(iid, GUID_NULL) then Exit;
  Result := DISP_E_UNKNOWNNAME;
  if cNames <> 1 then Exit;
  PropName := WideCharToString(rgszNames^[0]);
  rgdispid[0] := TDISPID(GetPropInfo(FObject.ClassInfo, PropName));
  if rgdispid[0] <> 0 then
  begin
    if PPropInfo(rgdispid[0])^.PropType^.Kind in ValidTypes then
      Result := NOERROR;
  end
  else if FObject is TComponent then
  begin
    Child := TComponent(FObject).FindComponent(PropName);
    if Assigned(Child) then
    begin
      rgdispid[0] := FirstComponentIndex + Child.ComponentIndex;
      Result := NOERROR;
    end
  end;
end;
```

OLE string data is always in Unicode (WideChar) format. Unicode is a double-byte character set that is used throughout Win32 to prevent the loss of information when transporting data across locale or language boundaries. This used to mean moving data between machines, but you can now even have applications on the same machine using different locale or language environment settings.

In GetIDsOfNames, the property name parameter (rgszNames) is a WideChar Unicode string. This is converted into an ANSI string for the rest of the routine to use. There is no loss of information here because valid Pascal identifiers (such as property names) can only contain the letters A through Z and 0 through 9 of the Latin alphabet. If the string contained user data, then you would have to worry about loss of information when you converted the Unicode string down to an ANSI string.

GetIDsOfNames calls GetPropInfo with the ClassInfo pointer of the IObjectDispatch object's captive VCL object and the name of the property desired. If GetPropInfo returns `nil`, we try to find a child component of the captive VCL object. If that succeeds, we return the component's index offset by our component name map base (FirstComponentIndex = 16).

IDispatch.Invoke

Now we come to the IObjectDispatch.Invoke method, shown in Listing 9.3. Invoke has a multitude of parameters, many of which may be null or empty depending on what the caller doesn't want. The most interesting parameter is the varResult variant. Variant is a data type similar to Pascal's variant record, which defines multiple fields overlaid on the same area of memory. Unlike Pascal variant records, though, variants support *type coercion*—implicit conversion of data in the variant from one data type to another. For example, the server may return an integer value in the varResult variant, but the client may want to view that data as a string instead. By typecasting the variant to a string, the client can get the data in the format that it wants without having to know what the data type was before or how to convert it. Internally, the compiler sees the typecast as a signal to call VariantChangeType, a Win32 API function that does the actual data coercion.

Listing 9.3 The Invoke method fetches property values and child components of the captive VCL object and sends the data to the caller in the varResult variant parameter.

```
procedure NewDispatch(var V: VARIANT; AObject: TObject);
begin
  if Assigned(AObject) then
    V := VarFromInterface(IObjectDispatch.Create(AObject));
end;
```

```
type
  TCardinalSet = set of 0..SizeOf(Cardinal) * 8 - 1;

procedure VariantOleStr(var Dest: Variant; const S: String);
begin
  Dest := S;
  VarCast(Dest, Dest, varOleStr);
end;

function IObjectDispatch.Invoke(dispIDMember: TDispID;
  const iid: TIID; lcid: TLCID; flags: Word;
  var dispParams: TDispParams; varResult: PVariant;
  excepInfo: PExcepInfo; argErr: PInteger): HResult;
var
  PropInfo: PPropInfo;
  W: Cardinal;
  TypeInfo: PTypeInfo;
  I: Integer;
  Temp: String;
begin
  Result := E_NOINTERFACE;
  if not IsEqualGUID(iid, GUID_NULL) then Exit;
  Result := E_INVALIDARG;
  if varResult = nil then Exit;
  VariantInit(varResult^);
  Result := E_NOTIMPL;
  if Flags and DISPATCH_PROPERTYGET <> 0 then
  try
    if (FirstComponentIndex <= dispidMember)
        and (dispidMember <= LastComponentIndex) then
    begin
      Dec(dispidMember, FirstComponentIndex);
      NewDispatch(varResult^,
        TComponent(FObject).Components[dispidMember]);
      Result := NOERROR;
      Exit;
    end;

    PropInfo := PPropInfo(dispidMember);
    Result := NOERROR;
    case PropInfo^.PropType^.Kind of
      tkInteger: varResult^ := GetOrdProp(FObject, PropInfo);
      tkEnumeration: varResult^ := GetEnumName(PropInfo^.PropType,
         GetOrdProp(FObject, PropInfo));
      tkFloat:   varResult^ := GetFloatProp(FObject, PropInfo);
      tkString, tkLString:
        VariantOleStr(varResult^, GetStrProp(FObject, PropInfo));
```

```
      tkSet: { build string of set contents: [one,two,five] }
        begin
          Temp := '[';
          W := GetOrdProp(FObject, PropInfo);
          TypeInfo := GetTypeData(PropInfo^.PropType)^.CompType;
          for I := 0 to (sizeof(Cardinal) * 8 - 1) do
            if I in TCardinalSet(W) then
              Temp := Temp + GetEnumName(TypeInfo, I) + ',';
          Temp[Length(Temp)] := ']';
          VariantOleStr(varResult^, Temp);
        end;
      tkClass:
        NewDispatch(varResult^,
          TObject(GetOrdProp(FObject, PropInfo)));
    else
      Result := E_NOTIMPL;
    end;
  except
    on EOutOfMemory do
      Result := E_OUTOFMEMORY;
    else
      Result := E_INVALIDARG;
    end;
end;
```

Variants are an artifact of weakly typed, often interpreted languages, where a variable can be manipulated as though it were almost any data type. Since the many flavors of Visual Basic have long been Microsoft's preferred OLE Automation scripting language, it's no surprise that variants should appear in the parameter list of OLE's IDispatch.Invoke method. The type ambiguity of variants can be handy at times but cumbersome as well.

When you declare a local variable of type Variant, the compiler will automatically generate code to initialize the variant prior to use and clear the variant when the procedure exits. However, when you receive a variant as a parameter, there's no guarantee that the variant has been initialized, particularly when the caller is outside your application. This is the case with varResult: Since it is an outgoing parameter, we must assume it has not been initialized and call VariantInit ourselves. If varResult contained garbage and we did not explicitly initialize it, an exception could occur when we later assign a value to the varResult. When you assign to a variant, the previous contents are first released. If the previous contents were garbage that looked remarkably similar to a string or an object pointer, the system would try to release the phantom pointer, which would raise an exception or potentially overwrite memory.

IObjectDispatch.Invoke first checks that iid is a null GUID (globally unique identifier) just as before, makes sure the caller has given us a varResult variant parameter to return our result in, and then tests the wFlags parameter to see whether this call to Invoke is a get request. This sample code doesn't support setting property values, but how to go about doing that should be pretty clear once you understand how the get process works. A third option, calling object methods via Invoke, is a bit more complicated since it usually requires extracting values from the DispParams array of variants. Delphi's built-in Automation Server object takes care of this for you, but it's far too complicated to get into here.

Next, Invoke tests the id (dispidMember) to see whether it's in the range of component name indices. If so, the Nth child component is drawn from the captive VCL object's component list and passed to NewDispatch, which creates a new IObjectDispatch object for the child component and inserts that dispatch into the variant.

If the id is not in the component name index range, it is assumed to be a property id. The id is typecast back to a property info record pointer, and the type indicated by that property record determines how we package the property value in the varResult variant.

The TypInfo function GetOrdProp gives us the value of integer, enumeration, and set-type properties of the captive VCL object. For enumerated types and sets, we go an extra step to build a string expression containing the enumeration name of the value or set members. This is easier to view and debug in client apps but adds overhead for string allocation and construction on the server end and string decomposition at the client end.

Notice the VariantOleStr helper routine. Normally, there is nothing wrong with assigning a Delphi string to a variant. However, this is bare-metal OLE we're dealing with here—hardly what you would call normal. A Delphi string is not the same as an OLE string, and the only string data that can be passed to other apps in a variant is an OLE string. The VariantOleStr assigns the Delphi string to the target variant and then uses the VarCast helper function to convert the variant's Delphi string into an OLE string. This is easier on the eyes than the more direct approach of calling StringToOleStr to perform the conversion and then cramming special values into the variant's internal fields. You should avoid touching the internals of a variant if only because direct manipulation of a variant is the most effective way to screw things up.

GetFloatProp retrieves the value of floating-point properties. OLE supports Single (4-byte) and Double (8-byte) precision values but not Extended (10-byte) precision values.

Finally, GetOrdProp is used to fetch the instance pointer value of class properties (i.e., Form1.Font). NewDispatch will create a new dispatch instance for the given object and stuff the dispatch into the varResult variant.

Notice the `try...except` block that surrounds all the real code in the Invoke method. Should an exception be raised in the business part of Invoke, you don't want that exception to propagate out past the Invoke call. Since Invoke is being called directly by OLE, there are no other Delphi exception handlers outside this Invoke routine. That means any unhandled exceptions escaping from Invoke will be routed to the Delphi RTL default exception handler, which will summarily terminate your server application (and possibly bring down the client app as well). It is imperative that we prevent exceptions from escaping from Invoke. The `try...except` block contains one on clause for out-of-memory errors and an unqualified `else` block to trap all other kinds of exceptions. The error handling and reporting here is not terrific—we just set the result to an error code. Filling in the ExcepInfo structure with descriptive info would be an improvement.

Notice also that GetIDsOfNames does not have a similar `try...except` block wrapped around it. If you consider the routines that GetIDsOfNames uses, you'll see that none of them will raise exceptions. GetPropInfo will always return a valid PropInfo pointer or `nil` if no match for the name string could be found. The IS operator doesn't raise exceptions, nor does the TComponent.FindComponent call. An exception handler around the statements of this routine wouldn't hurt, but it also wouldn't help much. If in doubt, go ahead and put in the exception handler.

We now have a functional implementation of an OLE Automation IDispatch interface that can return the values of the published properties of any VCL component and that can return interfaces for any named child components of a VCL component. All that's left to do is plug it in and turn it on.

Building a Factory

How does OLE create instances of your IObjectDispatch class? It doesn't. It asks you to create them for it. An OLE server typically creates one *class factory* for each OLE interface class type that the server exposes. In our case, we have only one—IObjectDispatch. You create one instance of the class factory class and register that instance with OLE, telling it what OLE interface class type(s) that class factory can produce. When OLE needs an instance of that type, it calls your class factory's CreateInstance method. Instances of IObjectDispatch will come and go as the client pokes around in your app, but the class factory instance will usually hang around as long as your app is open for business.

Listing 9.4 shows the declaration and implementation of IDispatchFactory, a descendant of IClassFactory, the OLE-defined interface for class factories. IDispatchFactory overrides all the abstract methods it inherits from IClassFactory and IUnknown. The IDispatchFactory constructor takes an IDispatch object for a parameter. The method IDispatchFactory.CreateInstance uses this object to obtain the interface type requested by OLE. In this scenario, there is really only one IObjectDispatch object that the factory provides on request. This scenario (like most) doesn't require creating a new object instance for each request. Reference counting allows us to hand out the same instance to multiple requests, possibly to multiple clients.

Listing 9.4 Class factories allow OLE to obtain instances of objects without knowing how the objects are created.

```
type
  IDispatchFactory = class(IClassFactory)
  private
    RefCount: Integer;
    FDispatch: IDispatch;
  public
    constructor Create(Dispatch: IDispatch);
    destructor Destroy; override;
    function QueryInterface(const iid: TIID; var Obj): HResult;
      override;
    function AddRef: Longint; override;
    function Release: Longint; override;
    function CreateInstance(UnkOuter: IUnknown; const riid: TIID;
      var ppvObject): HResult; override;
    function LockServer(fLock: BOOL): HResult; override;
  end;

constructor IDispatchFactory.Create(Dispatch: IDispatch);
begin
  RefCount := 1;
  FDispatch := Dispatch;
  FDispatch.AddRef;
end;

destructor IDispatchFactory.Destroy;
begin
  FDispatch.Release;
  inherited Destroy;
```

```
end;

function IDispatchFactory.QueryInterface(const iid: TIID;
                                        var Obj): HResult;
begin
  if IsEqualGUID(iid, IID_IUNKNOWN)
      or IsEqualGUID(iid, IID_IClassFactory) then
  begin
    TObject(Obj) := Self;
    AddRef;
    Result := NOERROR;
  end
  else
    Result := E_NOINTERFACE;
end;

function IDispatchFactory.AddRef: Longint;
begin
  Inc(RefCount);
  Result := RefCount;
end;

function IDispatchFactory.Release: Longint;
begin
  Dec(RefCount);
  if RefCount = 0 then Free;
  Result := RefCount;
end;

function IDispatchFactory.CreateInstance(UnkOuter: IUnknown;
              const riid: TIID; var ppvObject): HResult;
begin
  Result := FDispatch.QueryInterface(riid, ppvObject);
end;

function IDispatchFactory.LockServer(fLock: BOOL): HResult;
begin
  Result := NOERROR;
end;
```

Registering the Factory

Now let's plug in the class factory by registering it with OLE. As shown in Listing 9.5, the InitAutoServer procedure first constructs the root IObjectDispatch instance for the Delphi Application object. Next, a class factory instance is created for that root IObjectDispatch. The first OLE initialization step is to call OleInitialize. This pulls the various OLE DLLs into memory and lets them get situated before you do anything else. If you experience an Access Violation on the first call to an OLE function in your app, you've probably forgotten to call OleInitialize.

Listing 9.5 InitAutoServer notifies OLE that the application's automation object and class factory are open for business.

```
var
  AppDispatch: IDispatch;
  DispatchFactory: IDispatchFactory;
  RegDispatchFactory: Longint;
  RegApplication: Longint;
  AppGUID: TGUID;

procedure DoneDispatch;
begin
  RevokeActiveObject(RegApplication, nil);
  CoRevokeClassObject(RegDispatchFactory);
  OleUninitialize;
end;

procedure InitAutoServer(const AppGUID: TGUID);
begin
  AppDispatch := IObjectDispatch.Create(Application);
  DispatchFactory := IDispatchFactory.Create(AppDispatch);
  OleInitialize(nil);
  CoRegisterClassObject(AppGUID, DispatchFactory,
    CLSCTX_LOCAL_SERVER, REGCLS_MULTIPLEUSE, RegDispatchFactory);
  RegisterActiveObject(AppDispatch, AppGUID, 0, RegApplication);
  AddExitProc(DoneDispatch);
end;
```

Fun with Acronyms GUID, CLSID, and UUID are all names for the same thing. GUID is sometimes pronounced "goo-id," but I prefer "gwid" because it's monosyllabic—that is, easier to say—and because it reminds me of the large-tentacled sea creature that very nearly sank the mighty Nautilus. Not that tentacles, monsters sinking ships, or Victorian submarines masquerading as monsters sinking ships have anything to do with OLE, of course. Or do they?

The next step is to call CoRegisterClassObject, which takes a bunch of parameters. The first is the GUID of your OLE server object (IObjectDispatch). A GUID, or globally unique identifier, is a 128-bit number that uniquely distinguishes your

OLE object and application from all other software in the universe, past, present, and future. You can obtain a new GUID for new applications by running the GUIDGEN.EXE utility included in the OLE2 SDK or by writing a small program to call the OLE function CoCreateGUID.

Note that a GUID must be unique to each application that uses the IObjectDispatch. Here, the GUID identifies the application, or the root automation object of the application, but not a particular object interface within the application. Multiple applications can use IObjectDispatch objects internally to implement their Automation server support, but each application must have a unique GUID to distinguish itself from all others.

The InitAutoServer procedure in Listing 9.5 receives the application's GUID as a parameter. Add this AutoServ unit to a Delphi project and then add a call to InitAutoServer to the main form or project source file (.DPR) of the application, passing in the application's unique GUID. GUIDs are usually just declared as typed constants in the source code.

The second parameter to CoRegisterClassObject is the class factory instance for the indicated object. The third and fourth parameters indicate how the OLE server can be used, and the last parameter returns a value that should be used when unregistering the class at application shutdown.

Finally, a call to RegisterActiveObject informs OLE of the existence of your interface object. The last parameter returns a value that should be used when unregistering the object at application shutdown.

After everything has been registered with OLE, we register an exit procedure with the Delphi system unit so that our OLE unregistration code will be called when the app shuts down.

Automating the Application

For this exercise, we'll create a simple Delphi application (TESTAPP.DPR) containing a form with a few controls on it: a button, a label, an edit control, and perhaps a few checkboxes. We just need some targets to aim for in our automation test later.

In the TESTAPP.DPR project source file, add the AutoServ unit to the uses list, add a typed constant containing the application's automation GUID, and insert a call to InitAutoServer. See Listing 9.6.

Listing 9.6 This GUID and the call to InitAutoServer add OLE automation server support to this sample application.

```
program Testapp;
uses
  Forms, Ole2, AutoServ,
  Unit1 in 'UNIT1.PAS' {Form1};

{$R *.RES}

const
  AppGUID: TGUID = (D1:$57960ba0; D2:$b4f7; D3:$11ce;
    D4:($ba,$4c,$52,$41,$53,$48,$00,$01));

begin
  InitAutoServer(AppGUID);
  Application.CreateForm(TForm1, Form1);
  Application.Run;
end.
```

Registering the Application

That's all the registration that needs to occur at run time. If your application is already running when a client app requests a connection to it, everything will work fine. But what if your application isn't already running? You need to create entries in the Windows system registry so that OLE can find and launch your server app when a client asks for you and you're not already running.

Listing 9.7 (TESTAPP.REG) shows a sample REG file. Notice that the registry information includes the path to the application's EXE file, which could change when your end user installs your application. This is what install programs are for—configuring registry information to match the actual installation location. For this exercise, it's simple enough to edit the REG file to refer to the correct drive and directory containing the TESTAPP.EXE Automation server application and then run REGEDIT and select File:Merge to merge the TESTAPP.REG text file into the system registry. (In Windows NT 3.51, use the 16-bit REGEDIT program, not the 32-bit REGEDT32. The 32-bit version doesn't appear to support merging text REG files into the registry.)

Listing 9.7 Merging this REG file into the system registry allows OLE to play matchmaker between applications that request particular OLE objects and applications that implement those OLE objects.

```
REGEDIT
;;;;;;;;;;;;;;;;;;;;;;;;;;;;;;;;
; registration info Autoserv
HKEY_CLASSES_ROOT\TestApp.Application = Delphi Automation Server Test App
HKEY_CLASSES_ROOT\TestApp.Application\Clsid = {57960ba0-b4f7-11ce-ba4c-524153480001}
HKEY_CLASSES_ROOT\TestApp.Application.1 = Delphi Automation Server Test App 1.0
HKEY_CLASSES_ROOT\TestApp.Application.1\Clsid = {57960ba0-b4f7-11ce-ba4c-524153480001}
HKEY_CLASSES_ROOT\CLSID\{57960ba0-b4f7-11ce-ba4c-524153480001} = Delphi Automation Server Test App 1.0
HKEY_CLASSES_ROOT\CLSID\{57960ba0-b4f7-11ce-ba4c-524153480001}\ProgID = TestApp.Application.1
HKEY_CLASSES_ROOT\CLSID\{57960ba0-b4f7-11ce-ba4c-524153480001}\VersionIndependentProgID = TestApp.Application
HKEY_CLASSES_ROOT\CLSID\{57960ba0-b4f7-11ce-ba4c-524153480001}\LocalServer = C:\DCD\ch9\TestApp.exe /Automation
```

The TESTAPP Delphi application is now an OLE server, and it's plugged in. Let's turn it on.

Testing the Automation Server

To test the OLE Automation server we just plugged into the TESTAPP test application, we need to create an OLE Automation controller app. It's best to test your OLE code using other tools to avoid compatibility problems caused by "inbreeding" in your OLE development cycle. If you make a bad assumption in implementing your OLE server, you'll almost certainly carry that same assumption over to your OLE controller code as well. The result: Your apps work fine together, but they don't work with anything else.

The greater the difference between the tools you use to implement your OLE code and the tools you use to test the OLE compatibility of your code, the better the test. The Microsoft OLE SDK includes a lobotomized version of VB called DispTest, which is specifically designed to assist with testing OLE Automation server implementations. Less-lobotomized versions of VB will do, too.

In the interest of time, though, we'll just slap together an OLE automation control in a second Delphi application. After all, it takes only two lines of code.

First, make sure you've compiled the TESTAPP Automation server and merged its registration info into the system registry. Now, create a new project (MASTER.DPR) and drop a button and a label on the form. Double-click on the button to get into its OnClick event, and add to it the code shown in Listing 9.8.

Listing 9.8 OLE Automation in action: This button click fetches the contents of an edit control in the TESTAPP application using OLE Automation and the Automation server in TESTAPP.

```
procedure TForm1.Button1Click(Sender: TObject);
var
  OtherApp: Variant;
begin
  OtherApp := CreateOleObject('Testapp.Application.1');
  Label1.Caption := OtherApp.Form1.Edit1.Text;
end;
```

Compile and run the MASTER program, and click the button. If you got your registry information right, you should see TESTAPP magically pop up out of nowhere, and you should see that the label text in MASTER matches the text in the edit control in TESTAPP. Modify the text in the TESTAPP edit control and then punch the MASTER button again. The MASTER label picks up the new text. Congratulations! You've implemented your first OLE Automation server application from the ground up!

Not convinced of the significance of this event yet? OK, so there are a dozen and one ways to grab the text out of an edit control, even in another application, that don't require OLE. You could just send a WM_GETTEXT message to the edit control's window handle. No big deal.

Valid point, but easily belittled. Shut down both MASTER and TESTAPP and go back to the button click source code in MASTER. Change the code to grab OtherApp.Form1.Label1.Caption instead of Edit1.Text. Compile and run, and punch the button. The MASTER label's caption now shows the text of TESTAPP's label. What's so special about that? TLabel doesn't have a window handle—there is no way for an application to obtain a TLabel caption using Windows API functions or window messages. The TLabel doesn't have a window handle, so it simply doesn't exist as far as Windows and the rest of the universe is concerned. And yet here we have a two-line Delphi app that uses OLE Automation to obtain the caption of an internal object of TESTAPP. Since the transport layer is OLE Automation, a Visual Basic or any other application can obtain the same information.

Summary

In this chapter, we've examined the fundamentals of what OLE and COM are, how they operate, and the steps required to implement a standard OLE interface (IDispatch) to build a flexible and reusable (though crude) OLE Automation server engine. The OLE Automation server implementation presented here is too crude to deploy in a production application, but exploring its implementation in detail should give you some insight into how OLE objects in general are implemented. We've touched on most of the major areas of OLE implementation: abstract interfaces, reference counting, QueryInterface, parameter issues, class factories, OLE object initialization and registration, and registry information. Areas for further study include creating custom OLE interfaces, creating type libraries so that other applications can find out what your custom OLE interfaces have to offer, and exploring the network of standard interfaces provided by and required by OLE subsystems. For creating custom OLE interfaces, it's best to stick with OLE in-process server implementations so that you don't have to mess with creating proxies and stubs to marshall parameters of your custom interfaces. For interprocess communication, it's best to stick with OLE Automation since IDispatch allows you to call arbitrary methods and pass parameter data (through variants) without having to create marshaling stubs.

Like it or not, familiarity with OLE concepts and interface manipulations will only become more critical to Windows programming as more and more operating system services are exposed only as OLE interfaces, as more third-party components come to market in OCX (ahem, "ActiveX") form, and as the industry as a whole gains greater experience in improving the size and performance inefficiencies that originally plagued OLE. Delphi has already leapt to the top of the development tools heap in ease of use of OLE objects in applications and is on par with other compiled development tools for implementing OLE objects. Borland has never been known to rest on its laurels. Start reading up on OLE *now*.

Chapter 10

Optimization Techniques

Delphi was built for speed. Long before Delphi was a client/server product, before it was a RAD visual design tool, before Delphi even had a name, there was always one simple rule: Whatever this new thing would be, it had to be *fast*—with fast development, fast compilation, and fast execution. While Delphi's native code compiler does have a lot to do with the fast execution of Delphi applications (as compared to interpreted environments such as VB and PowerBuilder), the design of the VCL architecture also plays a major role in maintaining Delphi's high performance standards. This chapter examines the design techniques and programming strategies that VCL uses to minimize expensive operations and what you need to do in implementing your own components to get the most mileage from these strategies.

Levels of Optimization

There are basically three levels at which you can fine-tune the operation of a program: machine code instruction sequences, source code implementation, and general design. The benefit you can gain from time invested in each of these levels is usually inversely proportional to the level. That is, removing inefficiencies at the design level usually provides greater benefit than finding the optimum machine instruction sequence for a subroutine of a particular implementation of a particular design. After all, most of the code in your program is determined by your design. The scope of a design can be measured in millions of executable machine instructions; the scope of individual components and source code subroutines is in the thousands of machine instructions; the scope of hand-coded assembly language and compiler optimizations is typically less than a few hundred machine instructions.

As Anders Hejlsberg, chief architect of Delphi, is fond of saying, "If you take a program with an inefficient design and implement the whole thing in hand-coded assembler, all you'll get is a faster implementation of a slow design, which is never the same as a fast program." (Over time, this has been reduced to the "faster slow program" quip and is delivered with the same verve and obscurity as most Monty Python sound bytes.) If you start out with an efficient design, you don't need an expensive, complex implementation to reach your performance goals.

While machine capabilities should be considered throughout the design and implementation process, the discussion of optimization techniques for in-line assembler source code is beyond the scope of this book. Hand-coded assembly language should be reserved for very special circumstances, after you have honed your overall design and streamlined your source code implementation as far as you can and after you have obtained performance figures that show additional performance tuning in a particular routine will have a measurable benefit. I'll sometimes refer to machine capabilities to justify one particular source code implementation strategy over another. Even though we're not writing individual machine instructions, all source code must eventually be reduced to machine instructions. If you're familiar with how source code constructs map onto machine capabilities, you can organize your source code to make the compiler's job easier and more efficient. That adds up to code that is as efficient as hand-hewn ASM, but with all the robustness and flexibility of Pascal source code.

The Rosetta Code

You can see traces of code evolution from Pascal source to optimized assembler in some of the source code that accompanies this book, such as the TConsole components in console.pas. I tend to code something up in plain source code first to prove the viability of an idea and then test the working model in search of performance bottlenecks in the overall design. If the design is sound but the code needs further performance tuning, I may recode the one or two hot spots in in-line assembler. In the interest of documenting the algorithm for future maintenance, I usually keep the original Pascal code in comments right next to the ASM code that replaces it. This little insurance policy has saved my skin on a number of occasions, particularly when porting code between 16- and 32-bit environments or between major revisions of the compiler. ASM code is almost always directly tied to the specific implementation of the compiler, language, or RTL features of your development tools, and to the specifics of your hardware platform and operating environment (remember real-mode DOS?), so when you upgrade your tools or environment, you can expect to revisit some or all of your ASM code. With the original Pascal implementation of the routine sitting right there next to the ASM code, you can very easily fall back to the readable, debuggable, and infinitely more flexible Pascal code when the ASM code fails to survive some sort of migration. The first priority in a working system is to keep the system working. When time permits, you can always come back to the ASM code and play CPU for a few hours to figure out which bit went sour.

How Fast Is Fast Enough?

Probably the biggest misuse of time any programmer can make is to invest in improving the performance of something that doesn't matter—a body of code whose execution time is already well below the end user's perception threshold (such as submillisecond text redraw) or that is dwarfed by the costs of other operations that occur in the same context.

Frankly, it's a waste of time and talent to drop into assembly language to perform arithmetic operations on a few rectangles if the next step is to call BitBlt or DrawText to draw onto the screen. Almost all graphics output takes eons compared to normal data manipulations—on the order of tens of thousands of clock cycles. Let's say you spend an hour writing the ASM code and you eventually get the code down to half the clock cycles that would normally be required. This cuts the total time of your routine from 45,428 clock cycles all the way down to 45,350. Yee-hah. Even daydreaming would be a more rewarding use of an hour than this 0.1% cycle count improvement. At least with daydreaming, your subconscious has a chance to find a design change to eliminate the graphics operation entirely or find an implementation strategy that cuts the redrawn area in half.

Doing the rectangle math in plain old source code will produce the same results at the same performance level as the carefully crafted ASM code because the dominant performance factor is the graphics operation, not your source code. You're paying all the costs associated with ASM code (hard to write, hard to read, hard to debug, not portable—just a general liability for long-term maintenance) but realizing neither of ASM's benefits (smaller code size, faster execution) in any tangible way.

So, before you get all excited about an opportunity you've spotted to eliminate a few clock cycles, take a step back and consider the context in which that routine is used. Is the aspect of the routine you're trying to whittle down one of the three most expensive operations in the routine's context of execution? If not, throw back the little fish and refocus on catching the big fish. (In the performance pond, when all the big fish are caught, the little fish don't get bigger—the pond gets smaller!)

Appearance Is Everything

In the performance game, perception of speed is more valuable than actual completion time. A millisecond spent here and there to avoid a 500-millisecond expense is a very good trade off. Since most of the code in a graphical, interactive application executes in response to user input, the time it takes a program to respond to user input determines the user's perception of the program's performance. The user won't notice a millisecond here and there but will notice a hiccup longer than about half a second. There's little point in redrawing text on the screen several times each second when it takes at least half a second for the user to read and comprehend the text message.

A little sleight of hand goes a long way. A program that displays a splash screen within the first second of a 5-second application start-up will be perceived as faster than an application that starts up in 3 seconds with no splash screen. This is a classic perception paradox: A splash screen improves "performance" by adding more work to the application's start-up code!

The Fine Art of Procrastination

VCL incorporates a number of programming strategies to control expensive operations. Most of these strategies strive to either completely eliminate the expensive operation except when required by special cases, or reduce the profile of the expensive operation by breaking it up into smaller, less noticeable steps, or defer the expensive part of an operation as long as possible. Chuck Jazdzewski, lead programmer of the Delphi R&D team, refers to these strategies as "cost amortizations"—spreading out the cost of an expensive operation to minimize its immediate impact, even if spreading out the operation adds some overhead to the final tally.

One of the most expensive operations in Windows applications is, ironically enough, the creation of window handles. That's not to say that creating a window handle takes as long as printing a report. It's a matter of scale and volume. Because Windows applications create so many window handles so frequently, the little buggers tend to gang up on you.

One of the earliest innovations in the development of the VCL architecture was the on-demand Handle property of the TWinControl class. If the control hasn't yet created its window handle when you refer to its Handle property, the handle gets created right then and there. The Handle property (indeed, the entire notion of class properties) was originally created to solve the "When is my handle valid?" complexities of prior application frameworks such as OWL (Object Windows Library) and MFC (Microsoft Foundation Classes). However, as VCL grew in scope and feature set to eclipse (in its first release) the capabilities of the old frameworks, the development team's view of the Handle property changed from "It creates the handle as soon as you want it" to "It creates the handle only as soon as it is required." The distinction is subtle but extremely important: A component won't pay the performance cost of creating a handle until the handle is actually required. For many VCL controls, this means if you never make the control visible and you don't explicitly refer to its handle property, the control will never create its window handle. The on-demand Handle property evolved from a device for instant gratification into a device for procrastination.

Deferring Resource Creation

Virtually all VCL components own or use some sort of handle, be it a window handle, bitmap handle, device context handle, network socket handle, or whatever. Nearly every kind of system resource that is important enough to protect with an opaque handle (instead of a pointer to an application-readable data structure) is also complicated enough to incur some cost in creation. Consequently, nearly every kind of handle property in VCL incorporates some sort of creation deferral strategy. Components you write should employ similar deferral policies for their own expensive-to-create resources and (more importantly) should avoid forcing the creation of resources managed by ancestor classes or other components.

To implement support for creation of a resource on demand, you start by having a property with a property read function. When someone tries to read the value of the property, the read method can quickly check to see whether the resource (stored in a private field of the component) has already been allocated and can just return that value if it has. Otherwise, the read method can create the resource based on the current values of the properties of the component.

OK, so now you have a create-on-demand resource property. How can you (or your descendants) tell whether the resource has been created? You can't test the property because if the resource hasn't been created, referring to the property will cause it to be created (Heisenberg's Uncertainty Principle). Descendant classes will most likely not have access to the private field that stores the resource. The most common solution to this is to create a Boolean function in the component that indicates whether the resource has been created, without creating it. TWinControl.HandleAllocated is a classic example.

Making Hard-Shell/Soft-Shell Decisions

Depending on the nature of the resource you're handling and the ramifications of someone's accessing your resource through your component's property, you may need to distinguish between internal and external requests for the resource. For example, the TBitmap graphics class has a bitmap handle property. Grabbing a bitmap handle that is shared by multiple bitmap objects will force the bitmap object to make a private copy of the bitmap image and give you the handle to the private copy.

Creating a private copy of a shared image is a necessary evil when external users grab the bitmap handle, but you definitely do *not* want to clone the image every time your internal routines need the bitmap handle for nondestructive operations. There would be no point in even trying to share image data between bitmap objects if something as trivial as drawing the bitmap to the screen broke up the shared pool. This scenario calls for an internal routine that allows implementation methods of the component to reference the resource in a consistent manner, but without the costs of the safety checks that are required of the public Handle property. In TBitmap, HandleNeeded is the soft version; GetHandle is the hard version. This is an example of the hard-shell/soft-shell interface design issues discussed in Chapter 2.

Being a Good VCL Citizen

While implementing deferred resource creation in your own components is an honorable and worthwhile endeavor, it's actually more important that your components actively avoid forcing the creation of expensive resources in other components and in properties inherited from ancestor classes. You'll refer to other components' properties a thousand times more often than you'll implement your own on-demand resource creation properties.

Tenuous Beginnings

There are a lot of things going on during the construction of a component instance and during the loading of property data into an instance from a stream. Since the component, its siblings, and its ancestors are all usually in a partial state during these initialization processes, you should do whatever it takes to avoid forcing resource creation during the construction and loading of a component. Property write methods that perform other actions besides accepting a property value usually check for csLoading in the component's ComponentState property to decide whether to perform the side effect or not. Most of the time, when property values are being stuffed into your component from a stream, you do not want to perform peripheral actions such as giving sibling components change notifications or changing the value of other published properties.

Window Handle Avalanche

When a child control creates its window handle, it first must obtain the window handle of its immediate parent control. In a complex form with several nested layers of child controls, one poorly behaved child control that touches its window handle unnecessarily will set off an avalanche of window handle creation, starting from the component's parent form all the way down the containership tree. If the avalanche happens while loading a form from a stream and the form is going to be displayed immediately after loading anyway, the cost of the premature avalanche will probably be about the same as the normal cost of creating the window handles of the form and all its visible children when the form is first displayed.

However, if the form will remain invisible after it is loaded from the stream, the cost of the premature avalanche is significant. Since most forms are created at application start-up, this avalanche will adversely affect the time it takes the application to start up. If that one child control were a better VCL citizen and refrained from touching that handle while loading, the application would load more quickly.

There are worst-case scenarios where premature creation of window handles can double or triple form load time, usually caused by having to recreate the window handle of a control multiple times. For example, if a control "accidentally" forces the creation of its window handle when one of its properties is loaded from the stream, and a subsequent property read from the stream requires the control to destroy and recreate its window handle, the time spent creating the first window handle is wasted. If the window handle didn't exist when the second property was read from the stream, the control could just save the property value for use when the window handle is created later. Window class styles are an example of things that require destroying an existing window handle in order to effect a change. Changing a form's style to fsTopMost requires destroying the window handles of the form and all its controls so that the form window handle can be recreated with the topmost window class attribute.

Most of the time, creating the window handles for a form and its children takes the same amount of CPU time regardless of when that creation occurs. The advantage of cost deferral is that if you defer the cost long enough, you might not have to pay that cost at all.

Memory Allocation Strategies

Trading Memory for Speed

At first, you might think that keeping a program's memory allocations to a minimum is a great strategy for keeping your application running at peak efficiency. Trim, yes, but fast, no. Keeping memory use to a minimum at all times requires that memory be allocated at the moment it is needed and immediately freed afterwards. No matter how fast your memory allocation system is, allocating once or not at all will always be faster than allocating repeatedly on demand. The real question, then, is: Where can you afford to hoard RAM to improve speed?

Allocate Once and for All

One common strategy to maximize performance is to minimize the frequency of memory allocations. You could allocate a block on the first call to your routine and keep the memory block hanging around for subsequent calls to your routine to reuse. The cost for this performance gain is a larger memory footprint, or working set. If an application's working set is larger than the system's available RAM, your application spills over into the system's virtual memory swap file, and you lose all the performance gain (several times over) to swap file thrashing.

Overallocate to Prevent the Creeps

If you know you're about to begin an operation that will require growing a memory block multiple times, set the memory block's size prior to starting the operation. Overallocating once (and temporarily) is much better than reallocating and copying data multiple times in the same operation.

For example, TList uses an internal array of pointers to keep track of the items you put into it. As you add items, it grows its internal array of pointers. If you know (or even suspect) that you're about to add 10,000 items to the list, set the TList's Capacity property to 10,000 before adding the items. If it turns out that you didn't need 10,000 slots in the TList after all, you can simply set the capacity to match the actual item count after the items have been added.

Precalculate Data

Another memory-for-speed trade-off is to exchange run-time calculations for precalculated data stored in memory. This data could be calculated at compile time by declaring constant arrays containing the data or could be calculated at

MEMORY ALLOCATION STRATEGIES

application start-up or on the first call to your routine. For example, instead of using a `case` statement to decide which function result to return in response to a particular byte value, you could build an array of all possible byte values and their associated return values. The code-intensive `case` statement could then be replaced with a simple memory lookup operation. The byte value is the index into the array, and the data stored in that array location is the return value.

This technique is beneficial even to replace individual `if/then/else` statements. The machine code for an `if` statement requires a comparison and one or more conditional jump instructions. Conditional jump instructions can stall the multiple-instruction pipelines of superscalar processors such as the Pentium, which means a simple comparison may wind up costing you several clock cycles of pipeline restart penalties. Fetching the required result from a predefined array requires only one memory access instruction, with no pipeline-stalling jumps. This technique is best used in loops, where the cost of a few clock cycle penalties is multiplied by the number of loop iterations.

Logic Tables

Let's say you have some sort of special data comparison routine that accepts two string parameters and returns an integer value indicating whether the first string is greater than, less than, or equal to the second string (returning 1, –1, and 0, respectively). Let's say your special data comparison algorithm is optimized in such a way that it can't handle empty strings, but you also can't require or guarantee that empty strings won't be passed into this routine. You need a way of quickly determining whether one or both of the parameters are empty strings, and handling that separately from the actual data comparison algorithm. Compare the code and descriptions in Listing 10.1, Listing 10.2, and Listing 10.3, and you should begin to see how precalculated tables can eliminate a lot of code and minimize the impact of handling special cases.

Listing 10.1 This fictitious compare algorithm fillters out empty strings, with all the costs up front (four compares and four jumps before the main routine is reached).

```
function IsotetrimorphicCompare(const A, B: String): Integer;
begin  // Handle empty strings separately from main compare
  if (Length(A) = 0) and (Length(B) = 0) then
    Result := 0
  else if Length(A) = 0 then
    Result := -1
  else if Length(B) = 0 then
```

```
      Result := 1
   else
   begin
      // Main compare engine here.
   end;
end;
```

Listing 10.2 This filter version gets into the main code faster (two compares) but has about the same code size (four compares, four jumps) as Listing 10.1.

```
function IsotetrimorphicCompare(const A, B: String): Integer;
begin
   if (Length(A) > 0) and (Length(B) > 0) then
   begin
      // Main compare code here.
   end
   else if Length(A) = 0 then
      Result := -1
   else if Length(B) = 0 then
      Result := 1
   else
      Result := 0;
end;
```

Listing 10.3 This filter implementation uses one memory lookup, one compare, and one jump to handle all four possible cases but is not as easy to read or debug.

```
function IsotetrimorphicCompare(const A, B: String): Integer;
const Filter: array [Boolean,Boolean] of ShortInt = ((2,1),(-1,0));
begin
   Result := Filter[Length(A) = 0, Length(B) = 0];
   if Result < 2 then Exit;
   // Main compare engine here.
end;
```

Memory Addresses, Caches, and Locality of Reference

Be careful not to abuse precalculated data. It adds to your application's working set, and a larger working set can adversely affect performance. Remember that most modern CPUs run several times faster than main memory, so the CPU will sometimes have to wait several instruction clock cycles for a memory request to return data. Fast memory caches between the CPU and main memory help to keep these delays to a minimum, but a program that accesses a wide variety of memory addresses in a short period of time will exhaust the capacity of the secondary caches and leave the CPU sitting idle waiting for memory requests to complete. The rule here is to try to keep your memory accesses in clumps of neighboring addresses instead of scattered all over the map. If you're in a loop that accesses a two-dimensional array, for example, running through the array in row major order—(1,1),(1,2),(1,3),(2,1),(2,2), . . .—will hit the memory addresses in consecutive order (because that's how Delphi stores array data), which is as close to ideal as a secondary cache could ask for. Accessing the array in column major order—(1,1),(2,1),(3,1),(1,2), . . .—will jump around in the array's memory addresses and, if the array is fairly large, will wreak havoc on the secondary caches.

Allocate Uniform Block Sizes

If you know you're going to be allocating and freeing a high volume of memory blocks, try to make the memory blocks a uniform size so that your program can more efficiently reuse blocks recently freed. Keep in mind that the Delphi memory allocator rounds allocation sizes up to an even multiple of 8 bytes and is most efficient dealing with block sizes less than 1K. Memory allocation requests for blocks larger than 1K are forwarded on to Win32 memory routines like GlobalAlloc that have more overhead than Delphi's internal small-block suballocator.

Don't Allocate at All

You can avoid the costs associated with dynamic memory allocations by not allocating the memory dynamically. (Wow!) Constants, global variables, and local variables are all forms of storage that don't require the relatively expensive operation of carving up blocks of heap memory at run time. Memory for global variables and constants is set aside when the application is first loaded into memory. Initialized global variables and nonordinal constants consume space in the application's EXE file on disk; uninitialized variables do not. Ordinal constants are incorporated directly into the machine instructions that reference them, so, in a sense, ordinal constants are stored nowhere and everywhere. Local variables may be stored on the stack or just in CPU registers, depending upon how long their data values need to be retained in a routine.

Local Variables and Stack Memory

Learning to Live with Abundant Stack Space

In 16-bit Windows applications, the amount of memory that could be used for the stack (and therefore local variables) was extremely limited—a theoretical limit of 64K, with a real-world limit around 20K. Needless to say, stack space was a precious commodity in 16-bit Delphi applications.

Win32 applications, on the other hand, measure stack space in megabytes. Win32 allows an application's stack to grow on demand up to a preset limit. In Delphi 2.0, the `default` stack limit is 1 *megabyte*. Now, when you start up a Win32 app, it doesn't run off and actually allocate 1MB of physical RAM for its stack; few applications ever need more than 30K of stack. Instead, Win32 reserves a 1MB range of logical memory addresses for the stack and commits 8K or 16K of that range as the initial stack area. As the program uses the stack and runs past the end of the currently committed stack memory, it will trigger a page fault. The operating system responds to the page fault by committing more of the stack's address range into physical memory and resuming the program instruction that triggered the fault. The program is never aware that this happened.

The sum of all this trivia is that the stack is a very attractive memory resource in Win32 applications. The stack can now handle small-to-medium-sized chunks of data with less overhead than dynamic memory allocations and is more dynamic than permanent global variables. There are two main costs associated with stack allocations: Growing the stack by page fault isn't cheap, and the stack never shrinks for the lifetime of the app (or thread). Keeping these costs in mind, you can realize moderate performance improvements and source code simplification by favoring stack variables over heap allocations for small-to-medium-sized memory requirements—anything less than 8K or so.

Fixed-Size Temporary Storage

Global variables occupy a fixed amount of memory for the entire lifetime of the program, which, generally, is wasteful. Local variables, though, are stored on the stack, so they "occupy" memory only for the lifetime of the routine they're declared in. Local variables don't retain their values from one function call to the next (globals do), so locals aren't appropriate for storing long-term precalculated data. However, locals are ideal for storing a value that you calculate once and refer to several times in the routine. The stack is a memory area, but because it is accessed so frequently by normal procedure calls and returns, the top of the stack is almost always going to be in the fast CPU or secondary memory caches, so there's little fear of memory access delays with local variables.

Simplified Threading

Stack memory is inherently thread-safe. Each thread in a program receives its own stack, so there is no risk of two threads manipulating the same local variable. Each thread has its own copy of its local variables. Global variables, on the other hand, must be handled very carefully in multithreaded apps, lest one thread modify the variable while another is using its value.

Heap allocations can incur additional overhead in multithreaded apps. The memory manager uses a critical section to ensure that two threads can't modify the heap's lists of memory blocks at the same time. When a thread makes a request of the memory manager (GetMem or FreeMem), the thread acquires the memory manager critical section, does its heap allocation work, and releases the critical section. Any other threads that attempt to allocate memory while that critical section is owned by the first thread will wait, or *block*, until the first thread has finished and releases the critical section.

Thread blocking in heap allocations should be rare unless you have a lot of threads turning over lots of memory allocations continuously. Local variables are an easy way to reduce heap turnover and thread collisions in the memory manager and are the easiest way to keep thread-specific data local to each thread.

Simplified Source Code

Except for long strings and variants, local variables require no allocation or deallocation function calls in source code or machine code. Since the stack space used by the local variables of a routine will be recovered when the routine exits (by normal exit or by exception), you don't need `try...finally` blocks to clean up your local variables as you do for heap allocations. Using local variables instead of heap memory reduces your need for `try...finally` blocks to release the allocated memory, which simplifies your source code, which reduces your machine code size, which improves performance.

One-Size-Fits-All Schemes

Though there is plenty of stack space available, local variables are still primarily fixed-size allocations, so they aren't appropriate when the amount of memory you will need is completely determined at run time and is completely arbitrary. However, if there is an absolute maximum allocation size that your routine will ever need and that maximum is less than, say, 8K, you could declare a local variable with that maximum size and just use what you need of it in your routine. This saves you the overhead of allocating from the global heap and will reduce the inevitable heap fragmentation that results from repeated allocations of variable-sized temporary blocks.

For example, a common graphics operation is to build a color palette from a list of color values. Typically, you would count how many color values you have, allocate a temporary memory block to hold that many color values in a logical palette structure, copy the color values into the logical palette memory block, call the CreatePalette API, and then release the logical palette memory block—all wrapped in a `try...finally` block to guarantee the temporary allocation will be freed. Windows color palettes are, by definition, limited to 256 or fewer colors, so the largest logical palette memory block you'll ever need is 256 times the size of a logical palette entry (4 bytes), plus the size of the logical palette header—in all, a few bytes over 1K of memory. Instead of repeatedly allocating a memory block of the minimum-required size, you could declare a local variable containing the logical palette header and all 256 logical palette color slots. The steps to create a palette are now to copy the color values into the logical palette local variable, call CreatePalette, and exit. It sounds simpler. It is simpler. It's also just a little faster.

If the system has to grow the stack to hold your 1K logical palette local variable, the page fault and stack growth take a bit longer than an equivalent single heap allocation. However, once an application has found its comfort level of stack space, stack growth should be very rare (assuming no recursion), which makes this largest-needed local variable scenario similar to an allocate-and-reuse heap allocation scheme. Since stack memory is not released after its been committed, it's almost identical to an allocate-and-reuse scheme. However, stack memory can be reused by other routines when the current routine exits. The memory used by an allocate-and-reuse scheme can be used only by the code that allocated it or knows about it.

Reasonable Use

More than about 8K worth of local variables in a routine or cluster of routines is excessive, particularly in a component intended for general use. The Intel virtual memory system works in 4K pages, so when you bump up the stack by more than 8K, you are three times as likely to hit a page fault to grow the stack as when you have less than 4K of local variables. With individual variables larger than 8K, you're starting to hit the point of diminishing returns. The amount of stack memory left sitting around after that routine returns borders on wasteful. Using larger chunks of stack for larger local variables also diminishes the chances that the stack memory is already in a fast cache somewhere.

However, reasonable use is always determined by the situation. A 16K or 64K local variable might be justified if the routine is called frequently and uses the majority of that stack space on each call.

Costs of Value Semantics—Managing Strings and Variants

With the introduction of long strings, Delphi 2.0 shatters the long-standing 255-character limit on the Borland Pascal string type. Long strings are now allocated from the heap (instead of the stack) to support arbitrarily large chunks of string data, but they retain the value semantics of the original string type implementation. While long strings are semantically and syntactically equivalent to the old short-string implementation, the performance issues and cost control strategies are quite different.

Value semantics means that when you assign A := B, A behaves as though it received its own copy of the data stored in B. A is not affected by subsequent modifications to B, nor is B affected by modifications to A. How this is actually implemented is immaterial to the semantics of the operation. Long strings are implemented using pointers to heap-allocated data. The data is reference counted so that multiple string variables can refer to the same copy of the data and is protected with a copy-on-write scheme so that modifications are made only on unique (reference count = 1) strings.

Since short strings were almost always allocated from the stack (already a precious commodity in 16-bit Windows applications), cost control techniques for short strings focused mainly on reducing the amount of stack space consumed by string variables and compiler-generated temporaries and to a lesser degree on reducing the number of times string data is copied from one variable to another. Since long strings are implicitly allocated from the global heap, cost control techniques for long strings focus mostly on reducing the number times string data is reallocated—that is, copied, modified, or resized.

Variants also use value semantics, but their implementation is governed by the operating system. Variants are very similar to long strings in terms of the machine code steps required to initialize, assign to, and free the data owned by a variant or string type variable.

Overhead for Automatic Cleanup

String and variant variables are automatically initialized by compiler-generated code when the variables come into scope. That is, string and variant local variables of a routine are initialized by the prologue code of the routine, before execution reaches the first source code statement within the routine.

Since strings and variants can both own dynamically allocated resources (variants can contain OLE strings, IDispatch interface pointers, or heap-allocated arrays of data), variables of these types must be *finalized* (or deallocated) to release the associated resource when the variable goes out of scope. Local variables are finalized in the epilogue code of the routine, when execution reaches the closing `end;` statement of the routine.

To ensure that the local variables are finalized regardless of what happens in the routine, the compiler must generate an implicit `try...finally` block around the entire body of the routine and finalize the local variables in the `finally` portion. This extra overhead is negligible in most routines of any size or complexity but can be significant in very small utility routines. The implicit `try...finally` block requires that the compiler generate a stack frame for the routine and touches enough registers that you lose much of the advantage of register parameters in small routines.

Hidden Temporaries

When you concatenate multiple strings in a string expression like DoSomething(A + B); or when a function returns a string value, as in DoSomething(IntToStr(X)), a temporary location is needed to store the intermediate results of these multistep operations. The string result of the IntToStr function call must be stored somewhere so that it can be passed to the DoSomething procedure. Similarly, the result of (A + B) must be stored somewhere so that it can be passed as a parameter. The "somewhere" is a temporary variable created by the compiler. When the evaluation of the string expression is complete or after the procedure to which the result was passed returns, the compiler generates code to free the string memory referred to by the temporary variable.

Temporaries are just like any other local variable as far as the compiler is concerned. Thus, a routine that contains an expression that requires a string or variant temporary will get an implicit `try...finally` block wrapped around the routine to finalize the temporaries even if the routine declares no local string or variant variables.

To visualize how that implicit `try...finally` block impacts compiler optimizations and code generation, consider the code in Listing 10.4, which contains two button click event methods of a form. One calls a function GetInt to obtain an integer and passes that integer result to a procedure TestInt. The other button click does the same but with string data instead of integer. Compare the three machine code instructions for the integer button click routine shown in Listing 10.5 with the 32 machine code instructions for the string button click routine shown in Listing 10.6.

Listing 10.4 These two button click methods may look very similar, but the machine code they require is very different (see Listing 10.5 and Listing 10.6).

```
function GetInt: integer;
begin
  result := 10;
end;
procedure TestInt(I: Integer);
begin
end;
procedure TForm1.Button1Click(Sender: TObject);
begin
  TestInt( GetInt );
end;
function GetStr: String;
begin
  Result := 'test';
end;
procedure TestStr(const S: String);
begin
end;
procedure TForm1.Button2Click(Sender: TObject);
begin
  TestStr( GetStr );
end;
```

Listing 10.5 The machine code for TForm1.Button1Click (viewed with Turbo Debugger 4.0) contains no ebp stack frame or any other kind of overhead (compare this to Listing 10.6).

```
TForm1.Button1Click:    TestInt( GetInt );
:0041FE60 E8EFFFFFFF      call    Unit1.GetInt
:0041FE65 E8F2FFFFFF      call    Unit1.TestInt
Unit1.41: end;
:0041FE6A C3              ret
```

Listing 10.6 String temporaries force the compiler to build an implicit `try...finally` block around the routine, defeating stack and register parameter optimizations.

```
TForm1.Button2Click: begin
:0041FE94 55               push    ebp
:0041FE95 8BEC             mov     ebp,esp
:0041FE97 6A00             push    00000000
:0041FE99 53               push    ebx
:0041FE9A 56               push    esi
:0041FE9B 57               push    edi
:0041FE9C 33C0             xor     eax,eax
:0041FE9E 55               push    ebp
:0041FE9F 68D0FE4100       push    0041FED0
:0041FEA4 64FF30           push    fs:dword ptr [eax]
:0041FEA7 648920           mov     fs:[eax],esp
Unit1.55:     TestStr( GetStr );
:0041FEAA 8D45FC           lea     eax,[ebp-04]
:0041FEAD E8BAFFFFFF       call    Unit1.GetStr
:0041FEB2 8B45FC           mov     eax,[ebp-04]
:0041FEB5 E8D6FFFFFF       call    Unit1.TestStr
:0041FEBA 33C0             xor     eax,eax
:0041FEBC 5A               pop     edx
:0041FEBD 59               pop     ecx
:0041FEBE 59               pop     ecx
:0041FEBF 648910           mov     fs:[eax],edx
:0041FEC2 68D7FE4100       push    0041FED7
Unit1.56: end;
:0041FEC7 8D45FC           lea     eax,[ebp-04]
:0041FECA E81133FEFF       call    @LStrClr
:0041FECF C3               ret
:0041FED0 E98B2FFEFF       jmp     @HandleFinally
:0041FED5 EBF0             jmp     Unit1.56 (0041FEC7)
:0041FED7 5F               pop     edi
:0041FED8 5E               pop     esi
:0041FED9 5B               pop     ebx
:0041FEDA 59               pop     ecx
:0041FEDB 5D               pop     ebp
:0041FEDC C3               ret
```

This implicit `try..finally` block overhead is necessary for the stability of your programs. The best way to avoid this overhead is to avoid string or variant data types in your source code. When string or variant data is required, keep in mind that regardless of how many string or variant local variables are in a routine, only one implicit `try..finally` will be created around the body of the routine. To minimize the code size impact of implicit `try..finally` blocks, routines that handle string or variant data should do as much as practical in fewer, larger routines. Unlike integer utility routines, small utility routines that perform string or variant operations provide no compiler optimization advantages.

String Operations

When manipulating long strings, the most important facts to keep in mind are that you're dealing with heap-allocated memory and that long strings can contain arbitrarily large amounts of string data. The strategy for dealing with both of these realizations is simple: Avoid unnecessary copying of the string data. With reference-counted long strings, assignments between string variables are cheap—cheaper than assignments between short strings, which must actually copy the string data. Long string assignments just increment the reference count of the string data. It is modification of multireferenced string data that is expensive since the string data must be "unique-ified"—copied to a new string memory block so that the reference count is 1.

String Concatenation

Concatenating multiple strings to make one larger string is a common operation that the Delphi compiler pays special attention to. In a string expression like A := A + B + C where all are string variables, the compiler generates code that uses the existing A string data as the starting point and adds B to the end of it, followed by C. No string temporary is needed in this case. In the most complex string expressions involving multiple string-returning function calls and concatenation operations, the compiler generates at most two string temporaries: one to accumulate the concatenated string data across multiple function calls in the expression and another to receive the string result of the next function call in the series. For example, in a string expression like A := B + IntToStr(10) + IntToStr(40); one string temp (Temp1) is allocated to receive the function result of IntToStr(10) and another (Temp2) is allocated to hold (B + Temp1). Temp1 is then reused to receive the function result of IntToStr(40) and concatenated with Temp2. Regardless of how many function calls (at the same level) are in an expression, only two temps are needed. As an additional optimization, the accumulator in this example (Temp2) would actually be string variable A, so only one temp is actually created.

When you concatenate strings, one of the strings is going to have to grow its string data block in the heap in order to hold the additional string data. If there are four concatenation operations in a single expression, the accumulator may have to grow as many as three times. If a free memory block happens to be adjacent in memory to the current string data block, resizing the string data is a snap: Just annex the neighboring free block. If the string data block is fenced in by other allocated blocks, though, the only way to grow the string data is to allocate an entirely new block and copy all the string data to the new block. That's expensive, especially when done repeatedly on the same string.

Using Delete Instead of Copy

To reduce the frequency with which string growth causes full reallocation and copying, the Delphi string manager uses an allocation strategy that favors leaving unused memory at the end of the string. When the string needs to grow, chances are good that it can grow in-place without having to copy everything over to a new block. When data is deleted from a string, a "tail" of unused memory is left attached to the string to facilitate future in-place string growth.

It is for this reason that you should use the Delete( ) standard procedure to remove trailing data from a string instead of using Copy( ) to copy the data you want to keep into a new variable. Delete is far more likely to perform the operation in-place, with no memory (de)allocation overhead, than Copy. The statement Delete(A, EndPoint+1, Length(A)–EndPoint) is far more efficient than A := Copy(A, 1, EndPoint), particularly for very large strings.

Of course, it goes without saying that you can no longer assume 255 is the maximum length of the data in a string. Those of you who got into the habit of using Copy(A, Index, 255) to extract the data at the end of a string will just have to unlearn that 255 assumption. Instead, use Delete(A, 1, Index) if you can modify the original string or Copy(A, Index, Length(A)–Index) if you cannot.

Constant Arrays of Strings

Dynamically allocated string data includes a 4-byte string length count, a 4-byte reference count, and a 4-byte memory block size. These are located at offsets –4, –8, and –12 from the start of the string data, respectively. All strings have a minimum allocation size of 12 bytes.

String constants have the length and reference count fields but not the memory block size, so string constants use a minimum of 8 bytes each. The reference count field of a string constant is always $FFFFFFFF, or –1, to indicate the string data does not need to be reference counted because it does not need to be freed. String constants are aligned on 4-byte addresses, so a 2-character string constant requires 12 bytes of memory and EXE file space. Don't forget the null terminator that's always at the end of a long string: A 3-character string constant requires 12 bytes, but 4- and 5-character strings require 16 bytes because the null spills over into the next 4-byte block.

What this adds up to is that constant arrays of strings can add a lot more to your EXE size than you would expect. PChar string constants, on the other hand, have only a null terminator—no 8-byte headers to eat up space. Like native strings, PChar data is aligned on 4-byte boundaries. If you can use your string data in PChar form instead of native string form, you can save 8 bytes per string constant from your EXE file size and working set.

Don't try to be too clever with this, though. Syntax allows PChar strings to be used where native string values are expected, but that doesn't mean it's efficient. PChar-to-string conversion does just that—copies the PChar data into a string temporary and performs the operation using the temp. Is taking the memory allocation hit and implicit `try..finally` code associated with string temps worth saving 8 bytes per string constant? Probably not.

SetLength

Many Win32 API functions that return string data require that you provide a buffer for the function to copy the string data into and return a count of the bytes copied into the buffer. Most of these functions follow the convention that if you pass in a `nil` pointer for the buffer, the function will tell you how many bytes you need to allocate to receive all the data.

Just as you can no longer assume a 255-character limit on Delphi strings, you should not assume that Win32 API functions that return string data have a fixed limit on the amount of string data they can return, unless the Win32 API documentation specifically states a maximum. Instead of using fixed-size local arrays of char variables to receive the data and then copying that to a string, use the string as the receiving buffer to begin with. Call the Win32 API function with a buffer parameter of `nil` to find out how much you need to allocate; then call SetLength to set the size of the string. Call the Win32 API function again, this time passing the string variable (typecast to a PChar) as the buffer parameter. The Win32 API will copy the data directly into your string buffer, so you don't have to waste time copying it yet again in your own code.

If the Win32 API function doesn't fill the entire buffer you provide, you should call SetLength again after the Win32 API call to set the string's length counter to the actual end of data. The actual end of data may be indicated by the Win32 API function (bytes copied) or by a call to StrLen to scan for the null terminator.

Format's 4K Limit

The Format routine replaces escape codes in a formatting string with provided data values, expanding the result string as it goes. However, in the interest of speed, Format does not dynamically reallocate its output buffer as it is generating the output string data. Format uses a fixed 4K buffer on the stack as its output buffer and copies the final output string from that buffer to the function result string.

If you try to send too much data through Format in one pass, you'll get an out-of-memory exception in the Format routine. The solution to this is to Format in smaller chunks and concatenate the results into the final string.

Plain Old Dirty Tricks

No discussion of optimizations and clean coding would be complete without a few words on genuinely useful hacks and dirty tricks. When the square peg doesn't fit in the round hole, get a bigger hammer. These are the sledgehammers.

Typecasting Incompatible Types

The rules of typecasting allow you to take data of one type and typecast it to a type of equal size. The compiler will not allow you to typecast a 4-byte data type into a 3-byte data type or vice versa. That is, the compiler won't allow the typecast if it can *see* that the two types are different sizes. The address operator (@) is typeless, so taking the address of a 4-byte data type gives you a typeless pointer. You can then typecast that typeless pointer as a pointer to a 3-byte data type, and the compiler has no grounds to complain:

```
TripleVar := PTriple(@QuadVar)^
```

Accessing a Class's Protected Members

The methods, properties, and fields declared in a class's protected sections are accessible only to descendants of that class and to code in the unit where the class is declared. The same applies to the descendant classes—all the protected members of a descendant class (including its inherited protected members) are accessible to code in the unit where the descendant is declared. To gain access to the protected members of a class, then, all you have to do is declare an empty descendant of that class in your unit and typecast instances of that class to your stub descendant, as shown in Listing 10.7. While it goes without saying that you should not get into the habit of doing these kinds of hacks, they do come in handy every once in a great while.

Listing 10.7 A dirty trick to gain access to protected members of someone else's component.

```
type
  TWinControlCracker = class(TWinControl);
begin    // access a protected property of TWinControl
  X := TWinControlCracker(Edit1).WindowHandle;
end;
```

Summary

VCL's strategies for performance cost deferral improves application performance by avoiding the cost of creating a resource until the resource is actually needed. In many cases, the resource may never actually be required, so the deferral strategy eliminates the cost entirely. Your components should avoid touching handles or other expensive-to-create resources in properties of other components or inherited from ancestor components. If your component manages a resource that takes considerable time or memory resources to create, you should consider implementing your own deferred creation strategy for that component.

The more memory allocations your application makes, the more time your application will spend doing something other than its primary task. Memory allocation strategies strive to reduce the frequency of memory allocations by caching and reusing a single memory block, by enlarging the memory block to reduce the need to reallocate the block, or by using global or local variables to avoid memory allocation overhead entirely. In particular, the stack is an attractive, fast source of temporary memory, even for moderately large memory blocks.

At each step in building your component or application, consider the context in which it will be used. What volume of data will the component have to deal with regularly? What are the most time-consuming processes the component performs? These and similar questions will help you determine how important performance and resource analysis is to your component and how much effort will be required to raise your component's performance a notch higher. There's always room for improvement. The real question is: Where in your code can you get the most improvement for the least amount of effort and risk? Learning to distinguish between what counts and what doesn't is one of the most important skills in performance tuning and one of the most difficult to acquire.

PART III

Design-Time Support Tools

Chapter 11

Delphi's Open Tools Architecture

On the surface, the Delphi Integrated Development Environment (IDE) gives all the appearances of being a single executable module. Product features are so integrated that people assume they're all implemented by one monolithic body of code. Beneath the surface, what we perceive as the Delphi IDE is actually an interlocking set of distinct modules: the Delphi32.EXE program, the CMPLIB32.DCL module (a DLL), the editor, debugger, and compiler DLLs, and other modules. What makes these distinct modules function as a single application is a network of communication links in the form of abstract interface classes. The network of links that binds the modules together also allows you to add new modules to the set, expanding the feature set of the IDE without having to recompile the main EXE file—or, indeed, any source code at all.

This chapter discusses the IDE's modular architecture in broad strokes, taking inventory of the IDE's major subsystems, where their interfaces are defined, and how they interact with your components and the rest of the IDE. Following chapters examine in detail the three most common IDE subsystems you'll use to build customized design-time support for your special components: property editors, component editors, and experts.

The Big Picture

The IDE's modules and subsystems are cleanly divided into two camps: those that implement components and component design-time support and those that don't use components at all or that treat all components as generic equivalents. As shown in Figure 11.1, the component library DLL (CompLib for short) is the focal point of all component development and add-in tools interfaces. CompLib contains all components that can be dropped on the form designer or edited with the Object Inspector, all property editors and component editors, most experts, as well as the implementation of the form designer, menu designer, and form inheritance update manager. The IDE EXE module contains or manages all the component-independent subsystems, such as the compiler, debugger, editor, and module manager, and most of the major user interface pieces, such as the options dialogs, component palette, and Object Inspector.

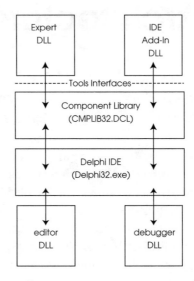

Figure 11.1 The network of modules that make up the Delphi IDE.

Though the IDE consists of many modules, component designers and add-in tools use the interfaces of only one module: the component library. Some of CompLib's published interfaces allow you to indirectly manipulate internal IDE subsystems. For example, through a virtual stream interface, you can get a copy of the text in the currently open editor window, modify it, and send it back to the editor. However, controlling the IDE is not CompLib's primary purpose. CompLib exists as a service to the IDE, not the other way around.

IDE, Compile Thyself

The main reason the Delphi IDE is split into EXE and CompLib camps is so that components can be added to the development environment. With the components and component design code placed in a DLL, the IDE EXE can unload the DLL, recompile the DLL with new components and design tools, and load the new DLL in one smooth operation. Compiling components into the component library DLL allows the IDE to benefit directly from all the RTTI property information and class information available from the compiler, making all components first-class citizens in the design-time environment. Compiling components into the IDE's execution environment vastly simplifies component editing and form design support, too. What you see on the form designer is not an approximation of a component's display; it is an actual instance of the component, running pretty much as it would in any Delphi application.

The Components of Component Design

TForm.Designer

When you load or create a form in the IDE, CompLib creates a form designer object to manage the form instance and escort it through the design process. The form designer object assigns itself to the form instance's Designer property. The Designer property is of type TDesigner, an abstract interface class defined in the Forms unit. The Designer class and property exist so that the normal run-time implementation of a form and its components can notify the IDE of internal state changes without having any knowledge of the design-time environment. If a component modifies its properties or state in response to design-time user input and the component owner's Designer property is not `nil`, the component should call the owning form's Designer.Modified method to notify the design-time environment that it needs to refresh its views of the component's properties.

For example, TDBGrid supports resizing grid columns with the mouse at design time. When a grid column is resized at design time by user input, the grid calls its parent form's Designer.Modified method. Actually, TCustomGrid implements this support; all TDBGrid does is enable the grid to see design-time mouse clicks by responding to the CM_DESIGNHITTEST internal message. Check out the Grids and DBGrids source files for specifics.

Property Browsing and Editing

When you select a component on a form at design time, the form designer (in CompLib) notifies the Object Inspector (in the IDE EXE) that the selection has changed. The Object Inspector then queries CompLib for a list of the selected component's property names, types, and corresponding property editor classes.

When you click on a property listed in the Object Inspector, the Object Inspector queries the property's associated property editor class to find out what style of property editor it should display. Note that the Object Inspector implements the actual user interface (the edit control) used to edit property values within the Object Inspector. The TPropertyEditor class you implement for a component's custom property type is a nonvisual descriptor of *how* your property should be displayed and edited; it is not the editor itself. However, a property editor class can implement a pop-up editor dialog to provide complete customization of complex property configurations. The standard property editors for TFont and TColor type properties, for example, bring up font and color-selection common dialogs when you double-click on the property edit control in the Object Inspector.

Component Editing

A component editor is a class that describes special actions that apply to a particular component type at design time. TComponentEditor can supply a list of actions, or *verbs*, that the designer adds to the component's design-time local menu. When you right-click on a component in the form designer and select one of these verbs from the pop-up menu, the designer tells the component's associated component editor class to execute that verb. For example, TPageControl has a component editor that provides New Page, Next Page, and Previous Page verbs to assist with page control navigation.

Double-clicking on the selected component in the form designer invokes the standard Edit action of the associated component editor class. Most component editors respond to the Edit verb by displaying a pop-up dialog containing additional information or configuration options for the component. For example, the TDataset component editor displays a Dataset Designer (Fields Editor) when you double-click on a TTable or TQuery component. Double-clicking on a TDBGrid displays the DBGrid Columns Editor.

Experts and Add-In Tools

An expert is a design tool that operates in a domain larger than an individual component or property. Most experts populate forms with components or even build entire projects based on information obtained by interviewing the Delphi user or obtained from some external source, such as third-party CASE tools. Delphi's tools interfaces allow add-in tools to insert their own menus into the Delphi IDE's menu tree, participate in file and project management, obtain information about the contents of a Delphi project, and manipulate the Delphi IDE to a limited degree. Delphi's Database Form Expert is an example of an expert that builds complex forms based on the structure of existing database tables. The PVCS version control system features of the Delphi Client/Server Suite are implemented using Delphi's tools interfaces.

Lines of Communication—Interfaces

The source code to CompLib's published interface classes is in the SOURCE\TOOLSAPI subdirectory of your Delphi installation. Extensive comments describing the purpose and requirements of each interface method make these files largely self-documenting. Just reading them will give you all sorts of exciting ideas. The interfaces are grouped by common function into separate source files, as follows:

- **DsgnIntf.** DsgnIntf contains the class declarations for the TPropertyEditor and TComponentEditor base classes, as well as implementations of property editors for all the standard property types. DsgnIntf includes the TFormDesigner interface class, a TDesigner descendant that provides a more detailed glimpse of the form designer's capabilities. Only component design tools used exclusively at design time can access the TFormDesigner class type. DsgnIntf also provides registration routines that make your custom property editor and component editor classes known to CompLib and a TComponentList class that is used to pass the form designer's list of selected components between the Object Inspector, CompLib, and property editors. For most property and component editors, DsgnIntf is the only IDE tools interface unit you need to reach your design-time goals.

- **EditIntf.** EditIntf contains interfaces to read from and write to the source code editor's editor buffer (TIEditorInterface, TIEditView, TIEditReader, TIEditWriter), as well as a plethora of project navigation interfaces, including TIModuleInterface, TIModuleNotifier, TIResourceFile, TIResourceEntry, TIFormInterface, and TIComponentInterface. These interfaces have little value to property and component editors, but they may be valuable to project-browsing experts and add-in tools.

- **ExptIntf.** ExptIntf defines the TIExpert interface. To build an expert or add-in tool, you create a descendant of TIExpert and implement all its abstract methods. Form and project experts appear in the IDE's Object Repository (in the File: New... dialog), while standard experts appear in the IDE's Tools menu. A fourth category of experts, add-in tools, takes full responsibility for merging their user interface elements into the Delphi IDE. ExptIntf also includes registration routines and DLL-exported function prototypes that allow you to implement experts and add-in tools in stand-alone DLLs.

- **FileIntf.** FileIntf is the home of the TIVirtualFileSystem interface class. A virtual file system is an abstract data storage interface that you can implement to store "files" in a variety of different ways—stored to files on disk, checked into a version control system, or written into a database blob or a component property. The IDE editor and Project Manager support virtual file systems so that the IDE can read and write files and whole projects to version control systems or enterprise repositories and so that the editor can edit or view data presented in a text representation. For example, the standard string list property editor has an option to move the string list editing into a code editor window, allowing you to edit the text of a string list property with all the conveniences of your preferred editor key bindings and editor macro capabilities. Thanks to the string list virtual file system, you can edit SQL statements for the TQuery.SQL property in the IDE editor, complete with SQL syntax highlighting!

- **VirtIntf.** VirtIntf defines the TInterface base class, the ancestor of all CompLib abstract interfaces. TInterface implements reference counting, much like OLE's IUnknown interface. VirtIntf also defines TIStream, an abstract interface used to pass stream data between DLL modules, particularly DLLs that are not written in Delphi.

- **IStreams.** IStreams provides TIStream implementations supporting the two main stream types: memory streams (TIMemoryStream) and file streams (TIFileStream). When you have to provide a TIStream to an interface, create a TIMemoryStream or TIFileStream instance, associate it with your actual TStream instance, and pass it to the interface that requires a TIStream. IStreams also provides a TStream implementation that uses a TIStream as its source. When you receive an IStream and need to access it as a TStream, create a TVirtualStream to bridge the gap.

- **ToolIntf.** ToolIntf is the heart of the IDE's add-in tools support. Through the TIToolServices interface, you can open and close projects and files, create modules, insert add-in tools menu items into the Delphi menu tree, enumerate the forms and units of a project, enumerate the units and components installed in the component library, register or access a virtual file system, access module interfaces, and install notification hooks so that your add-in tool can be notified of key IDE events (opening/closing projects, files, and so on). ToolIntf also provides string-handling routines for add-in tools not written in Delphi.

- **VCSIntf.** VCSIntf defines the TIVCSClient interface, which version control systems vendors can implement to add support for their version control systems into the Delphi IDE. The TIVCSClient interface is a simplification of the general notifications and services available through TIToolServices and will probably fall farther behind the capabilities of TIToolServices in future Delphi releases.

General Design-Time Issues

When Is the csDesigning ComponentState Set?

When a component executes at design-time, its ComponentState Property includes the csDesigning flag. There has been a bit of confusion as to *when* the csDesigning flag is set when a component is created at design time. At what point in your component's construction can you rely on the csDesigning flag of the ComponentState property?

When a component is created, memory is allocated from the heap for the component's instance data, and the instance data is filled with zeros. Next, the component's constructor is called. If you override your component's Create constructor (don't forget the `override`), execution enters your constructor code before anything has touched the instance data. Therefore, the ComponentState property is empty; the csDesigning flag is not set.

When you call the inherited Create constructor, execution makes its way up to TComponent.Create. TComponent.Create inserts the component into the provided Owner. The Owner's InsertComponent method inserts the component into its child list, sets the component's csDesigning flag to match its own ComponentState, and then calls Notification to notify all its children that it has inserted a new component. Notification is a virtual method of TComponent, and it is the first virtual method that is called after the csDesigning flag has been set. Therefore, csDesigning will be set appropriately when the call to the inherited constructor returns.

Nevertheless, some folks insist that their components need to know whether they're being constructed at design time *before* the call to the inherited constructor. If you're one of these people, you'll be pleased to know that this isn't a big deal. Notice that the component's csDesigning flag is set according to the passed-in owner's csDesigning flag. You can test the owner parameter's ComponentState (not the owner property!) for csDesigning before your own component has been initialized.

Design-time form construction is a special case that CompLib handles slightly differently. The form designer handles all form instances by proxy. Since form designing involves modifying the form class type, you obviously can't have a compiled instance of the actual form class running around in the IDE. Part of this special design-time handling of forms sets the proxy form instance's csDesigning flag before the form's properties and children are loaded from file. This ensures that the form's csDesigning flag is set appropriately before any of its child components are created and read from the stream.

Modifying VCL Source Code

The VCL source code files, included in the Delphi Developer and Delphi Client/Server Suite products, contain the source code for everything that goes into your executable program. Though Borland advises against it, it is within your power to modify the VCL source code to change implementation details or even interface details. If you modify a class type, a function declaration, or some other symbol declared in the interface section of a unit source file, all units that depend upon that symbol will have to be recompiled from source. If you don't have the source to those other units, you can't recompile.

This is not a new issue. Unit versioning has been around as long as Borland's Pascal compilers have had compiled units (Turbo Pascal 4.0, 1987). However, the notion of compiled units is new to Delphi's many converts from C and interpreted programming tools. Slipping into old source code habits that were tolerated in loosely structured interpreted languages or C headers can lead to disastrous results in Delphi. You can get away with modifying C header files without necessarily invalidating the binary OBJs that the header files describe. While you can modify the VCL unit interfaces and recompile your programs with those modifications, you have tainted your VCL DCU files and made them incompatible with all other Delphi installations and DCU files.

The VCL source code does not include the source code to Borland proprietary technology in the IDE and component library. CompLib consists of several Borland-compiled DCU files that contain the implementation of the form designer and design-time support code. If you taint your VCL units with interface modifications, the unit signatures in the precompiled CompLib DCUs will not match the unit signatures of your modified VCL units, and you will be unable to recompile the component library DLL.

The rules here are simple:

1. Don't modify the Borland RTL or VCL source code.

2. Don't modify the interface sections of RTL or VCL source units.

The first rule is a recommendation. The second is not.

Summary

The Delphi IDE's modular design makes it possible to recompile new components and design tools literally into the IDE's own executable code. Modular design requires well-defined interfaces of communication between modules, and well-defined interfaces make it easy to add more modules to the system. CompLib is the focal point of all design-time interfaces, supporting the creation of new property editors, component editors, experts, and sophisticated project management add-in tools. As we'll see in the next chapters, the dizzying array of options and opportunities presented by Delphi's design-time interfaces is topped only by what you can do with them.

Chapter 12

Property Editors

The DsgnIntf unit contains the TPropertyEditor base class type, plus no less than 21 property editor descendants that implement support for all the Object Pascal standard types and most VCL property types. DsgnIntf also contains nearly three pages of documentation in comment blocks, describing each property editor method and its use. This chapter augments the DsgnIntf documentation with an overview, correlations, and examples.

TPropertyEditor

Listing 12.1 shows the class declaration of the TPropertyEditor base type. Note that TPropertyEditor is not an abstract base class. When implementing your own property editors, you only have to override the methods you want to change.

Listing 12.1 The TPropertyEditor base class.

```
TPropertyEditor = class
  private
    FDesigner: TFormDesigner;
    FPropList: PInstPropList;
    FPropCount: Integer;
    constructor Create(ADesigner: TFormDesigner;
      APropCount: Integer);
    function GetPrivateDirectory: string;
    procedure SetPropEntry(Index: Integer; AInstance: TComponent;
      APropInfo: PPropInfo);
  protected
    function GetPropInfo: PPropInfo;
    function GetFloatValue: Extended;
    function GetFloatValueAt(Index: Integer): Extended;
    function GetMethodValue: TMethod;
    function GetMethodValueAt(Index: Integer): TMethod;
```

PROPERTY EDITORS

```
      function GetOrdValue: Longint;
      function GetOrdValueAt(Index: Integer): Longint;
      function GetStrValue: string;
      function GetStrValueAt(Index: Integer): string;
      function GetVarValue: Variant;
      function GetVarValueAt(Index: Integer): Variant;
      procedure Modified;
      procedure SetFloatValue(Value: Extended);
      procedure SetMethodValue(const Value: TMethod);
      procedure SetOrdValue(Value: Longint);
      procedure SetStrValue(const Value: string);
      procedure SetVarValue(const Value: Variant);
   public
      destructor Destroy; override;
      procedure Activate; virtual;
      function AllEqual: Boolean; virtual;
      procedure Edit; virtual;
      function GetAttributes: TPropertyAttributes; virtual;
      function GetComponent(Index: Integer): TComponent;
      function GetEditLimit: Integer; virtual;
      function GetName: string; virtual;
      procedure GetProperties(Proc: TGetPropEditProc); virtual;
      function GetPropType: PTypeInfo;
      function GetValue: string; virtual;
      procedure GetValues(Proc: TGetStrProc); virtual;
      procedure Initialize; virtual;
      procedure Revert;
      procedure SetValue(const Value: string); virtual;
      function ValueAvailable: Boolean;
      property Designer: TFormDesigner read FDesigner;
      property PrivateDirectory: string read GetPrivateDirectory;
      property PropCount: Integer read FPropCount;
      property Value: string read GetValue write SetValue;
   end;
```

The following text is an excerpt of the DsgnIntf documentation for the TPropertyEditor class.

TPropertyEditor

Edits a property of a component, or list of components, selected into the Object Inspector. The property editor is created based on the type of the property being edited as determined by the types registered by RegisterPropertyEditor. The Object Inspector uses a TPropertyEditor for all modification to a property. GetName and GetValue are called to display the name and value of the property. SetValue is called whenever the user requests to change the value. Edit is called when the user double-clicks the property in the Object Inspector. GetValues is called when the drop-down list of a property is displayed. GetProperties is called when the property is expanded to show sub-properties. AllEqual is called to decide whether or not to display the value of the property when more than one component is selected.

The following methods can be overridden to change the behavior of the property editor:

Activate
Called whenever the property becomes selected in the Object Inspector. This is potentially useful to allow certain property attributes to only be determined whenever the property is selected in the Object Inspector. Only paSubProperties and paMultiSelect, returned from GetAttributes, need to be accurate before this method is called.

AllEqual
Called whenever more than one component is selected. If this method returns true, GetValue is called, otherwise blank is displayed in the Object Inspector. This is called only when GetAttributes returns paMultiSelect.

Edit
Called when the ellipsis ('...') button is pressed or the property is double-clicked. This can, for example, bring up a dialog to edit the property in some more meaningful fashion than by text (example: Font or Picture properties).

GetAttributes
Tells the Object Inspector how to display the editor tools for this property. GetAttributes returns a set of type TPropertyAttributes, which can contain a combination of the following values:

paValueList:
The property editor can return an enumerated list of values for the property. If GetValues calls Proc with values, then this attribute should be set. This will cause the drop-down button to appear to the right of the property in the Object Inspector.

paSortList:
The Object Inspector sorts the list returned by GetValues

paSubProperties:
The property editor has sub-properties that will be displayed indented and below the current property in standard outline format. If GetProperties will generate property objects, then this attribute should be set.

paDialog:
Indicates that the Edit method will bring up a dialog. This will cause the '...' button to be displayed to the right of the property in the Object Inspector.

paMultiSelect:
Allows the property to be displayed when more than one component is selected. Some properties are not appropriate for multi-selection (example: TComponent.Name).

paAutoUpdate:
Causes the SetValue method to be called on each change made to the editor instead of after the change has been approved (example: TLabel.Caption).

paReadOnly:
Value is not allowed to change.

paRevertable:
Allows the property to be reverted to the original (inherited form) value. Things that shouldn't be reverted are nested properties (e.g., Fonts) and elements of a composite property such as set element values.

GetComponent
Returns the Index'th component being edited by this property editor. This is used to retrieve the components. A property editor can only refer to multiple components when paMultiSelect is returned from GetAttributes.

GetEditLimit
Returns the number of characters the user is allowed to enter for the value. The in-place editor of the Object Inspector will have its text limit set to the return value. By default this limit is 255.

GetName
Returns the name of the property. By default the value is retrieved from the type information with all underbars replaced by spaces. This should only be overridden if the name of the property is not the name that should appear in the Object Inspector.

GetProperties
Should be overridden to call PropertyProc for every sub-property (or nested property) of the property being edited, passing a new TPropertyEditor for each sub-property. By default, PropertyProc is not called and no sub-properties are assumed. TClassProperty will pass a new property editor for each published property in a class. TSetProperty passes a new editor for each element in the set.

GetPropType
Returns the type information pointer for the property being edited.

STANDARD PROPERTY EDITORS

GetValue
Returns the string value of the property. By default this returns '(unknown)'. This should be overridden to return the appropriate value.

GetValues
Called when paValueList is returned in GetAttributes. Should call Proc for every value that is acceptable for this property. TEnumProperty will pass every element in the enumeration.

Initialize
Called after the property editor has been created but before it is used. Many times property editors are created but because the property is not present in all the selected components the property editors are thrown away. Initialize is called after it is determined the property editor is going to be used by the Object Inspector and not just thrown away.

SetValue(Value)
Called to set the value of the property. The property editor should translate the string and call one of the SetXxxValue methods. If the string is not in the correct format or not a valid value, the property editor should raise an exception describing the problem. SetValue can ignore all changes and allow all editing of the property be accomplished through the Edit method (example: TImage.Picture).

Standard Property Editors

The 21 standard property editor classes implemented in DsgnIntf run through just about every possible combination of options supported by the Object Inspector and TPropertyEditor base class. When making plans to create a new property editor, you would do well to find a similar standard property editor and study its DsgnIntf implementation. In many cases, you'll probably find you don't need to implement a new property editor at all.

Keep in mind that these 21 property editor classes are just the core set that happen to live in the DsgnIntf unit. There are more property editors nestled in other VCL units, closer to the components they support or the forms they display.

TOrdinalProperty

TOrdinalProperty is the base class for all ordinal value property editors. It overrides the AllEqual method to return True if GetOrdValue returns the same longint value for all the selected components. TOrdinalProperty is an abstract base class that serves as the ancestor of TIntegerProperty, TCharProperty, TEnumProperty, and TSetProperty.

TIntegerProperty

TIntegerProperty is the default editor for all Longint properties and all subtypes of Longint, such as Integer, Cardinal, Word, Byte, and subranges such as 1..10. TIntegerProperty automatically restricts the value entered into the property editor to the range of the subtype. For example, TIntegerProperty.SetValue will not allow negative values to be entered into a property of type Cardinal, Word, or Byte. Properties TForm.Top, Left, Width, and Height are just a few examples of properties that use the TIntegerProperty editor.

TCharProperty

TCharProperty is the default editor for all Char properties and subtypes of Char, such as the subrange type 'A'..'Z'. None of the standard VCL components publish properties of type char, so this property editor doesn't see much action.

TEnumProperty

TEnumProperty is the default editor for all enumerated properties, such as type TShape = (sCircle, sTriangle, sSquare). It obtains the names of the enumeration elements from the property's RTTI structures (provided by TPropertyEditor.GetPropType) to populate the GetValues list and to convert between ordinal values and text in SetValue and GetValue. TEnumProperty overrides GetAttributes to include [paValueList, paSortList] in the return value so that the Object Inspector will display the enumeration values in a sorted drop-down list. TForm.FormStyle and TForm.BorderStyle are examples of enumerated properties.

TFloatProperty

TFloatProperty is the default editor for all floating-point properties, including Single, Double, Comp, and Currency types. It implements GetValue and SetValue to use the GetFloatValue and SetFloatValue methods provided by TPropertyEditor. None of the standard VCL components publish floating-point properties, but you may run across these types in financial or scientific data analysis components or in OCX controls, such as TGraphicsServer.YAxisMin and YAxisMax.

TStringProperty

TStringProperty is the default editor for properties of type string and its subtypes, such as string[20] or TFilenameString. It implements GetValue and SetValue to use the standard GetStrValue and SetStrValue methods provided by TPropertyEditor. TStringProperty overrides GetEditLimit to restrict input to the number of characters supported by the string subtype. TForm.Hint and TOpenDialog.FileName are examples of properties that use the TStringProperty editor. TCaptionProperty, TComponentNameProperty, TFontNameProperty, and TMPFilenameProperty are descendants of TStringProperty that add special behaviors.

TCaptionProperty

TCaptionProperty is a simple descendant of TStringProperty that overrides GetAttributes to include paAutoUpdate in the return value. This makes the Object Inspector refresh the property editor—and therefore the component property—after every keystroke in the Object Inspector's edit control. TCaptionProperty is used by most Caption and Text properties so that you can see the results of your edits in the component as you type.

TComponentNameProperty

A component's name must be unique within the scope of its immediate owner. TComponentNameProperty is a TStringProperty descendant that enforces this rule by preventing Name properties from showing up in the properties listed for a set of selected components. TComponentNameProperty also limits the edit length to 63 characters, the maximum number of significant characters in an Object Pascal identifier.

TFontNameProperty

TFontNameProperty is a TStringProperty that provides a list of the names of all the fonts installed on the system.

TMPFilenameProperty

TMPFilenameProperty is a TStringProperty that displays an OpenFile common dialog as its Edit action. This was originally created for the TMediaPlayer.FileName property (thus, the "MP" in the class name), but there is nothing media-player-specifc about this property editor. This property editor configures the OpenFile common dialog with the ofShowHelp, ofPathMustExist, and ofFileMustExist options.

TSetProperty

TSetProperty is the default editor for all set-type properties. It implements set elements as subproperties by overriding GetAttributes to include paSubProperties in the return value and by overriding GetProperties to create a TSetElementProperty instance for each of the elements in the set's base type. Form.BorderIcons and Font.Style are examples of set properties.

TSetElementProperty

TSetElementProperty is the property editor created to handle individual set elements in an expanded set property. TSetElementProperty treats each element in the set as a Boolean value.

TMethodProperty

TMethodProperty is the default property used to edit all event properties. An event is simply a property whose type is a method pointer type. The TMethodProperty keeps track of the value of the method pointer but has to work with the form designer to do most of its work. From the form designer, it can get the source code name of the method in the form, get a list of form methods that are type compatible with the property's method type, and insert and display the source code of the form method when you double-click on the property in the Object Inspector. TMethodProperty overrides GetAttributes to include [paValueList, paSortList] in the return value so that the Object Inspector will display a drop-down list in the edit control. TMethodProperty overrides GetValues to call Designer.GetMethods to obtain a list of type-compatible methods in the currently selected form. TMethodProperty.SetValue negotiates with the Designer to decide whether to rename the currently associated form method to the new string value or to create a new method with the string value as its method name. TMethodProperty.Edit asks the Designer to create a method in the form and display it in the source code editor.

TClassProperty

TClassProperty is the default property editor for all properties whose type is a class that descends from TPersistent but not TComponent. It overrides GetAttributes to include paSubProperties in the return value and overrides GetProperties to enumerate the properties of the object instance the property refers to. Font, Brush, and Pen properties are all examples where TClassProperty is used, as well as TForm.HorzScrollbar and TForm.VertScrollbar.

TComponentProperty

TComponentProperty is the default property editor for all properties whose type is a class that descends from TComponent. Recall from Chapter 6 that the streaming system treats component-type properties as references to objects whose lifetimes may be independent of the current component. If the referenced component is not streamed out with the current component, the property will be `nil` when the current component is streamed in later. Therefore, TComponent-Property needs only to allow you to reference other components on the form or, through form linking, other components on other forms in the project.

To do that, TComponentProperty overrides GetAttributes to include [paValueList, paSortList], GetValues to list the names of components on the current form, GetValue to display the name of the associated component, and SetValue to search for a component by name. All the component searching and enumeration are performed by the form designer.

TColorProperty

TColorProperty is an interesting combination of three property editing options: direct input, drop-down list, and pop-up dialog. Colors are essentially just integer RGB values, but VCL defines a number of constants for standard colors and for system color indices. TColorProperty returns a list of these color constant names in GetValues. TColorProperty.Edit displays a color-selection common dialog to assist in selecting just the right shades and hues. TColorProperty.GetAttributes includes [paDialog, paValueList] in its return value but not paSortList. The color identifiers in the drop-down list are organized by color value and system color group, not by alphabetical sort of the identifier names.

TCursorProperty

TCursorProperty provides a mapping between constant identifiers for system cursors and their ordinal values. This is similar to the color identifier mapping performed by TColorProperty.

TFontProperty

TFontProperty is another double-dipper: It is a TClassProperty that displays a dialog as its double-click Edit action. This allows you to expand a Font property to edit its subproperties (thanks to TClassProperty) as well as bring up a font common dialog to select a font configuration.

TModalResultProperty

TModalResultProperty is yet another identifier-to-ordinal-value mapper. This time, the identifiers are the standard modal result constants that can be assigned to TForm.ModalResult to close a modal form. Since any integer is a valid modal result, TForm.ModalResult cannot restrict its range to a predefined enumeration. Thus, we have a series of mrXXX integer constants (mrOK, mrCancel, and so forth) and a TModalResultProperty to manage them at design time.

TShortCutProperty

TShortCutProperty translates between text descriptions of keystroke combinations and their ordinal value virtual key code equivalents. This editor is used by the TMenuItem.ShortCut property. TShortCutProperty uses the ShortCutToText and TextToShortCut utility routines in the Menus unit to perform the actual value translation.

TTabOrderProperty

TTabOrderProperty is a TIntegerProperty that overrides GetAttributes to exclude paMultiSelect from its attribute set. Like a component's Name property, a component's TabOrder must be unique. Excluding paMultiSelect from the property editor's attribute set prevents TabOrder properties from appearing in the list of properties common to a group of selected components.

Registering Property Editors

Before we get into the depths of implementing a property editor, it's important to understand how CompLib selects and creates property editors. How you register a property editor determines CompLib's options in using that property editor, so we'll start with registration. Listing 12.2 shows the procedure declaration of RegisterPropertyEditor from the DsgnIntf unit.

Listing 12.2 The procedure declaration of RegisterPropertyEditor.

```
procedure RegisterPropertyEditor(PropertyType: PTypeInfo;
  ComponentClass: TClass; const PropertyName: string;
  EditorClass: TPropertyEditorClass);
```

The first three parameters to RegisterPropertyEditor limit the scope in which CompLib will use your property editor class type, given in the fourth parameter. There are three scopes at which you can register property editors: global, component, and property-specific.

Global-Scope Registration

```
RegisterPropertyEditor( TypeInfo( string ), nil, '',
TMyStringProperty);
```

This statement passes only a property type and property editor class to RegisterPropertyEditor. This makes TMyStringProperty the default property editor for all string-type properties in all components, replacing the built-in string property editor and any other editors that were registered for the string-type prior to this call. With this registration, TMyStringProperty would be used to edit any string property that does not have a component-scope or property-specific editor registered for it. This would include TForm.Hint and TOpenDialog.FileName but not TForm.Name (uses TComponentNameProperty editor) or TLabel.Caption (uses TCaptionProperty editor).

Component-Scope Registration

```
RegisterPropertyEditor( TypeInfo( string ), TEdit, '',
TMyStringProperty);
```

This statement registers TMyStringProperty as the preferred property editor for all string-type properties of TEdit and descendant components. This takes precedence over any global-scope registrations for the string type. With this registration, TMyStringProperty will be used to edit the TEdit.Hint property, for example, but not TForm.Hint because TForm isn't a descendant of TEdit. Also, this registration would not affect TDBEdit, TMemo, or TDBMemo. Their common ancestor is TCustomEdit, not TEdit. If you change the registration to use TCustomEdit instead of TEdit, all TCustomEdit descendants would be covered by TMyStringProperty.

Typed Types

TEdit.Text is not affected by this TMyStringProperty registration because the Text property is declared as a *typed string* type—TCaption. (Caption and Text are really the same property; after all, you never see them together.) In Controls.pas, TCaption is declared as

```
type TCaption = type string;
```

This type declaration makes TCaption a unique string type as far as RTTI property information is concerned but still a normal string as far as the compiler is concerned. The type of TEdit.Text (TCaption) is not identical to the type that this example registers TMyStringProperty to edit (string), so this registration won't affect the property editing of TEdit.Text.

TEdit.Name is not affected by this TMyStringProperty registration. TComponentNameProperty is registered with property-specific scope (examined next), which takes precedence over this component-scope registration example.

You can create "typed types" of types other than string. TDateTime, for example, is a unique Double type.

Property-Specific Registration

```
RegisterPropertyEditor( TypeInfo( TComponentName ), TComponent,
'Name', TComponentNameProperty);
```

This is the property registration statement CompLib uses to register TComponentNameProperty as the editor of the Name property (of type TComponentName, a typed string) in all TComponents. Using a typed string adds extra insurance that no one will replace this vital property editor accidentally.

Property-specific registrations take precedence over component-scope and global-scope registrations. The only way to usurp a property-specific property editor registration is with another property-specific registration that uses the exact same property type, component type, and property name as the editor registration you're trying to replace. At all levels, the most recently registered property editor takes precedence over prior registrations on the same level.

These multiple levels of property editor registration make it easy to provide (or replace) blanket coverage for a widely used property type as well as provide pinpoint precision in placing specialized property editors on specific component properties.

Implementing Property Editors

When implementing your own property editor from scratch, these are the methods you will probably need to override and implement, in priority order:

1. SetValue—Convert string text into the property's native data format.

2. GetValue—Convert the property's native data format to text.

3. GetAttributes—Indicate how you want the Object Inspector to edit your property.

4. GetValues—If GetAttributes includes paValueList, return all the string values you want to appear in the editor's drop-down list.

5. Edit—If GetAttributes includes paDialog, display your modal form and then apply the modifications to the property or underlying component.

Of course, if you inherit from an existing property editor class, you only have to override the parts you want to change. You will probably never need to override the other TPropertyEditor virtual methods.

Example: TVerboseStringProperty In Delphi 1.0, the only way to handle string data larger than 255 bytes in a published property was through a TStringList. With Delphi 2.0's long strings, that is no longer the case. For string properties whose data is often longer than a dozen characters, wouldn't it be nice to be able to edit that text in something larger than the 1-inch-wide Object Inspector edit window? (Yes, I know you can resize the Object Inspector to make the edit control wider, but that's beside the point: It's still too small for some string data.) Let's make a simple string property descendant that pops up a memo editor in its Edit action to give you more elbow room to edit the property's string data. The name TLongStringProperty carries too many implications that it does something special for the long-string type, so let's call this property editor TVerboseStringProperty instead.

Listing 12.3 shows the complete source code for the TVerboseStringProperty and its pop-up memo form. This vstrprop.pas source file and its sidekick DFM file are included on the CD-ROM that accompanies this book. Figure 12.1 shows the pop-up memo editor in action.

> **Warning: TStringList Defeats Word-Wrap**
>
> There are distinct advantages to moving string data as a single string instead of breaking it up into a list of little strings (a string list). For example, extracting the text data from a multiline TMemo into a string list will break the text lines where they happen to word-wrap in the TMemo control. When you assign that string list data back to the TMemo, each string in the TStringList becomes a separate line ending with a hard line break in the TMemo. Your large word-wrapped paragraph is now sliced up into individual lines that no longer word-wrap as a paragraph when you resize the memo.

To use this new property editor in your Delphi installation, install vstrprop.pas into your component library. Select Component: Install, click the Add button, click the Browse button, and locate and select the vstrprop.pas source file. Close all the dialogs to recompile the component library with the new property editor. The vstrprop unit registers the TVerboseStringProperty editor to replace the TEdit.Text property editor.

Listing 12.3 The vstrprop.pas unit implements a string property editor that includes a pop-up memo editor for editing lengthy strings.

```
unit vstrprop;
interface
uses Windows, Messages, SysUtils, Classes, Graphics, Controls,
    Forms, Dialogs, StdCtrls, ExtCtrls, DsgnIntf;

type
  TMemoForm = class(TForm)
    Memo1: TMemo;
    Panel1: TPanel;
    Panel2: TPanel;
    OK: TButton;
    Cancel: TButton;
  private
    procedure WMGetMinMaxInfo(var Msg: TWMGetMinMaxInfo);
      message WM_GetMinMaxInfo;
  end;

type
  TVerboseStringProperty = class(TStringProperty)
  public
    function GetAttributes: TPropertyAttributes; override;
    procedure Edit; override;
  end;
```

```pascal
  procedure Register;

implementation
{$R *.DFM}

var
  MemoForm: TMemoForm = nil;

procedure TMemoForm.WMGetMinMaxInfo(var Msg: TWMGetMinMaxInfo);
begin
  if csLoading in ComponentState then Exit;
  with Msg.MinMaxInfo^.ptMinTrackSize do
  begin
    X := Panel2.Width;
    Y := Y + Panel1.Height * 2;
  end;
end;

function TVerboseStringProperty.GetAttributes:TPropertyAttributes;
begin
  Result := inherited GetAttributes + [paDialog];
end;

procedure TVerboseStringProperty.Edit;
var
  CompName: string;
begin
  if MemoForm = nil then
    MemoForm := TMemoForm.Create(Application);
  if PropCount = 1 then
    CompName := GetComponent(0).Name
  else
    CompName := '*';
  MemoForm.Caption := 'Editing '+CompName+'.'+GetName;
  MemoForm.Memo1.Text := GetStrValue;
  if MemoForm.ShowModal = mrOk then
    SetStrValue(MemoForm.Memo1.Text);
end;

procedure Register;
begin
  RegisterPropertyEditor(TypeInfo(TCaption), TEdit, 'Text',
    TVerboseStringProperty);
end;
end.
```

TVerboseStringProperty overrides GetAttributes to include paDialog in the attribute set and overrides Edit to display the pop-up memo editor form. This code uses a global variable to hold onto the memo edit form instance once it has been created so that user modifications such as form size and screen position are retained from one invocation to the next. The memo form will be destroyed when the application (Delphi) is shut down. The Edit method sets the memo form's caption to include the component name (if only one component is selected) and the property name. (I find this helpful to remind me what I was doing between interruptions.) The Edit method assigns the property's string value to the form's memo text property and executes the form as a modal dialog. If the form was closed by clicking the OK button, the Edit method assigns the memo's text to the property's string value.

The TMemoForm includes a WM_GETMINMAXINFO message handler to prevent the form from being resized smaller than the button panel at the bottom of the form (see Figure 12.1). Most modal dialogs and main forms aren't (or rather, shouldn't be) resizable, so you usually don't have to worry about this sort of thing. You could achieve the same result using the form's OnResize event, but that event happens after the form has been resized. WM_GETMINMAXINFO comes through as soon as the user starts dragging the form's frame rectangle, long before the form is resized or redrawn, which makes for a cleaner, more professional form.

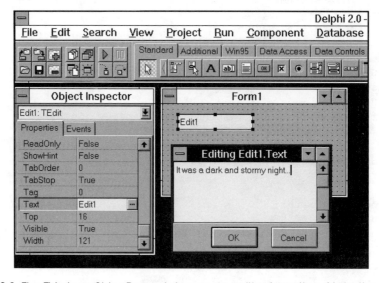

Figure 12.1 The TVerboseStringProperty's pop-up editor in action: Note the ellipsis button in the TEdit.Text property in the Object Inspector.

Property Editor Rules of the Road

Property editing is a very focused activity having well-defined boundaries. There are limits to what property editing was intended to do, and your options in implementing new property editors follow those design parameters. Here are the rules of the road:

- **A published property represents a distinct unit of data—an actual value or a reference to another object.** You might be able to represent that data as text in a number of ways or not at all, but the data itself is atomic. Consequently, property editors deal only with atomic data. The only exceptions to this are the built-in set property and class property editors, which expand to reveal nested properties.

- **The Object Inspector deals only with published properties.** The Object Inspector and TPropertyEditor specification were not intended to handle ambient or nonpersistent attributes of a component. A property editor's sole purpose for being is to configure property data that will be written to the form's DFM file so that it can be read from file at run time to determine a component's behavior or appearance.

- **CompLib determines the selection and lifetime of a property editor.** CompLib decides which property editor class to use for each component property, based on how the property editors were registered. CompLib creates property editor instances when the design environment needs them and destroys them when they are no longer needed.

Some of the consequences of these rules include:

- **You don't create property editor instances.** You may have noticed in the TPropertyEditor declaration at the start of this chapter that the constructor is a private member of the class and is the only way to initialize several of the class's private data fields. This is deliberately done to ensure that property editors are only created in the proper context— by CompLib.

- **You can't define property editors that create their own subproperty classes, like TSetProperty and TClassProperty.** Implementing GetProperties requires creating TPropertyEditor instances, which is not allowed outside the DsgnIntf unit. The only reasons for creating subproperties are to represent the different data elements of a compound data type and to represent something that isn't persistent data at all. If you feel a desperate need to create subproperties, it's likely that your property type is already in violation of the published property rules—it's not atomic. To represent compound data in published properties, use sets or TPersistent helper classes, just as VCL does.

- **The data a property editor handles must be concrete and must be persistent.** Object Inspector property editors are not the place to put design-time conveniences that have no bearing on the persistent data of the component. Tools to help you manipulate only the design-time representation of a component are best implemented as verbs in a component editor or, for big jobs, as an expert. For example, TPageControl has a component editor that adds Next Page, Previous Page, and New Page to the TPageControl's design-time pop-up menu.

Summary

Delphi's property editor system allows you to add special design-time support for your own components' special properties as well as replace the default property editors on a global, component, or property-specific scale. Three levels of property editor registration allow you to install blanket coverage for a particular property type or target only certain components or certain properties with pinpoint precision. The Object Inspector takes care of all the user interface details of editing properties on behalf of the property editor. A property editor is primarily responsible for telling the Object Inspector what display options it supports (simple edit, drop-down list, pop-up dialog, or combinations) and for converting the property's native data to and from the generic string representation the Object Inspector requires. Most of the time, the dozens of VCL standard property editors will handle your component's properties with aplomb. For the rare occasion when you need more specialized editing of a custom property, customizing an existing property editor through inheritance makes creating sophisticated property editors a snap.

Chapter 13

Component Editors

A component editor is a design-time tool that has a broader range of options to manipulate a component than an individual property editor. Property editors can only edit published properties and should restrict themselves to manipulating information that is stored in the component's persistent data. Component editors have no such restrictions. All of a component's public properties and methods as well as its published properties are available to a component editor.

Component editors use this access to provide one or more of the following design-time services:

- **Manipulation of aspects of a component that are not part of the component's persistent data.** These aspects usually involve the design-time appearance of the component, such as providing pop-up menu items to switch between pages in a notebook control.

- **Configuration of persistent data managed by defined properties.** Defined properties (implemented in a component's DefineProperties method) have no RTTI type information, so they cannot be edited in the Object Inspector. For example, you could use a component editor to edit the data behind a component's public array property. Array properties cannot be published or edited in the Object Inspector.

- **Shortcuts for common component configuration tasks.** For example, using pop-up menus to switch notebook pages is more convenient than changing the notebook component's ActivePage property.

- **Pop-up dialogs to configure complex data or relationships in the component.** Examples include TDataset's component editor invoking the Fields Editor design window and TDBGrid's component editor invoking the Columns Editor dialog.

Most component editors exist primarily to provide *access* to design-time component-specific editing tools. You can visualize a component editor as the brains behind the pop-up menu that appears when you right-click on the component at design time. The component editor class determines the contents of the pop-up menu and acts as a springboard to launch specialized component configuration dialogs. It's a bit ironic that most TComponentEditor implementations don't actually edit components but, instead, redirect edit actions to more specialized code or visual pop-up configuration dialogs. Like property editors, component editors are nonvisual conductors of the editing process.

TComponentEditor

The TComponentEditor class lives in the DsgnIntf unit, almost lost in the sea of standard property editors. Since a component editor's tasks are fairly few and well defined, the class declaration is much simpler than that of TPropertyEditor. As shown in Listing 13.1, TComponentEditor only needs methods to support two things: definition and handling of pop-up menu items and handling of the double-click component Edit action.

Listing 13.1 The TComponentEditor base class.

```
TComponentEditor = class
private
  FComponent: TComponent;
  FDesigner: TFormDesigner;
public
  constructor Create(AComponent: TComponent;
    ADesigner: TFormDesigner); virtual;
  procedure Edit; virtual;
  procedure ExecuteVerb(Index: Integer); virtual;
  function GetVerb(Index: Integer): string; virtual;
  function GetVerbCount: Integer; virtual;
  procedure Copy; virtual;
  property Component: TComponent read FComponent;
  property Designer: TFormDesigner read FDesigner;
end;
```

TComponentEditor.Create

The constructor for the component editor class receives a component and a form designer as parameters. These are available to descendants and other users of the class through the Component and Designer properties, respectively. This constructor is virtual so that component editors can be constructed polymorphically using class references. Don't forget to use `override` when declaring your descendant contructors. (Compiler warnings will remind you, but only if you have warnings enabled.)

Note that while a property editor can edit the same property in multiple selected components (if the property editor includes paMultiSelect in its attributes), a component editor can only deal with a single component at a time.

Pop-up Menu Items

TComponentEditor's GetVerbCount, GetVerb, and ExecuteVerb methods define the contents of the pop-up menu that the form designer displays when you right-click on a selected component. Each menu item is a *verb*, an action that your component editor can perform. Override GetVerbCount to return the total count of menu items you want to insert in the pop-up menu. Override GetVerb to return the caption string to display in each menu item. The verb indices are consecutive and start at zero. The first item index is 0; the last is GetVerbCount–1. Override ExecuteVerb to respond to mouse clicks on your menu items by performing the actions associated with the menu items.

Most component editors implement pop-up menu verbs either to tweak a design-time display aspect of the component or to display a modal dialog to configure defined property data or some complex aspect of the component. Such dialogs must be modal to prevent the form designer's component selection from changing while the dialog is active.

If you decide to extend an existing component editor in a descendant class, the index range of any new verbs your descendant defines should start at the end of the ancestor's verb index range.

TComponentEditor.Edit

The form designer calls the Edit method when you double-click on a selected component at design time. If you don't override Edit, the default Edit implementation will call ExecuteVerb(0), which corresponds to the first menu item in the component editor's pop-up menu definition. Since most component editors also provide access to their component-editing dialog(s) through the first menu item in the component's pop-up menu, few component editors need to override the Edit method.

> **Conveniently Obvious**
>
> As a matter of style, it's a good practice to provide redundant access points for features whose most convenient (primary) access point is not obvious. Anyone who has faced traffic symbols in a foreign land or tried to edit text in someone else's editor knows firsthand that *convenient* is rarely synonymous with *obvious* and that *intuitive* really means *obvious* to the well-informed. Since there is no visual indication that double-clicking on a selected component will do something special, you should also include your double-click behavior in a menu item in the component's pop-up menu. Pop-up menus are, of course, the most obvious software feature to grace Windows since the immaculate conception of Alt+Tab and Ctrl+Alt+Del.

Modifying the Component

Whenever your component editor or one of its delegate configuration dialogs modifies the persistent state of a component, you must call FormDesigner.Modified to notify the design environment that the component has been changed. Failing to notify the IDE of component changes may cause projects to be closed without saving changes, prevent components from redrawing themselves to reflect the modified state, and prevent the change from propagating through the form inheritance update mechanism. Property editors contain standard get and set methods for all the standard types, which automatically call Designer.Modified. In component editors, you have to remember to call FormDesigner.Modified yourself. When in doubt, call Modified.

For a modal configuration dialog, it's not strictly necessary to call FormDesigner.Modified for every little change you make to the component. It's sufficient to call Modified when the modal dialog is closed before returning control to the design environment. It's still better to call Modified as soon as possible after each individual change (so that things that rely upon those changed values, such as form inheritance, will update immediately in the design environment), but calling Modified once when the dialog is closed is the bare minimum required to keep the system working correctly.

Registering Component Editors

To associate a new component editor with a particular component type, call the RegisterComponentEditor procedure in the DsgnIntf unit. RegisterComponentEditor simply takes a component class reference and a component editor class reference and stores that association in an internal list. A component editor registered for component TFoo will be used to edit component instances of TFoo and all descendants of TFoo, except for descendants that have their own component editors.

The form designer calls GetComponentEditor (also in DsgnIntf) to locate an appropriate component editor for a particular component type. GetComponentEditor returns the most specific and most recently registered component editor for the component type. You can replace an existing component editor simply by registering your new component editor for the same component type after the existing component editor is registered. Order of registration is usually determined by the order in which units are added to the component library, so just make sure your unit is listed after the unit that registers the component editor you want to replace.

Coordinating Component and Editor Registration

RegisterComponentEditor should be called only at design time, in a Register procedure declared in the interface section of your unit. The component library calls (and expects) Register procedures in all units installed into the component library. There are two ways to package your component editor:

1. Bundle it with your component. There is no penalty for including component (or property) editors in the same unit as your component implementation, as long as the design-time classes are referenced only by the unit's Register procedure. Applications should never refer to a unit's Register procedure, so neither the procedure nor anything it refers to gets linked into the final EXE or DLL. The component library does reference the unit's Register procedure, so the code is linked into the component library, where it is needed. The advantage of this approach is that all the code is in one place. The disadvantage is that all the code is in one place—it's easy to overlook flaws in your component's interface when all the code that manipulates the component is in the same unit, and it's easy to accidentally reference a design-time support class from inside your component's implementation.

2. Place the design-time support code in its own unit with its own Register procedure and have that unit use the component's unit. All design-time registration chores for the component are handled by the design-time support unit, so the component unit wouldn't need a Register procedure at all. Delphi programmers install your design-time support unit in the component library to install the component into the IDE's component palette. This technique has the advantage of keeping design-time support cleanly separated from the component implementation. The disadvantage is that a component editor in a separate unit won't have as much access to implementation details of your component as a component editor implemented in the same unit as a component. If your design-time code includes one or more forms, you should package the design-time code separately from the run-time code to prevent the DFMs from being linked into your run-time apps.

Almost all of VCL's standard property and component editors are implemented in support units separate from the component implementation units. StdReg.pas, for example, contains most of VCL's specialized property and component editor classes, uses the core VCL component units, and registers the core VCL component classes for inclusion in the component library. DBReg.pas performs a similar function, registering all the VCL database classes and design-time support tools. For simple component or property editors, it's easiest to just put the editors in the component's unit. For complex design-time support, though, it's best to separate all the design-time support code from the component implementation.

TDefaultEditor

When you double-click on most components, the default edit action is to insert or select a particular component event handler into the form and switch focus to the IDE code editor window. This behavior is implemented by TDefaultEditor, which handles all TComponent and descendant classes that don't have their own component editors. TDefaultEditor overrides the Edit method to select an appropriate default event handler for the component. The Edit method looks for an OnCreate, OnChange, or OnClick event property in the component's published properties, in that order of preference. If a component contains both an OnClick and OnCreate property, for example, the default component editor selects OnCreate for the default edit action for that component. If the component contains none of these three event properties in its published property list, the default component editor selects the first published event property listed in the component's RTTI for the default edit action.

If you want to change the default event property of a component, create a component editor that inherits from TDefaultEditor and override its protected virtual method, EditProperty. Implement EditProperty to filter out all event properties except the property you want to be your component's default event property. Allowing only that property to reach the inherited EditProperty method ensures that it is the first and only property the inherited code sees, which guarantees that the inherited code will select it for the component's default edit action. For example, Listing 13.2 shows a component editor that makes a component's OnPayday property the default edit action. Note the use of CompareText to perform a case-insensitive string comparison. RTTI identifier strings retain the case of the symbols as they were originally declared in source code, and Pascal source code is case insensitive, so the case of source code symbols is pretty arbitrary.

Listing 13.2 This component editor makes OnPayday the default event property drawn up in the code editor when you double-click on a TPayrollComponent in the form designer.

```
type
  TTaxManComponentEditor = class(TDefaultEditor)
  protected
    procedure EditProperty(PropertyEditor: TPropertyEditor;
      var Continue, FreeEditor: Boolean); override;
  end;

procedure TTaxManComponentEditor.EditProperty(
  PropertyEditor: TPropertyEditor;
  var Continue, FreeEditor: Boolean);
begin
  if (PropertyEditor is TMethodProperty) and
    (CompareText(PropertyEditor.GetName, 'OnPayday') = 0) then
    inherited EditProperty(PropertyEditor, Continue, FreeEditor);
end;

begin
  RegisterComponentEditor(TPayrollComponent,
    TTaxManComponentEditor);
end;
```

Note that if you register this component editor to handle a component type that doesn't contain a published OnPayday event property, no default event property will be selected and the component will have no default edit action. In other words, don't do that.

If you want to add verbs to a component's design-time pop-up menu but want to retain the default double-click behavior, derive your new component editor from TDefaultEditor and override GetVerbCount, GetVerb, and ExecuteVerb.

Implementing Component Editors

Example: TConsoleAboutBox. Listing 13.3 shows a complete component editor that implements an About box for the TConsole and TColorConsole components that accompany this book. The TConsoleComponentEditor defines a new verb for the component's design-time pop-up menu, 'About...', which displays a simple form containing credits and copyright notices for the components. The CnslReg unit also takes care of all design-time component registration chores for the console classes.

Listing 13.3 The CnslReg unit implements a component editor to display an About box at design time for the TConsole and TColorConsole components.

```
unit CnslReg;
interface
uses
  Windows, Messages, SysUtils, Classes, Graphics, Controls, Forms,
  Dialogs, StdCtrls, ExtCtrls, Console, DsgnIntf;

type
  TConsoleAboutBox = class(TForm)
    Memo1: TMemo;
    Panel1: TPanel;
    Button1: TButton;
  end;

  TConsoleEditor = class(TDefaultEditor)
  public
    procedure ExecuteVerb(Index: Integer); override;
    function GetVerb(Index: Integer): string; override;
    function GetVerbCount: Integer; override;
  end;

procedure Register;

implementation
{$R *.DFM}

procedure TConsoleEditor.ExecuteVerb(Index: Integer);
```

```
begin
  if Index <> 0 then Exit;
  with TConsoleAboutBox.Create(Application) do
  try
    ShowModal;
  finally
    Free;
  end;
end;

function TConsoleEditor.GetVerb(Index: Integer): string;
begin
  if Index = 0 then Result := 'About...';
end;

function TConsoleEditor.GetVerbCount: Integer;
begin
  Result := 1;
end;

procedure Register;
begin
  RegisterComponents('Additional', [TConsole, TColorConsole]);
  RegisterClasses([TFixedFont]);
  RegisterComponentEditor(TConsole, TConsoleEditor);
end;
end.
```

Summary

Component editors allow you to insert menu items into a component's design-time pop-up menu and implement behaviors for those menu items. Those behaviors can change the design-time (nonpersistent) display of the component, modify the persistent data of a component's public (nonpublishable) properties, or perform other design-time–related tasks without burdening the component with code that is never used at run time. After modifying the persistent state of a component (changing a published property or changing a public property that affects streamed data), your component editors should always call FormDesigner.Modified so that the rest of the design-time environment will know about your modifications.

Chapter 14

Experts and Add-in Tools

The Delphi IDE's support for add-in tools extends far beyond property and component editors. Through the ToolIntf unit, you can gain access to a variety of the IDE's major subsystems, such as IDE menus, project mangement, and module management. While the IDE's tools interfaces specifically disallow disabling or replacing the standard IDE subsystems, you can use the tools interfaces to build software development support tools of arbitrary complexity to enhance the IDE's native features. Many of the IDE native features you're already familiar with (such as the database form expert, component expert, and PVCS version control system) are implemented using these tools interfaces.

Explanation of Terms

Expert versus Add-in Tool

An *expert* is a utility that assists with the creation or configuration of a component, form, or project. Experts are helpers that simplify the number of steps required to reach a specific goal. You could reach the same goal by simply using the Object Inspector, source code editor, and form designer, but the expert automates most of the steps. Experts are generally one-shot operations: Once the expert has helped you create a complicated form or project, it usually cannot go back and edit the thing it created.

When installed into the IDE, experts should take up residence on the File:New... dialog. In your expert, all you have to do to achieve this is indicate that you're a normal expert, and the IDE tool services will do the rest.

Experts generally do not add new features to the IDE, other than their ability to streamline existing processes. *Add-in tools*, on the other hand, add new project management features to the IDE that are usually independent of component or form property configuration chores. Add-in tools generally insert themselves into the IDE main menu tree and plug themselves into the tool services notification system to keep track of the status of the open project. You implement an add-in tool using expert interfaces, but you mark it as a nonstandard expert to prevent the IDE from supplying the standard expert UI support. We'll see how to do this later in this chapter.

For example, consider a utility to edit Windows version information resources in your project. It would be inappropriate to set this up as an expert because version information resources are independent of components and forms (version info is a distinct Windows resource type that cannot be embedded inside a form resource) and because configuring version information is not a one-shot operation (you'll need to edit the version information in the future). A version resource editor would work best when accessed through a menu item inserted into, say, the IDE's Project menu. When no project is open, you will want to disable this menu item, so your add-in tool will need to listen to project status notifications.

The scopes of experts and add-in tools are disjoint. The only thing they have in common is that they both implement the TIExpert interface. TIExpert is the only representation the IDE has for external modules, so *expert* should be treated as a general term that encompasses all uses of the TIExpert interface. Use the terms *form expert* or *project expert* to refer to a configuration expert implementation and *add-in tool* to refer to an add-in tool expert implementation.

Modal versus Modeless Windows

While an expert is almost always displayed as a modal form, add-in tools are more likely to use nonmodal forms. Modal forms are easier to write because the rest of the IDE is disabled while the form is modal, so the only way to change the project is through that modal form. Keeping a modeless form up-to-date is more difficult because the Delphi user can switch away from the form and change the project using other IDE tools. Since add-in tools have to hook into the IDE's notification systems anyway (as part of defining their own UI), the additional work required to make an add-in work as a modeless form is relatively minor.

Deciding whether to use a modal or modeless form is usually pretty easy. If your expert or tool has a singular task to perform, such as building a new form module, it should probably use a modal form. If the tool's purpose is more open-ended, where the Delphi user will want to return to the tool frequently during the development of a project, it should use a modeless form. Modeless forms do add clutter to the desktop, but they also provide Delphi users the greatest freedom of movement and flexibility.

Non-VCL Expert DLLs

Delphi IDE experts and add-in tools can be implemented in Delphi or in any other language that can produce Win32 DLL modules, such as C or C++. You will have to translate the Delphi IDE's tools interface classes into equivalent C++ pure virtual classes or C arrays of function pointers. The IDE's tool services provide several functions to help non-Delphi DLLs manage pointers to Delphi's dynamically allocated long strings. The IDE also has a few messaging and window handle requirements that are automatically handled by VCL but require special attention in non-VCL DLLs. If you choose to write an expert DLL with Delphi, but not using VCL forms, you fall into the non-VCL expert DLL category as well. These special requirements and support functions for non-VCL expert DLLs are explained in the function descriptions in the next section.

TIToolServices—Gateway to the IDE

The TIToolServices interface is the root of the IDE's design-time interfaces. If something can't be reached through TIToolServices, it's not available to experts and add-in tools. Listing 14.1 shows the TIToolServices class from ToolIntf.pas.

Listing 14.1 The TIToolServices class, the root of all access to IDE internal services.

```
type
  TCreateModuleFlag = (cmAddToProject, cmShowSource, cmShowForm,
    cmUnNamed, cmNewUnit, cmNewForm, cmMainForm, cmMarkModified,
    cmNewFile, cmExisting);
  TCreateModuleFlags = set of TCreateModuleFlag;

  TIToolServices = class(TInterface)
  public
    { Action interfaces }
    function CloseProject: Boolean; virtual; stdcall; abstract;
    function OpenProject(const ProjName: string): Boolean;
      virtual; stdcall; abstract;
    function OpenProjectInfo(const ProjName: string): Boolean;
      virtual; stdcall; abstract;
    function SaveProject: Boolean; virtual; stdcall; abstract;
    function CloseFile(const FileName: string): Boolean;
      virtual; stdcall; abstract;
    function SaveFile(const FileName: string): Boolean;
      virtual; stdcall; abstract;
    function OpenFile(const FileName: string): Boolean;
```

```
      virtual; stdcall; abstract;
    function ReloadFile(const FileName: string): Boolean;
      virtual; stdcall; abstract;
    function ModalDialogBox(Instance: THandle; TemplateName: PChar;
      WndParent: HWnd; DialogFunc: TFarProc;
      InitParam: LongInt): Integer; virtual; stdcall; abstract;
    function CreateModule(const ModuleName: string;
      Source, Form: TIStream;
      CreateFlags: TCreateModuleFlags): Boolean;
      virtual; stdcall; abstract;
    function CreateModuleEx(const ModuleName, FormName,
      AncestorClass, FileSystem: string; Source, Form: TIStream;
      CreateFlags: TCreateModuleFlags): TIModuleInterface;
      virtual; stdcall; abstract;

    { Project/UI information }
    function GetParentHandle: HWND; virtual; stdcall; abstract;
    function GetProjectName: string; virtual; stdcall; abstract;
    function GetUnitCount: Integer; virtual; stdcall; abstract;
    function GetUnitName(Index: Integer): string;
      virtual; stdcall; abstract;
    function EnumProjectUnits(EnumProc: TProjectEnumProc;
      Param: Pointer): Boolean; virtual; stdcall; abstract;
    function GetFormCount: Integer; virtual; stdcall; abstract;
    function GetFormName(Index: Integer): string;
      virtual; stdcall; abstract;
    function GetCurrentFile: string; virtual; stdcall; abstract;
    function IsFileOpen(const FileName: string): Boolean;
      virtual; stdcall; abstract;
    function GetNewModuleName(var UnitIdent,
      FileName: string): Boolean; virtual; stdcall; abstract;

    { Component Library information }
    function GetModuleCount: Integer; virtual; stdcall; abstract;
    function GetModuleName(Index: Integer): string;
      virtual; stdcall; abstract;
    function GetComponentCount(ModIndex: Integer): Integer;
      virtual; stdcall; abstract;
    function GetComponentName(ModIndex, CompIndex: Integer): string;
      virtual; stdcall; abstract;

    { Virtual File System interfaces }
    function RegisterFileSystem(
      AVirtualFileSystem: TIVirtualFileSystem): Boolean;
      virtual; stdcall; abstract;
    function UnRegisterFileSystem(const Ident: string): Boolean;
      virtual; stdcall; abstract;
    function GetFileSystem(
```

```pascal
    const Ident: string): TIVirtualFileSystem;
    virtual; stdcall; abstract;

  { Module interfaces }
  function GetModuleInterface(
    const FileName: string): TIModuleInterface;
    virtual; stdcall; abstract;
  function GetFormModuleInterface(
    const FormName: string): TIModuleInterface;
    virtual; stdcall; abstract;

  { Menu interface }
  function GetMainMenu: TIMainMenuIntf;
    virtual; stdcall; abstract;

  { Notification registration }
  function AddNotifier(AddInNotifier: TIAddInNotifier): Boolean;
    virtual; stdcall; abstract;
  function RemoveNotifier(
    AddInNotifier: TIAddInNotifier): Boolean;
    virtual; stdcall; abstract;

  { Pascal string handling functions }
  function NewPascalString(Str: PChar): Pointer;
    virtual; stdcall; abstract;
  procedure FreePascalString(var Str: Pointer);
    virtual; stdcall; abstract;
  procedure ReferencePascalString(var Str: Pointer);
    virtual; stdcall; abstract;
  procedure AssignPascalString(var Dest, Src: Pointer);
    virtual; stdcall; abstract;

  { Error handling }
  procedure RaiseException(const Message: string);
    virtual; stdcall; abstract;

  { Configuration access }
  function GetBaseRegistryKey: string; virtual; stdcall; abstract;
end;
```

The IDE creates the ToolServices object and passes it to your expert DLL during DLL initialization. Note that the IDE is responsible for implementing, creating, and freeing the TIToolServices interface object, so you should never free this interface yourself.

Action Methods

CloseProject

This function closes the IDE's currently open project, prompting the user to save modified files if necessary. CloseProject returns False if the user cancels the close operation by clicking the Cancel button on a file save confirmation dialog. If the IDE sucessfully closes the project or if no project was open to begin with, CloseProject returns True.

OpenProject

This function opens the named project in the IDE, after first closing the currently open project. To create a new project and empty main form, pass an empty string as the project name. If the user cancels the prerequisite close operation or if an error occurs while opening the specified project, this function returns False. If the IDE successfully opens the specified project, OpenProject returns True.

OpenProjectInfo

OpenProjectInfo returns True if the IDE successfully opens the named project. This routine bypasses all the normal project load features (such as loading a desktop file, showing the source code, and so forth) and simply opens the .DPR and .DOF files. Avoid using this routine since it doesn't completely open the project.

SaveProject

SaveProject instructs the IDE to save the currently open project as well as any modified files that belong to the project. The IDE will prompt the user to give names to unnamed modules in the project. If the IDE successfully saves the project, or if the project doesn't contain any modified files, or if there is no project open, SaveProject returns True. If the user cancels the save operation or if an error is encountered in saving a file, this function returns False.

CloseFile

This function returns True if the IDE successfully closes the specified file or if the file is not currently open.

OpenFile

This function returns True if the IDE successfully opens the specified file or if the file is already open.

ReloadFile

ReloadFile discards any modifications made to a file and reloads the file data from the file's original disk image. The IDE will *not* prompt the user for confirmation prior to discarding the modifications. This function returns True if the file is already open and the IDE successfully reloads the file data, False if the file is not open or if an error occurs while reading the file data.

ModalDialogBox

Non-VCL expert DLLs must call this function to display a modal dialog box. This is necessary so that the IDE main message loop can continue to provide idle-loop services such as status line messages and tooltip hints. Note that expert DLLs written with Delphi need only assign the GetParentHandle result to the DLL's Application.Handle property and then simply call their form's ShowModal method. (See GetParentHandle description given shortly.)

CreateModule

CreateModule opens a new unit source file in the code editor window and, optionally, a corresponding form in a form designer. There are a multitude of variations in how you can use this method. Here are just a few examples:

```
ToolServices.CreateModule('MyUnit', nil, nil, [cmNewForm]);
```

This creates a new unit named MyUnit.pas, a corresponding blank form, and the form class declaration in the unit. This new form is not added to the current project.

```
ToolServices.CreateModule('MyUnit', nil, nil,
  [cmAddToProject, cmExisting, cmShowSource]);
```

This opens an existing MyUnit.pas file (and corresponding form, if any), adds it to the current project, and brings the code editor window to the front to display the unit source.

```
ToolServices.CreateModule('MyUnit', CodeIStream, nil,
  [cmShowSource, cmMarkModified]);
```

This creates a new unit named MyUnit.pas containing the source code provided by the CodeIStream, brings the code editor window to the top to display the source file, and marks the source as modified. No form is associated with this unit.

```
ToolServices.CreateModule('',CodeIStream, FormIStream,
  [cmAddToProject, cmMainForm, cmUnNamed, cmShowForm]);
```

This creates a new unnamed unit using the source code provided by CodeIStream and the form file provided by FormIStream, adds the form to the project, makes the form the project's main form, and shows the form.

CreateModule's stream parameters are IStream interfaces, not real TStream classes. Create an instance of TIMemoryStream (from the IStreams unit), write your source code or form resource to its MemoryStream property, and then pass the TIMemoryStream instance in the Source parameter of the CreateModule call. Free the TIMemoryStream instance after the call, and it will free the real memory stream it created internally. TIFileStream provides a similar stream interface wrapper for disk files. Don't forget to reset the stream positions to zero (or wherever the data you want the IDE to look at exists in the stream) before calling CreateModule.

Note that Delphi will create the neccessary unit source code when you tell it to create a new form, but, in all other cases, you are responsible for synchronizing the source code and form you provide. Delphi won't synthesize a unit given a DFM, and it won't synthesize a DFM given a unit containing a form declaration.

CreateModuleEx

This method is an extended version of CreateModule that adds support for virtual file systems and form inheritance (introduced in Delphi 2.0). All CreateModule options are supported, with the addition that the cmExisting flag will cause the IDE to load the specified module from the specified virtual file system. The file system name must be a valid file system previously registered through RegisterFileSystem. Pass an empty string for the file system parameter to use the default file system.

The additional AncestorClass parameter allows you to specify an existing form class name in the project to be the ancestor of the form you're creating. The ancestor form's module must be added to the current project prior to this call.

Project/UI Information

GetParentHandle

GetParentHandle returns the window handle of the Delphi IDE's application window, which should be used as the parent window for any windows created by non-VCL expert DLLs. For expert DLLs implemented in VCL, just assign this handle to the DLL's Application.Handle property at DLL initialization, and all subsequent forms and windows in the DLL will automatically use the proper parent window. Initializing the DLL's Application.Handle also enables other services in the DLL's VCL forms, such as pop-up hint windows, status line updates, and F1-context-sensitive help.

Failing to use the proper parent window for your windows will cause user interface problems in the IDE. For example, minimizing the IDE main window hides all windows that were created with the IDE's application window as their parent. If your expert windows don't set the parent window correctly, your expert windows will remain visible when the IDE is minimized.

GetProjectName

GetProjectName returns a fully qualified path name of the currently open project file or an empty string if no project is open.

GetUnitCount

This function returns the number of units belonging to the currently open project. Project membership is determined solely by the `uses` list in the project's .DPR file.

GetUnitName

GetUnitName returns the fully qualified file name of the Nth unit belonging to the currently open project.

EnumProjectUnits

This function calls the provided EnumProc procedure pointer once for each unit belonging to the currently open project.

GetFormCount

GetFormCount returns the number of forms belonging to the currently open project. Since every form must have its own unit, but units don't have to have forms, this value will always be less than or equal to GetUnitCount.

GetFormName

This function returns the fully qualified file name of the Nth form in the project.

GetCurrentFile

GetCurrentFile returns the fully qualified file name of the currently selected module. This could be a unit or a form file, and *only* a unit or form file. If no module is currently selected, this function returns an empty string. To get the file name of an arbitrary file open in an editor window, use TIEditorInterface.FileName, defined in EditIntf.pas.

IsFileOpen

This function returns True if the named module (unit or form file) is currently open in the IDE.

GetNewModuleName

This function generates a new module unit file name and unit identifier pair, guaranteed to be unique within the currently open project—for example, Unit1.pas, Unit2.pas, and so on.

Component Library Information

GetModuleCount

GetModuleCount returns the number of modules (units) currently installed in the component library.

GetModuleName

This function returns the unit name of the Nth module installed in the component library.

GetComponentCount

GetComponentCount returns the number of component classes registered by a particular module installed in the component library.

GetComponentName

This function returns the class name of the Nth component in the Mth module in the component library.

Virtual File System Registration

RegisterFileSystem

Call this function to register a new virtual file system implementation for use in the IDE. If the file system's unique name conflicts with another file system already registered, the registration fails and the function returns False. (The file system's GetIDString method provides its unique name.)

UnRegisterFileSystem

Call this function to remove your virtual file system implementation from the IDE. This only prevents new files from being opened with this file system; it does not affect files already open with this file system.

GetFileSystem

GetFileSystem returns a TIVirtualFileSystem interface to a file system implementation registered under the specified name. This function returns `nil` if no file system has been registered with the specified name.

Module Interfaces

GetModuleInterface

This function returns a module interface for the specified unit file name. Multiple calls to this function for the same module name return the same module interface instance, with only the reference count adjusted. You must call Release when finished with the module interface returned by this function, and *only* Release (not Free or Destroy). TIModuleInterface is defined in EditIntf.pas. From the module interface, you can get to the module's source code, form designer, ancestor module, file system, and change notification interfaces.

GetFormModuleInterface

This function returns a module interface for the specified form. Note that this looks at the form identifier, whereas GetModuleInterface looks at the unit file name.

Menu Interface

GetMainMenu

This function returns an interface to the IDE's main menu. As with all interfaces, you should call Release when you no longer need the interface. From the TIMainMenuIntf interface, you can locate individual menus in the IDE menu tree and insert new menu items for your add-in tools. See ToolIntf.pas for more detail.

Project Notifications

AddNotifier

Call this method to register an instance of a TIAddInNotifier implementation. TIAddInNotifier receives project status change notifications through its sole FileNotification method, allowing add-in tools to keep track of when the IDE starts to close a project, starts to open a project, and finishes opening a project; when the IDE opens and closes individual files; and when modules are added to or removed from the project. The FileNotification method can also abort these actions by setting the Cancel parameter to True.

To implement a TIAddInNotifier to support your add-in tools, create a descendant of TIAddInNotifier and override the FileNotification method. The body of this method either can act on the notifications independently (for example, to disable your add-in tool's menu item when the project is closed and to enable it when a project is opened) or can simply forward the notifications on to a more capable method in your add-in tool's main class.

If you only want to track status changes to a specific module or file, implement TIModuleNotifier instead, and register it with the particular TIModuleInterface. See EditIntf.pas for more detail.

RemoveNotifier

Call this method to remove a previously registered instance of a TIAddInNotifier. Before destroying your notifier implementation instance, you *must* remove it from the tool services' notifier list. You could do this in your notifier's destructor, for example.

Utilities for non-Delphi DLLs

The following methods allow non-Delphi expert DLLs to allocate, release, and copy Delphi long strings. Experts implemented with Delphi will never need to use these methods.

NewPascalString

This function allocates and returns a pointer to a Delphi long string built from the provided PChar (char *, in C-speak) parameter. The return value can be passed tools interface methods that require a string parameter. The function returns `nil` when given a PChar parameter that is an empty string or `nil` pointer. To release your reference to the Delphi long string, you must call FreePascalString. Never allocate memory for Delphi long strings yourself. Long strings must be managed by the Delphi system unit.

FreePascalString

This function decrements the internal reference count of the indicated Delphi long string. If the reference count drops to zero, the memory allocated to the string is released. Never dispose of a Delphi long string pointer directly or modify the internal reference count of the string. Note that you are responsible for freeing strings returned by IDE tool services' function calls.

ReferencePascalString

This function increments the reference count of the given Delphi long string. This allows a non-Delphi DLL to "keep" a string passed to it by a Delphi routine without making a copy of the string data. For example, the EnumProjectUnits method calls a function address you provide. That callback function has three string parameters that your expert may want to retain for use after the callback returns. To extend the string pointer's lifetime beyond the scope of the function the string was created in (in this example, the callback function), you must call ReferencePascalString. Every call to ReferencePascalString must have a corresponding call to FreePascalString to actually release the string's memory.

AssignPascalString

This function assigns one Delphi long string to another by incrementing the reference count on the source string and decrementing the reference count on the destination string. Never directly assign Delphi long string pointers to each other.

This will cause a memory leak, and the imbalance in reference counts could lead to heap corruption and a crash.

Error Handling

RaiseException

RaiseException tells the IDE to raise an exception. Execution will not return from this method call. This method is a carryover from the 16-bit Delphi days when exceptions were an application feature (not an operating system feature) that couldn't easily cross DLL boundaries. It shouldn't be necessary for 32-bit Delphi expert DLLs to call this method, but experts written in other languages may find it easier to call this than to raise their own exceptions.

Implementing TIExpert

Just as TIToolServices is your expert's gateway into the IDE, TIExpert is the IDE's gateway into your expert. Delphi experts and add-in tools must implement TIExpert in a descendant class and register that expert class with the IDE tool services. First, let's look at what you need to do to implement a TIExpert descendant class, and then we'll see how to initialize and register the expert. Listing 14.2 shows the class declaration of TIExpert in Delphi's ExptIntf.pas unit.

Listing 14.2 TIExpert, the IDE's link to your expert or add-in tool.

```
type
  TExpertStyle = (esStandard, esForm, esProject, esAddIn);
  TExpertState = set of (esEnabled, esChecked);

  TIExpert = class(TInterface)
  public
    { Expert UI strings }
    function GetName: string; virtual; stdcall; abstract;
    function GetAuthor: string; virtual; stdcall; abstract;
    function GetComment: string; virtual; stdcall; abstract;
    function GetPage: string; virtual; stdcall; abstract;
    function GetGlyph: HICON; virtual; stdcall; abstract;
    function GetStyle: TExpertStyle; virtual; stdcall; abstract;
    function GetState: TExpertState; virtual; stdcall; abstract;
    function GetIDString: string; virtual; stdcall; abstract;
    function GetMenuText: string; virtual; stdcall; abstract;
```

```
  { Launch the expert }
  procedure Execute; virtual; stdcall; abstract;
end;
```

GetStyle

GetStyle indicates what kind of expert this TIExpert implementation represents and determines how the IDE treats your expert module. The return value can be esStandard, esForm, esProject, or esAddIn. For esStandard experts, the IDE inserts a menu item into its Tools menu and calls the expert's Execute method when the menu item is clicked. For esForm and esProject experts, the IDE inserts the expert's icon into a page of the File:New... dialog and calls the expert's Execute method when the user double-clicks on the expert's icon. In the IDE's Tools:Repository dialog, the Delphi user can select an esForm expert as the default source for new forms (File:New Form) and can select an esProject expert as the default source for new projects (File:New Application). For esAddIn experts, the IDE performs no user interface setup for the module. AddIn tools are responsible for setting up their own IDE user interface hooks, usually by inserting menu items into the IDE main menu.

You must override and implement every abstract method defined in TIExpert, but your expert's style determines which expert methods must provide meaningful responses. For example, esStandard, esForm, and esProject style experts must implement the Execute method to perform their designated task. Since the IDE doesn't provide any UI for esAddIn style experts, the IDE never calls their Execute methods, so esAddIn style experts don't need to do anything in their Execute methods. Similarly, esAddIn style experts can ignore most of the UI string methods of TIExpert and just return an empty string.

GetName

GetName must return a unique descriptive name identifying this expert. This is a display string, so it may be shown to the Delphi user. This method is required in all styles of experts.

Translating Display Strings

If you intend to translate your expert into other languages (English, French, German, Tagalog, Urdu—whatever), all display strings will need to be translated, so you should store display strings in easy-to-translate string resources instead of in hard-to-translate source code constants. Internal strings that are never shown to the end user, such as component names, don't need to be translated or resourced.

GetAuthor

GetAuthor should return the name of the person or company that created the expert. This string is required in esForm and esProject experts and will appear in the author column of the Object Repository's detail view.

GetComment

GetComment should return a one- or two-sentence description of what the expert does. This string is required in esForm and esProject experts and will appear in the description column of the Object Repository's detail view.

GetPage

GetPage should return the name of the tab page in the Object Repository dialog in which this esForm or esProject expert should appear. If a page with this name does not already exist, a new page will be created. This is a display string. If an esForm or esProject style expert's GetPage method returns an empty string, the IDE will place the expert in a generic Object Repository page called "Experts." Note that the Delphi user can override this page name request using the Tools: Repository configuration dialog.

GetGlyph

In esForm and esProject experts, GetGlyph should return an icon handle for the IDE to display in the Object Repository. If GetGlyph returns zero, the IDE will use a stock icon for the expert. The icon handle must be valid for the entire lifetime of the expert interface instance.

GetState

In esStandard style experts, GetState determines the state of the menu item the IDE created for this expert. If the return value includes esEnabled, the menu item is enabled; otherwise, the menu is disabled. If the return value includes esChecked, the menu item is drawn with a check mark. Note that this method may be called frequently—each time the expert's name or icon is shown in a menu or listbox. This method is required in esStandard, esForm, and esProject style experts.

GetIDString

GetIDString must return a string name identification for the expert that is unique across all possible experts produced by software tools vendors. This is an internal string used only to distinguish this expert from others installed in the IDE. This string is not displayed to the end user. The recommended format for this string is CompanyName.ExpertFunction, such as Borland.VersionInfoEditor or Mobius.SpriteAnimator. All experts must implement this method to return a unique identification string.

GetMenuText

In esStandard style experts, the IDE calls GetMenuText to get the text to display in the menu item the IDE maintains for the expert prior to displaying the menu. This method is called each time the IDE menu item is displayed, which makes it possible for the menu item's text to reflect the current state of the expert or other context information.

Execute

Execute is the method that does all the real work of an esStandard, esForm, or esProject expert. Usually, the Execute method creates and shows a modal form. An expert's form might only display and edit options to control the operation of the expert and let the expert's Execute method do the actual dirty work of manipulating IDE tool services interfaces to poke and prod the project.

Installing and Initializing an Expert

Once you have implemented a TIExpert descendant for your expert, along with a form and code to use the IDE tool services to actually build or modify parts of a project, how do you get the IDE to use your expert? Simple. You can compile the expert into into its own DLL and modify the system registry to tell the IDE where to find the DLL, or you can simply compile the expert into the component library (which is a DLL, after all, that the IDE already knows about).

To DLL or Not To DLL

Compiling an expert into the component library offers a few big advantages over compiling into a separate DLL. CompLib experts require less code to set up, and the total size contribution of the expert to CompLib is fairly small. CompLib already contains everything in VCL (and then some), so adding your expert to the mix grows CompLib only by the amount of code you actually write. The main disadvantage to putting experts in CompLib is that they will make rebuilding the component library take a little longer. Every unit added to CompLib adds to its link time. It's also a little inconvenient to have to rebuild CompLib just to install or remove an expert.

Compiling one or more experts into a stand-alone DLL takes you out of the CompLib compile and link cycle but at a cost in code size, memory use, and programming simplicity. As a stand-alone DLL, your expert doesn't have to be unloaded from memory and reloaded every time the Delphi user reconfigures the component library (which, for me, occurs several times daily—on slow days), but your expert will use more disk and memory space for that independence. A DLL that contains an expert must include not only the expert's code and data but also any VCL code that the expert makes use of, such as the Forms unit. VCL's minimum code footprint to support a form with a few buttons and labels is about 150K. An expert that uses forms, database tables, and DBGrids will quickly find itself pushing 300K. The same expert compiled into CompLib might add only 12K to the CompLib DLL since CompLib will very likely already include all the VCL and database controls. You can reduce the per-expert DLL overhead cost by putting multiple experts in the same DLL, but that tends to complicate product packaging (it's hard to sell just a third of a DLL). CompLib experts have greater economy; DLL experts have greater autonomy.

Experts in DLLs also have slightly different initialization code requirements. As we'll see shortly, it's quite manageable, but it's still more than what's required for experts compiled into CompLib.

Compiling an Expert into CompLib

An expert needs only three things in its IDE life to be a happy camper: The expert needs to be created, it needs to be registered with the IDE, and it needs access to an instance of the IDE's TIToolServices interface.

The only requirement for compiling a unit into the component library is that the unit must expose a Register procedure in its interface section. CompLib doesn't care what a unit contains, as long as it has that Register procedure. When the unit is compiled into CompLib, its Register procedure will be called shortly after the IDE loads CompLib into memory.

To allow your expert unit to be compiled into CompLib, then, all you have to do is declare a Register procedure in your expert unit's interface section. In the body of that Register procedure, create an instance of your TIExpert implementation class and notify the IDE of its existence with a call to RegisterLibraryExpert (a function defined in ExptIntf). ExptIntf also defines a global ToolServices variable that, when your unit is compiled into CompLib, is automatically initialized

INSTALLING AND INITIALIZING AN EXPERT

with an instance of the IDE's TIToolServices interface prior to the execution of the Register procedures of the installed units. If your expert is an add-in tool, the Register procedure or your TIExpert constructor is also your jumping-off point for creating and registering project notification interfaces and setting up shop in the IDE UI.

That's it! In your expert unit's Register procedure, you have constructed an instance of your expert interface, have registered it with the IDE, and have gained access to the IDE tool services interface. Now you just kick back and wait for the IDE to call you back, either in the methods of your TIExpert class (for esStandard, esForm, and esProject experts) or in the callback methods of your add-in tool's inserted menu items and project notification interfaces.

Building an Expert in a DLL

Building an expert in a separate DLL requires only a few more steps than compiling an expert into CompLib. You have to define a project file that begins with `library` instead of `program`, and you have to export a function with the name InitExpert0016 from the DLL. That name is stored in the ExpertEntryPoint string constant in the ExptIntf unit. The exported function must have a parameter list compatible with the TExpertInitProc procedure type defined in ExptIntf. Listing 14.3 shows the DLL initialization routine in the ExptDemo.dpr project found in Delphi's DEMOS\EXPERTS directory.

Listing 14.3 A stand-alone DLL expert must export an initialization function like this InitExpert.

```
library ExptDemo;
uses
  ShareMem,
  ExptIntf,
  ToolIntf,
  { ... etc. };

procedure DoneExpert; export;
begin
  { Put any general destruction code here.  Note that the Delphi IDE
    will destroy all registered experts automatically. }
end;

function InitExpert(ToolServices: TIToolServices;
  RegisterProc: TExpertRegisterProc;
  var Terminate: TExpertTerminateProc): Boolean; export; stdcall;
```

331

```
begin
  { Make sure we're the first and only instance }
  Result := ExptIntf.ToolServices = nil;
  if not Result then Exit;

  ExptIntf.ToolServices := ToolServices;
  if ToolServices <> nil then
    Application.Handle := ToolServices.GetParentHandle;

  Terminate := DoneExpert;

  { Register the experts }
  RegisterProc(TDialogExpert.Create);
  RegisterProc(TApplicationExpert.Create);
end;

exports
  InitExpert name ExpertEntryPoint;
begin
end.
```

The InitExpert function shown in Listing 14.3 performs all the initialization steps unique to initializing an expert DLL. It assigns the ToolServices parameter to the DLL's ToolServices global variable (in the ExptIntf unit) so that all the code in the DLL will have easy access to the ToolServices interface. InitExpert assigns ToolServices.GetParentHandle to the DLL's Application.Handle property so that all VCL forms and dialogs will be properly owned by the host application (the Delphi IDE) and so that the DLL's components can benefit from the host application's main message loop idle processing (pop-up hint windows, status line updates, and mouse-enter/mouse-leave notifications).

InitExpert assigns the DLL's DoneExpert procedure to the Terminate procedure variable parameter so that the IDE will call DoneExpert before unloading the expert DLL. This ExptDemo project doesn't do anything in its DoneExpert procedure, but it shows you how to do it if your expert does need an opportunity to release global resources prior to DLL shutdown.

Finally, InitExpert does the most important part. It creates instances of the two experts the DLL implements and registers them with the IDE by calling the RegisterProc procedure variable parameter.

In both CompLib experts and DLL experts, the best place for an add-in tool to set up shop in the IDE UI, create and register callback notifications, and so on, is in the expert's constructor. Minimizing expert setup code that lives outside the methods of an expert class will make it much easier to switch an expert from a

DLL configuration to a CompLib configuration and back again. (You know you're going to make the switch at least once, just out of curiosity.)

Installing an Expert DLL into the IDE

Once you have your expert built in a stand-alone DLL, you need to tell the IDE that it exists and where to find the DLL on disk. The IDE looks for this information in the system registry, under the registry key HKEY_CURRENT_USER\Software\Borland\Delphi\2.0\Experts. Each IDE expert DLL module has its own key value under this Experts key. The name of the value isn't important, but it should be unique and easily recognized as belonging to your expert. "CompanyName.ExpertName" is a good pattern to follow. The data of the registry entry is a string containing the fully qualified file name of the expert DLL as installed on your system. You'll need to create or update this registry entry when installing your expert DLL on customers' machines.

The next time you fire up the Delphi IDE, it will find the new registry entry, load your expert DLL, and call the DLL's InitExpert0016 initialization function. This level of automation is great for the Delphi user but makes developing and testing expert DLLs a bit of a pain: To recompile the expert DLL, you have to unload the DLL from memory, and to do that you have to exit the IDE.

Implementing the Rest of the Expert

Once you have your TIExpert interface implemented, you can focus on building the real expert—the forms, support code, and ToolServices manipulation code that makes your expert actually do something useful. Many experts, such as the Dialog Expert and Application Expert implemented in ExptDemo, operate in an interview/execute model. The interview part queries the Delphi user in one or more steps to gather information needed to build the appropriate form or project. When the user clicks the OK button on the last such query, the execute part builds the components or source code needed and submits that material to the IDE for incorporation into the current project.

Many add-in tools use a simple modal options dialog or present themselves as a nonmodal browser or manipulator of project information. The Project Explorer expert (DEMOS\EXPERTS\ProjExpl.dpr) is an excellent example of a modeless project-browsing add-in tool. The Project Explorer is an add-in tool implemented in a stand-alone DLL that inserts its own menu item into the IDE's View menu and registers project change notification handlers to keep track of what's going on in the current project.

When you select its View:Project Explorer menu item, it displays a nonmodal window containing an outline of the contents of the project, as shown in Figure 14.1. The project's modules, forms, and components are arranged hierarchically in the order of project, unit, form, component. Once you reach the form level, the arrangement of components in the outline reflects the visual containment (Parent/Child relations) of components on the form. A form may contain a notebook control, which contains page controls, which contain components. You can use the Project Explorer to change the component shown by the Object Inspector, show the source code editor for a particular unit, and even change the names of components.

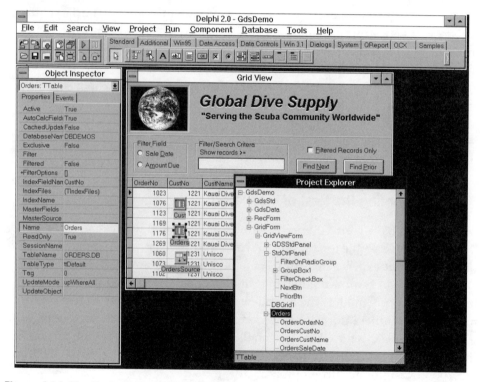

Figure 14.1 The Project Explorer demo expert shows how to navigate the module interfaces of the project, bring editor windows to the front, change the Object Inspector selection, and much more!

The Project Explorer sample code packs a wealth of information on how to navigate the TIModuleInterface, TIFormInterface, and TIComponentInterface interfaces defined in the EditIntf unit; how to construct a modeless form to listen for and respond to project change notifications; how to open and display modules in a project; how to get and set component properties through the tool services interfaces; and a variety of other useful implementation details. If you're considering writing a modeless-style add-in tool for the Delphi IDE, you most certainly should sit down and study the Project Explorer source code.

Summary

The Delphi IDE's tool services interfaces offer a rich array of information and control points with which you can browse, manipulate, and create components, forms, units, and projects. While this chapter focused on the services offered by the root TIToolServices interface and the tasks necessary to implement the required TIExpert interface and to build and install your experts in either CompLib or in stand-alone DLLs, you should now have a pretty good idea of the nature of the many other tool services categories and classes provided by the IDE. Once you know that something exists and you know where to begin looking for it (TIToolServices is the root of everything), finding the specific information you need is simply a matter of following leads to their source.

Appendix

Win32 Review

Since many 32-bit Delphi 2.0 programmers have a background in 16-bit Delphi, it's a good idea to review the major differences between the 32-bit and 16-bit Windows environments and between the 32-bit and 16-bit Delphi products. This list is by no means exhaustive; if something in the following summary is news to you, look it up in the Delphi 2.0 documentation or other Win32 reference.

Address Spaces

In the Win32 environment, each application (process) has its own private virtual address space, meaning that pointers and addresses valid in one process are meaningless in other processes. There are techniques for sharing memory between processes, but this must be done explicitly. In general, any 16-bit code you have that passes pointers to other applications will have to be rewritten before it will work at all in 32-bit Windows. Private address spaces completely isolate multiple processes from one another, making it impossible for an errant program to overwrite memory owned by another process, including the operating system. (Windows 95 is less protective of system memory areas than Windows NT, but the same principles apply.)

A 32-bit Dynamic Link Library (DLL) is loaded into the private address space of each process that uses it. This means that each instance of the DLL and all its global variables and memory allocations are contained in a separate address space from all other instances of that DLL. This is very different from 16-bit DLLs, whose global variables are shared across all applications that use the DLL. A 16-bit DLL could easily be used as a communication bridge to exchange information between applications (intentionally or not); this will not work in 32-bit DLLs—at least not without a lot of additional work.

In the 16-bit environment, memory was addressed in 64K-byte chunks, called *segments*. To traverse logical memory blocks larger than 64K, you had to manipulate the pointer to hop between segments at each physical 64K boundary.

The 32-bit environment still has segments, but since each segment can address up to 4GB (gigabytes) of memory, nobody really cares about segments. Instead, a 32-bit application uses only one "segment" to define its entire address space. All pointers in the application are merely 32-bit offsets within that private 4GB address space. Pointers in 16-bit Delphi apps are the same size as in 32-bit Delphi apps (4 bytes), but you no longer need to monkey around with the pointer contents to traverse huge memory blocks. Any 16-bit code that performs such pointer arithmetic *must* be deleted from 32-bit programs.

Preemptive Multitasking

Each process can contain multiple threads of execution that run concurrently with one another and with the rest of the system. Execution time is distributed across available threads using preemptive multitasking. Unlike 16-bit Windows, where other applications get execution time only when your application yields to the system by processing messages, Win32's preemptive multitasking requires no cooperation from the application and is completely invisible to the application. When a thread has exhausted its execution timeslice, it is suspended by the operating system until other threads have had an opportunity to execute. This means that one program caught in an infinite loop (or just a very long calculation) will not adversely affect the stability of the operating system or other applications. On a single-processor machine, only one thread can execute at a time; on multi-processor machines (supported by Windows NT), multiple threads can execute simultaneously. This is important to keep in mind when writing code that manages or communicates between multiple threads.

Long Strings

Probably the most significant new feature in Delphi 2.0 (as pertains to the topics in this book) is long strings. The 16-bit Delphi native string type was limited to storing a maximum of 255 characters per string because the length of the string was stored in a byte. Delphi 2.0 extends the native string type to use a 32-bit string length, providing essentially unlimited storage capacity in native strings. The price for this expansion, though, is that string variables can no longer store their data on the stack. In 16 bits, it was a simple matter to toss string variables onto the stack since the largest string could be only 256 bytes long. With the absurd capacity of long strings, though, those assumptions break down, so long strings are always allocated from the global heap. The long string variable itself is just a 4-byte pointer to the heap-allocated string data. You can still use byte-length strings in Delphi 2.0 by declaring your string variable with the ShortString type or by specifying an explicit string length in the type declaration.

Long strings are the standard string type used in all Delphi components and run-time library routines and are used exclusively in the public interfaces of source code that accompanies this book. PChar (null-terminated) variables and short string variables may be used in the implementation of certain methods to avoid the performance hits associated with heap-allocated strings where assumptions about the maximum length are allowed, but long strings are always the preferred type for parameter and property types exposed to the programmers using your classes and units.

32-Bit Integers

Since the native register size of the 32-bit Intel processor is 32 bits and operations on native-sized integers are faster and less complicated than non-native sizes, the Integer type grows from 16 bits in Delphi 1.0 to 32 bits in Delphi 2.0. For most 16-bit code that uses Integers for calculations, loop variables, and parameters, this size change has no effect on the execution of the code. Code that reads integers from binary files written by 16-bit programs or that contains assumptions about the size of data structures will need to be reviewed when porting to 32-bit Delphi. If a specific data type size is required, use ShortInt, Byte, Word, SmallInt, or Longint. If the physical size of the data is not critical or if optimum execution speed is more important, use the native-sized Integer or Cardinal types. All these types are already defined in 16-bit Delphi. SmallInt is equivalent to Integer, and Cardinal is equivalent to Word in 16-bit Delphi. In 32-bit Delphi, SmallInt remains a 16-bit signed integer data type, while Integer grows to 32 bits. Word remains a 16-bit unsigned integer, while Cardinal grows to 32 bits. Note that while Integer, Cardinal, and Longint are all the same size, they are not equivalent types. Longint is a signed integer type whose data size is larger than or equal to the native integer type. This means Longint could be larger than Integer in some future implementation of Delphi, and, therefore, you cannot pass an Integer variable to a Var Longint parameter, or vice versa.

Index

A

Abstract interfaces, 88-90
  crossing language boundaries, 90
  exporting objects from DLLs, 90
  importing objects from DLLs, 89
  linking user and implementor, 90
Add-in-tools defined, 313-315
Address spaces, 337-338
Aggregates, instantiation of, 65
Aggregation defined, 49
Algorithms, code, 25-26
AllocateHWnd, 200-201
APIs (Application Programming Interfaces), 6, 11, 23, 27, 32
  and messaging knowledge, 30
Application.HookMainWindow, 201
Application.OnMessage, 181-182
Application Programming Interfaces (APIs); *See* APIs (Application Programming Interfaces)
Applications, *See also* TApplication.
  automating, 243-244
  registering, 244-245
  shutdown, 187
  start-up, 187
Application writing
  characteristics, 24-26
  opportunities, 26-28
  skill set, 21-23
Assign and AssignTo, TPersitent, 205-210
AssignTo turnabout, 208
  direct field access, 210
  implementing assign, 207-208
  making the assignment, 206
  non-self class tests, 208-209
  smart linking, 208-209
  transferring data via properties, 210

B

BDE (Borland Database Engine), 20

Binary component streams, converting between text and, 172-173
  32-bit integers, 339
Bitmaps, using, 216-217
Blueprints, 3-4
Bonding, component-window, 188-189
Borland Database Engine (BDE), 20
Broadcasting messages, 200

C

CASE tool approaches, 14
Class
  accessing protected members, 270-271
  illuminated, 127
  implementation of private and protected methods, 62-63
Class declaration, reading a, 38-47
  class methods, 46-47
  nonpublished event properties, 46
  private sections, 41-42
  protected sections, 40-41
  public sections, 40
  published event properties, 44-46
  published sections, 39-40
  static methods and properties, 43-44
  virtual methods, 42-43
Class factories
  building, 239-241
  registering, 241-243
Class methods, 46-47
Class references, 98-100
Class-type properties, writing, 161-162
Clipboard support, 210-211
Code algorithms, 25-26
COM (Common Object Model), 90
  abstract interfaces, 226-228
  in-process servers, 228
  interfaces, 225-247
  proxies, 227-228
Common Object Model (COM); *See* COM (Common Object Model)

INDEX

Components
  coordinating, 307-308
  designing, 35-69
    abstraction, 36-38
    balancing priorities, 35-38
    cost of design factors, 38
    design-time support, 67
    extensibility, 36
    identifying tasks and parts, 47-61
    operating within the implementation bubble, 62-63
    usability, 36
  editing, 278
  editors, 303-311
    implementing, 310-311
    registering, 307-308
    TComponentEditor, 304-306
  modifying, 306
  reading, 171
  scope registrations, 295-296
  Window bonding, 188-189
Component writers
  component provider, 28-33
  skill set, 28-30
Component writing
  characteristics, 30-31
  opportunities, 31-33
Contractless programming, 24-25
Convergence, iterative, 47-48
Cross-links defined, 156
csDesigning ComponentState, setting the, 281-282

D

Data, persistent user, 143-151
Database operations, SQL database access, 19-20
DCU (Delphi Compiled Unit), 97
DDB (device-dependent bitmap), 216
Decomposition, 48
DefaultHandler; TObject, 194
DefineProperties; TPersistent, 175
Delphi
  10 year history of, 4-7
  application writer, 21-28
  lessons learned, 7-12
  programming model, 3-33

  solutions, 12-21
    automatic design-time component editing, 16-17
    automatic object persistence, 16
    components easily incorporated into the visual environment, 17
    continuous gradient of experience, 20-21
    contractless programming, 13-14
    custom behaviors through delegation, 12-13
    database operations, SQL database access, 19-20
    graphics and control encapsulation, 18-19
    memory allocation and pointers hidden, 17-18
    property streaming, 16
    structured exception handling, 18
    visual program design merged with programming environment, 14-16
Delphi Compiled Unit (DCU), 97
Delphi component writer, 28-33
Design-time issues, 281-283
  support, 67
Device-dependent bitmap (DDB), 216
DIB (device-independent bitmap), 216
Dispatch, TObject, 200
DLLs (Dynamic Link Libraries), 32
  building experts in, 331-333
  exporting objects from, 90
  importing objects from, 89
  non-VCL experts, 315
  utilities for non-Delphi DLL experts, 325-326
DMT (Dynamic Method Table), 83-85, 192
DsgnIntf unit, 279
Dynamic Link Libraries; See DLLs (Dynamic Link Libraries)
Dynamic method
  inside calls, 84-85
  table, 83-85

E

Editing
  component, 278
  property, 277-278
EditIntf unit, 279

Editor registration, 307-308
Editors
  component, 303-311
  property, 285-302
Error-handling systems, fire brigade, 105-106
Event properties, published, 44-46
  isolating helper classes with aggregation, 45-46
  using helper methods to fire events, 45
Exception handlers, implementing, 117-120
Exception handling, 105
Exceptions, 105-123
  changing one's assumptions, 114-117
    allowing separation of tasks, 116-117
    simplification improves performance, 115-116
    simplifying source codes, 115
  communication systems, 105-108
    automatic notifications, 106-108
    fire brigade, 105-106
  raising, 120-123
  syntax, 108-114
Experts, design-time
  and add-in tools, 278, 313-335
  defined, 278, 313-315
  implementing, 333-334
  installing and initializing, 329-334
    building experts in DLLs, 331-333
    compiling experts into Complib, 330-331
  to DLL or not to DLL, 329-330
  versus add-in tool terms, 313-315
ExptIntf unit, 279
Extensibility
  maximum extensibility equals minimum functionality, 64
  setting the degree of, 64-67
Extensibility inhibitors
  implementation details, 65
  instantiation of aggregates, 65
  monolithic methods, 65
  published properties, 66
  sets and enumerated types, 64
  what makes a class more extensible?, 66-67
Extensibility enhancers
  deferrable decisions, 66
  implementation details, 67
  planning, 66
  second opinions, 66-67
  simple, clear opportunities, 66

F

Factory, class
  building a, 239-241
  registering the, 241-243
FIF (Fractal Image File), using, 219-224
FileIntf unit, 280
Fire brigade error-handling systems, 105-106
FreeNotification, TComponent, 203-205
  establishing the link, 204
  receiving notifications, 204-205

G

GDI (Graphics Device Interface), 11
GetEnumName, 142-143
GetEnumValue, 142-143
GetPalette, 211-212
GetPropInfo, 140
GetPropInfos, 141
GetPropList, 141
GetTypeData, 143
Global-scope registrations, 295
Graphical user interface (GUI) design tools, 10
Graphics, 213-224
  decorating components with fonts, pens, and brushes, 215-216
  file format extensions, 217-224
  fractal image file graphics class, 218-219
  sharing resources, 213-215
  using bitmaps, 216-217
    file format preservation, 216-217
    performance tradeoffs with DIB versus DDB, 216
  using FIF, 219-224
Graphics Device Interface (GDI), 11
GUI (graphical user interface) design tools, 10

H

Handle avalanches, window, 255
Handles, windowless window, 200-201
HAS relationships, identification of, 48-49
HookMainWindow, TApplication, 201

I

IDE (Integrated Development Environment), 5, 275
  design-time subsystems, 277-278
    add-in tools, 278
    component editing, 278
    experts, 278
    property browsing and editing, 277-278
    TForm.Designer, 277
  EXE and CompLib camps, 276-277
  installing an expert DLLs, 333
  modules and subsystems, 275-278
  TIToolServices, 315-326
IDispatch, implementing, 229-239
  mapping child component names to unique IDs, 233-235
  mapping names to unique dispatch IDs, 232
  mapping property names to unique IDs, 232-233
IDispatch.Invoke, 235-239
Illuminated class, 127
Integers, 32-bit, 339
Integrated Development Environments (IDEs); *See* IDEs (Integrated Development Environments)
Interfaces
  abstract, 88-90
  lines of communication, 279-281
IsDlgMsg, TApplication, 183
IsHintMsg, TApplication, 182
IsKeyMsg, TApplication, 182
IsMDIMsg, TApplication, 182
IS relationships, identification of, 48-49
IsStoredProp, RTTI function, 143
IStreams unit, 280
Iterative convergence (spiral development process), 47-48
IUnknown, 229

L

Language directives, 74
Local message loops, 185-187
Local variables, 260-263
Logic tables, 257-258

M

Marshaling defined, 227
Memory
  addresses, caches, and locality of reference, 258-259
  allocate uniform block sizes, 259
  allocating once and for all, 256
  allocation strategies, 256-263
  don't allocate at all, 259
  overallocate to prevent the creeps, 256
  precalculate data, 256-259
  trading memory for speed, 256
    fixed-size temporary storage, 260
    stack, 260-263
Message loops, 179-187
  running the gauntlet of filters, 181-183
Message methods, 192-193
  DefaultHandler, 194
  implicit message cracking, 193-194
  marking a message as handled, 195
Messages
  previewing keystrokes, 183
  receiving, 188-195
    component-window bonding, 188-189
    message methods, 192-193
    three message-handling opportunities, 189-195
  sending, 195-200
    external, 195-196
    internal, 196-200
Messaging, 177-202
  drawbacks, 202
  Win32, 177-179
Methods
  class, 46-47
  static, 43-44
  virtual, 42-43
Modal versus modeless windows, 314
Modeling defined, 3
Multitasking
  preemptive, 338
Multithreading, simplified, 261

N

Non-VCL expert DLLs, 315

INDEX

O

Object linking and embedding (OLE); *See* OLE (object linking and embedding)
Object oriented programming (OOP) 5-6, 21
OLE (object linking and embedding), 88, 199
  automation servers, 228-239
  IDispatch, 229-239
  interfaces, 225-247
  IUnknown, 229
  interprocess communication, 225-226
  marshaling, 227
OnIdle state machines, 185
OOP (object oriented programming), 5-6, 21
Open tools architecture, 275-283
  DsgnIntf, 279
  EditIntf, 279
  ExptIntf, 279
  FileIntf, 280
  IStreams, 280
  ToolIntf, 280
  VCSIntf, 281
  VirtIntf, 280
Optimization, levels of, 249-252
  appearance, 252
  how fast is fast enough?, 251
  Rosetta code, 250-251
Optimization techniques, 249-271
OWL (Object Windows Library), 6

P

PaletteChanged, 211-212
Pascal, 4-6
Perform, 199-200
Pointers, sibling, 156-157
Polymorphism
  in action, 75-81
  virtual methods, 73-103
PostMessage, asynchronous messaging using, 197-198
Procrastination, 252-255
  being a good VCL citizen, 254-255
  deferring resource creation, 253
Programming
  contractless, 24-25
  model defined, 3

Properties, 43-44
  browsing and editing, 277-278
  get routines, 141-142
  published, 66, 173-174
  set routines, 142
  specific registrations, 296
Properties reading, 170-171
Property editors, 285-302
  implementing, 297-300
  registering, 294-296
    component-scope, 295-296
    global-scope, 295
    property-specific, 296
  rules of the road, 301-302
  standard, 289-294
  TCaptionProperty, 291
  TCharProperty, 290
  TClassProperty, 292-293
  TColorProperty, 293
  TComponentNameProperty, 291
  TComponentProperty, 293
  TCursorProperty, 293
  TEnumProperty, 290
  TFloatProperty, 290
  TFontNameProperty, 291
  TFontProperty, 294
  TIntegerProperty, 290
  TMethodProperty, 292
  TModalResultProperty, 294
  TMPFilenameProperty, 291-292
  TOrdinalProperty, 289-290
  TPropertyEditor, 285-289
  TSetElementProperty, 292
  TSetProperty, 292
  TShortCutProperty, 294
  TStringProperty, 291
  TTabOrderProperty, 294
Public interface of components, 40
Published properties, 66, 173-174
  default values, 173
  order of streaming, 174
  stored options, 174

R

RAD (rapid application development), 105
Reading components from streams, 171

INDEX

Reading properties from streams, 170-171
ReadState, 175
Redeclaring virtual methods, 86-88
RegisterComponentEditor, 307
RegisterWindowMessage, 196
Registering design-time property editors
  component-scope, 295-296
  global-scope, 295
  property-specific, 296
Remote Procedure Calls (RPC), 199, 227
RES (Windows resource) file, 158
Roots, choosing the right, 49-54
  existing components: TCustomxxx, 51
  TComponent, 52-53
  TGraphicControl, 53
  TObject, 51-52
  TPersistent, 52
  TWinControl, 53-54
Rosetta code style, 250-251
RPC (Remote Procedure Calls), 199, 227
RTL (Run-Time Library), 106
RTTI (Run-Time Type Information), 125-151
  advantages, 128
  data structures, 131-139
  disadvantages, 128-130
  example project, 143-151
  non-RTTI types, 130
  routines, 140-143
    GetEnumName, 142-143
    GetEnumValue, 142-143
    GetPropInfo, 140
    GetPropInfos, 141
    GetPropList, 141
    GetTypeData, 143
    IsStoredProp, 143
    property get routines, 141-142
    property set routines, 142
    TObject.ClassInfo, 140
    TypeInfo function, 140
  structures, 16-17
  supported types, 130
  TPropInfo, 131-136
  TTypeData, 137-139
  TTypeInfo, 136
  TTypeKind, 136
  TypInfopseudostructures, 131-139
  TypInfo unit, 125-126

Rules of thumb for
  implementing exception handlers, 117-120
  raising exceptions, 120-123
Run-Time Library (RTL), 106
Run-Time Type Information (RTTI); *See* RTTI (Run-Time Type Information)

S

SendMessage
  blocking, 199
  pitfalls, 198-199
  synchronous messaging using, 198
Servers
  loading in-process, 228
  OLE automation, 228-239
  testing automation, 245-246
Sets and enumerated types, 64
Sibling pointers defined, 156
Smart linking, enhancing, 92-98
Source code
  modifying VCL, 282-283
Spiral development process, 47-48
SQL database access, 19-20
Stacks
  learning to live with abundant space, 260
  memory management benefits, 260-263
  one-size-fits-all schemes, 261-262
Static methods, 43-44
Streams
  reading with TReader, 168-172
    starting the read process, 168
    TComponent.ReadState, 169-170
    TReader.ReadData, 170-171
    TReader.ReadRootComponent, 169
    TStream.ReadComponent, 168-169
    winding down the read process, 171-172
  writing with TWriter, 158-168
    initiating output, 158-159
    TComponent.WriteState, 160
    TWriter.WriteComponent, 159-160
    TWriter.WriteData, 161
    TWriter.WriteDescendent, 159
Streaming, 153-175
  opportunities for component writers, 173-175
  property-based, 153-155

INDEX

component ownership, 156
cross-links, 156-157
parentage, 156
property deltas, 155-156
sibling pointers, 156-157
visual form inheritance, 155-156
tools, 157-158
Strings
long, 338-339
managing, 263-270
optimization techniques, 267-270
constant arrays of strings, 268-269
format's 4K limit, 270
SetLength, 269
string concatenation, 267-268
using delete instead of copy, 268
and variants
hidden temporaries, 264-267
overhead for automatic cleanup, 263-264

T

Tables, logic, 257-258
TApplication.Idle, 183-185
TApplication.OnIdle event, 184-185
TApplication.OnMessage, 181-182
TCaptionProperty, 291
TCharProperty, 290
TClassProperty, 292-293
TCollection, 58-61
TColorProperty, 293
TComponent, 52-53
TComponentEditor, 304-306
  pop-up menu items, 305
TComponentEditor.Create, 305
TComponentEditor.Edit, 305-306
TComponent.GetChildren, 166-167
TComponentNameProperty, 291
TComponentProperty, 293
TComponent.ReadState, 169-170
TComponent.WriteState, 160
TControl.Perform, 199-200
TCursorProperty, 293
TCustomxxx conventions, 51
TDefaultEditor, 308-310
TEnumProperty, 290
Text component streams, converting between binary and, 172-173
TFiler.DefineBinaryProperty, 166

TFiler.DefineProperty, 163-165
TFloatProperty, 290
TFontNameProperty, 291
TFontProperty, 294
TForm.Designer, 277
TGraphicControl, 53
TIExpert, implementing, 326-329
TIntegerProperty, 290
TIToolServices, 315-326
  action methods, 318-320
  component library information, 322-323
  error handling, 326
  menu interface, 324
  module interfaces, 323-324
  project information, 321-322
  project notifications, 324
  utilities for non-Delphi DLLs, 325-326
  virtual file system registration, 323
TList, 55
TMethodProperty, 292
TModalResultProperty, 294
TMPFilenameProperty, 291-292
TObject, 51-52
TObject.ClassInfo, 140
TObject.Dispatch, 191-192
ToolIntf unit, 280
Tools
  add-in, 278, 313-335
  graphical user interface (GUI) design, 10
  implementation, 54-61
TOrdinalProperty, 289-290
TPersistent, 52
TPersistent.DefineProperties, 162
TPropertyEditor, 285-289
TPropInfo, 131-136
  Default, 135
  GetProc, 135
  Index, 135
  NameIndex, 136
  PropType and Name, 134-135
  SetProc, 135
  StoredProc, 135
TPW (Turbo Pascal for Windows), 6
TReader, 168-172
TReader.ReadData, 170-171
TReader.ReadRootComponent, 169
TSetElementProperty, 292
TSetProperty, 292
TShortCutProperty, 294

TStream.ReadComponent, 168-169
TStream.WriteComponent, 158
TStream.WriteComponentRes, 158
TStream.WriteDescendent, 159
TStringList, 58
TStringProperty, 291
TStrings derivatives, 56-57
TTabOrderProperty, 294
TTypeData, 137-139
TTypeInfo, 136
TTypeKind, 136
Turbo pascal, 4-6
Turbo Pascal for Windows (TPW), 6
Turbo Vision, 5-6
TVerboseStringProperty, 297-300
TWinControl, 53-54
TWinControl.Broadcast, 200
TWriter, 158-168
TWriter.WriteComponent, 159-160
TWriter.WriteData, 161
TWriter.WriteDescendent, 159
Typecasting incompatible types, 270
TypeInfo function, 140
Types, typecasting incompatible, 270
TypInfo unit, 125-126

U

Utilities for non-Delphi DLLs, 325-326

V

Variables, local, 260-263
Variants, managing, 263-270
VCL (Visual Component Library), 4, 35
  architecture, 29
  modifying source code, 282-283
  subsystems, 203-224

VCSIntf unit, 281
VirtIntf unit, 280
Virtual methods, 42-43, 73-103
  inside calls, 83
  redeclaring, 86-88
  structure of, 81-82
  syntax review, 74
  table, 81-83
Virtuals
  defeat smart linking, 91
  enhancing smart linking, 92-98
  reviewing what's really in one's executables, 97
  smart linking, inverse, 97-98
Visual Component Library (VCL); *See* VCL (Visual Component Library)
VMT (Virtual Method Table), 81-83
  inside calls, 83
  structure of the, 81-82

W

Waterfall development process, 47-48
Win32 messaging, 177-179
Window handle avalanches, 255
Windowless window handles, 200-201
Windows
  API and messaging knowledge, 30
  Application Programming Interface (API), 6, 11
  Graphics Device Interface (GDI), 11
  handling registered messages, 196
  modal versus modeless, 314
WndProc, 191
WriteComponentResFile, 158
WriteDescendentRes, 159
WriteState, 175

Addison-Wesley warrants the enclosed disc to be free of defects in materials and faulty workmanship under normal use for a period of ninety days after purchase. If a defect is discovered in the disc during this warranty period, a replacement disc can be obtained at no charge by sending the defective disc, postage prepaid, with proof of purchase to:

Addison Wesley Developers Press
Editorial Department
One Jacob Way
Reading, MA 01867

After the ninety-day period, a replacement will be sent upon receipt of the defective disc and a check or money order for $10.00, payable to Addison-Wesley Publishing Company.

Addison-Wesley makes no warranty or representation, either express or implied, with respect to this software, its quality, performance, merchantability, or fitness for a particular purpose. In no event will Addison-Wesley, its distributors, or dealers be liable for direct, indirect, special, incidental, or consequential damages arising out of the use or inability to use the software. The exclusion of implied warranties is not permitted in some states. Therefore, the above exclusion may not apply to you. This warranty provides you with specific legal rights. There may be other rights that you may have that vary from state to state.